BREAKTHROUGH
divine revelations

by Open

Openhand Press

BREAKTHROUGH: divine revelations
by Open

First edition: printed 1st September 2016
Published by Openhand Press

ISBN 978-0-9556792-6-1

Cover design & layout: Trinity Bourne

for the real people…

"You've no idea how hard I've looked for a gift to bring You.
Nothing seemed right.
What's the point of bringing gold to the gold mine,
or water to the Ocean.
Everything I came up with was like taking spices to the Orient.
It's no good giving my heart and my soul
because you already have these.
So, I've brought you a mirror.
Look in it, and remember yourself."
(adapted from Rumi).

Contents

Foreword

It seems to me that just about everyone in the world is searching for something - some kind of fulfilment, peace, joy or love. Yet all too often, all that's found, are dancing veils in a world of disillusion.

Many people are close, tantalisingly close, to what they're really looking for. The problem is one of confusion: it's not a destination, something to be achieved or acquired. No, the real 'goal' is a feeling, a sense of completeness, a connection to the eternal Source of life and a free-flowing liberated expression of that - your very own soul. When you truly find this sweet spot of life itself, all the lights in the Universe come on at once; it is priceless, beyond value or even definition. You can't bottle it up and sell it, yet when you can access it, you'll ultimately discover there's an unlimited streaming flow of this abundance. There is simply nothing else to compare with it.

Many people - including those consciously on the spiritual path - are close, tantalisingly close, to this priceless prize. So how do you access it, and keep doing so?

From observation through countless lifetimes, I believe it's straightforward and simple. However it does require persistence, patience and commitment, so it's not easy. But if you know what you're looking for, and most importantly, how to look, then breakthrough into your deepest spiritual self - life's stupendous prize - is open to every single person who is honestly committed.

Breakthrough is about recognising the often conflicting impulses of the moment, which tangle people up in knots internally. There are essentially two impulses taking place in every situation you'll ever face: that of the ego, which is trying desperately to justify, placate, protect or elevate itself; and the soul - your true sense of self - which is only ever looking for a liberated expression in the moment.

Here's the secret that many approaches to this conundrum are missing: you cannot simply drop the ego to access the fullness of the soul, like dropping hot coals. It's only ego that does this. What you can do however, is seize the moment, feel honestly into the contractions of the ego, recognise there are nuggets of soul gold in this tightness - *in this heat* - then work through the fire of transformation, reclaim the lost fragments of soul, and break through with lightness.

Your very soul is liberated on the outstretched wings of the divine. You've hit the jackpot, the sweet spot of life itself, and there is nothing like it. This is "Breakthrough".

Did I say it was easy?

Easy it is not. But with persistence, and a basic understanding of how to work through your tightness, you can, and will, break through.

Don't worry. You're getting bags of help. The whole Universe is conspiring to reveal yourself to yourself. Whatever you may think you're engaged in - jobs, relationships, entertainment - actually the only thing ever going on, the singular purpose of the moment, is this 'self-realisation'. Some call it 'self-actualisation', because in those intimately lucid moments of crystal clear clarity, you are literally making yourself real.

And that's the only thing truly going on.

Not only is the natural flow of the Universe constantly conspiring to reveal this to you, but also you have an abundance of soul family and guides, working diligently in the dimensions to support and assist you. As in the case of the story I'm about to share with you.

It is the story of a 'seeker', Chris Bourne: a person who, maybe like you, didn't even know what exactly he was seeking. Sharing his story is sure to offer invaluable reflections and insights into your own journey, for there are moments in life when you're on the verge of Breakthrough, and even manage to achieve it, before life's tantalising temptations lure you back into the darkness once more.

That's the challenge indeed of being in dense, physical incarnation. It's profoundly beautiful yes, the sense of relativistic separation creates a myriad of exquisite forms, yet these temptations all too easily attach you to an illusionary goal or need - that you must have, and then cannot live without. If you can witness these allurements of life, recognise how and why they're owning you, then you have the chance to truly break through.... you can have your 'cake' and eat it too. That is exactly what happened for Chris.

I have been his guide, through this and previous incarnations, working behind the scenes to help activate his awareness, just as you all have guides working often unseen for you. Chris spent the best part of his life searching for the deeper meaning of life, and frequently breaking through, before being swallowed up once more by desire, sense of lack or neediness. Finally, through an earth-shattering sequence of events, Chris did indeed wake up and stayed that way, before ascending into a higher vibration of being - the New 5D Paradigm - a heaven, which ultimately awaits everyone.

Chris left me these memoirs before passing on. I felt compelled to share them, because I know without a doubt, that they will offer powerful reflections - *divine revelations* - to situations and circumstances happening in your life - in your career, relationships and general aspirations. Truly breaking through into your Cosmic Self, is not about throwing the baby out with the bathwater. Although dumping the ego in this way might initially feel peaceful, it only leads to frustration, as you discover a fundamental part of yourself is missing. No, to truly liberate your soul and thereby attain lasting fulfilment in life, is to penetrate this tightness and break through it. Thus you reclaim that missing aspect of yourself, to which the Universe is conspiring to bring you.

You cannot ultimately avoid this intense confrontation of life. As this story will share, humanity's very ignorance of the divine is driving him and society to the precipice of oblivion, as the Earth's ecosystems are literally being torn apart. All realities come and go. In a Universe of constant change, change is the only constant. Right now, society is bleeding the life out of the people and the planet. But it won't last much longer. It's simply not sustainable. So why not - like Chris - dive full-on, all-in, and embrace the challenge of each moment, so that you may break through into the sweet spot of your soul. It leads to an immortal life, as a cosmic being, on a renewed Earth, in a New Paradigm of existence, in the Fifth Density.

This book is the first in the Openhand series of the "5D Shift Project", which is a framework of exploration for your own evolutionary inquiry. I suggest you take your time when you read it, pausing at key explorations that resonate for you and work to apply the revelations contained within the text to the situations you're currently facing. That way, it becomes much more than just reading a book, but rather powerful inspiration for your shift into a higher consciousness.

BREAKTHROUGH is an epic, true account of what actually took place (although some of the names have been changed so as to protect privacy). I know that it will inspire you to recognise what this earth-shattering transformation of life is truly presenting to everyone right now. It demonstrates that by regressing through your own life experiences, you can reclaim lost nuggets of 'soul gold' buried in the sediment of life. It reveals how, in each moment, you can seize the real prize, and break through into your True, Cosmic Self.

Although it is not easy, ultimately it is simple. It's straightforward. So why don't we begin...

Namaste

Open

1

A Shoulder to Cry on

"Embrace and express your ancient inner pain."

It couldn't possibly be her, could it? The woman with the long dark hair was several places up ahead of me in the queue waiting to check-in at the Las Vegas Hilton. Could it really be her? The one I'd been having those erotic dreams about the last several months? Soon I'd find out, the long queue, which was snaking through the lobby toward the reception desk, would turn back toward me, and I would get to see her face. But what if it is HER?

My marriage had been on the rocks for several years. Unlike the tired Friday night movies, we were not "living life happily ever after". We had long since lost genuine interest in each other and the vacuum of true soul connection had been filled by predictable mutual dependency. My life was determined by pleasing others, because, in truth, I lacked the courage to be genuine and speak my honest feelings: pleasing my children on a Saturday at Wacky Warehouse because I had lost the ability to do something original with them; pleasing my friends by fulfilling their conditioned expectations of me; pleasing ridiculously demanding customers because I needed that ever-burgeoning pay cheque. I was truly lost in the rat race, climbing the endless property ladder to nowhere. Something just had to give... and finally, just when all hope seemed to be lost, life did give. It gave more than I could ever - in my wildest dreams - imagine possible.

It had begun a few weeks earlier with an email, "the chance of a lifetime", an all-expenses-paid trip to Comdex, the international technology conference in Las Vegas. There was just one more vacant place available to the first suitable applicant. The thought of winning never entered my mind, but something deep within caused me to apply anyway. Surprise, surprise! I won the last place and a few weeks later, like Alice, I was whisked off to a magical wonderland. As the plane steadily climbed out of the dark, billowing clouds shrouding Heathrow International Airport, there was a deepening sense that I was leaving the darkness and density of my past behind.

Mid-flight entertainment was the film "The Bourne Identity", the story of a betrayed man, shot several times in the back and cast adrift in the ocean. Miraculously discovered by the crew of a passing fishing trawler, he is rescued and healed, but left suffering amnesia, unaware of his true identity. Comfortably numb I may have been, but even so, I could not miss the startling synchronistic parallel with my own life. Indeed, from the very beginning, there was a sense of magic in the air, a presence, seemingly able to shape events and circumstances with benevolent purpose. Just like the one unfolding right now, in the basement of the Las Vegas Hilton.

Another step; she's beginning to turn. The sense of expectation is escalating, which seems to slow the hands of time, delivering my soul onto the teasing precipice of now. Slowly, but surely, her features reveal themselves tentatively, through cascades of wavy hair, and as the light shines in, steadily, it seems to me, her whole face is lighting up, like some angel from another dimension.

My God. Yes. *It is her!*

I rub my eyes to look again. Perhaps I'm just tired and jet-lagged. Maybe it just looks like her? But no. There is no mistaking, there she is, standing in front of me, the exact likeness of the woman in my dreams - receptive, compelling, giving, angelic. I find myself wondering how do things like this happen? And as she draws closer, my heart begins to pound. Then our eyes meet, for a brief moment, that seems to stretch to eternity. Was that a faint smile?

My reality was thrown into instant turmoil. Suddenly I realised just how dead and depressed I'd been - how sadly devoid of real chemistry my life was. All it had taken was a glance and the subtlest of smiles to light up my life. Why had I let that spark of real living get away from me? Yes, there was some kind of magic in the air, like angel dust, that simply lit up the impossibly ordinary. Would I see the woman again? Somehow, somewhere, deep inside of me, I just knew I would.

That evening I went with my roommate, a fellow entrepreneur called John, to the opening event of the conference, which was to be presented by Bill Gates. As we made our way into the stadium, some strange 'pull' seemed to engage me, steering us both in a particular direction, parting the swathes of moving people, until two seats revealed themselves in front of us: *right next to the woman with the long dark hair.* "Are these free?" I asked, slightly shy and embarrassed... "They are indeed," she smiled back. If this was a dream, I definitely did not want to wake up!

We introduced ourselves. Her name was Maria. She had a ready smile, a warm heart, and an empathic receptiveness that so made me want to melt into her. Our exchanges began politely and it turned out we were on the same trade mission, but even as the mighty Bill began his opening address, I could find no interest in his words. I was totally captivated by the real chemistry of the evening – that which seemed to be igniting right next to me. At one point my knee brushes hers, although it's not intentional, I guess something deep inside is longing to initiate something more intimate. She doesn't retract. Such a feather light gesture and yet my heart is flying. How can this be? Just a day earlier, I was still smothered under a thick blanket of depression, and yet now, after a short stream of apparently inconsequential events, my life has ignited. At the time, the greater significance was lost on me. The last thing I wanted to do was analyse. My life was way too analytical. Time for the heart to take over.

The lacklustre 'main event' drew wearily to a close, but for me, it had long since dissolved into some far distant galaxy. Where would it go from here? I was just beginning to ponder when John piped in… "A drink then?" Good man. "Yes, what a great idea. What about you, Maria?" Yes, she'd join us. Life was quickly getting better and better.

John was a lovely guy, and under any normal circumstances, I'd have got on well with him and found him great company. But these were far from normal circumstances. A dream was unfolding, with Maria taking centre stage, which I wanted to follow and never wake up from. John definitely didn't fit the 'theatre', but from the wings, he made a suggestion that definitely did blend with the drama - it seemed to pop out of the ordinary greyness and colourise the moment. Strange. It was as though my soul was somehow 'spiked' by an increase in energy, an increased acuteness of awareness. It was as if he'd touched something in the ether all around us, and suddenly animated a flow, which began to sweep up all around it… "Hey guys, did you know the Grand Canyon is just a short plane ride from here? How'd you like to skip the conference tomorrow and fly out there?" I had to pinch myself. Really? Could this be possible? Do wonderful things like this simply happen in life? There was a pregnant pause from both myself and Maria. She looked at me for a moment. Perhaps she was wondering the same thing? "Sure!" we echoed together. And, with teenage giggling smiles, "Yes, what a great idea." So we resolved to meet up the next morning at the ticket office in the lobby. As we all said goodnight, my eyes engaged Maria's once more. Just a fleeting glance, yet held long enough for us both to realise something significant was happening between us. It's amazing isn't it, how much can be said, yet without even exchanging a word!

The next morning, yet again, I found myself wondering if this was some kind of dream from which I would soon awake. No, Maria would not show up. She was just some figment of an over active imagination. But now the lift doors are opening and there she is, resplendent in a white dress. There it is again: the welling up of anticipation and sheer joy inside of me. It was a chemistry I'd missed for simply too long. As she walks over and greets us, my thoughts race into overdrive…If only we could get rid of John, I found myself ungraciously thinking. Somehow the Universe must have been listening though, because as the three of us stood at the kiosk about to pay, his mobile phone burst into song. It transpired there was some kind of confusion at his company's Comdex stand in the main hall, which required his urgent attention. I found myself reluctantly saying "Well it's okay, we'll go another day," which carried no energy whatsoever! Fortunately John was a considerate guy and insisted we went on without him: "Don't worry, this could last a while, I'll go another day". Yet again that pregnant pause followed, where the moment seemed to stretch to an eternity, where somehow, the workings of the Universe seemed to be purposefully configuring themselves with some deeper mission. Even amidst the heady cocktail of emotive chemistry, something in me was beginning to recognise this sense of deeper significance. It was as if somehow, I was dropping through layers of a tired, surrendering mind, and touching the moment with a sudden lucidity, a more expanded awareness.

More important than her angelic features and yielding sensuality, it turned out Maria was an incredible, empathic listener. Within minutes of the plane's departure, somehow, although I'd been deeply suppressed and repressed by life's sad disappointments, I was now pouring my heart out to her, as she listened attentively. It was as though in the ether all around us, I'd handed her a thread, that she was now unwinding and unravelling deep within me. I couldn't remember the last time I'd really cried. Perhaps not since a boy? But now, as we stood on the north side of the canyon alone together, I was blubbering like a baby.

It had all been bottled up inside: the struggling, the efforting, to achieve something, to find happiness or security. *Some kind of goal that would fill that aching emptiness inside.* And all the while, through all the struggling, me, the real me, had been squashed down, trampled on, by the stampede of the matrix – a meaningless tide of nothingness, which had beaten me down, and from which there was seemingly no escape. And yet now, just a conversation, with a caring stranger, was enough to begin unravelling all that compacted inner density. At the time, there was no time to marvel at the awesome healing simplicity of the human ear and heart.

Eventually, the torrent of tears subsided. And the seemingly ceaseless flow of words ceased. For the first, genuine time, my eyes reached out into the canyon. You see that's it. Behind these veils of compacted denseness we hold inside, we never really see anything at all. We're looking at things through tired and hazy memories of reality - judgments of what we expect it to be. Behind this wall of separateness, we can't really touch reality at all. The penny was dropping for me. My mind had given up, and my heart was rapidly softening, melting, as if into everything around it. That's when it happened: as I stare into the majestic void, I find myself not just looking at it; instead, *I am immersed within it.* I've become one with it. I'm no longer just *seeing* the colours, but *feeling* their vibration inside. I find this stillness has an incredible, indefinable quality, which draws me through the canvas separating me from the truth of it, and like Alice, sends me tumbling down the rabbit hole. It is as though I've fallen into the landscape, totally merging and at one with it.

The stillness was breathtaking, and my senses had suddenly 'quantum jumped'. It was as if 'God' had magically turned up the brightness, colour, sound and focus buttons all at the same time. Every sense had come alive, intense, as if suddenly more pure.

And then, in the space between the spaces, a voice appears. Although in truth, I can't really call it a voice, that's just how my mind needs to comfortably pigeonhole it. It's more a presence. And it doesn't speak. Somehow, it can exchange 'knowing' with me. Yes, there is definitely a conversation - there is definitely an exchange between two separate beings. But it's somehow all around me. How curious. At the same time, there's absolutely no concern as to the invasiveness. I instantly know its benevolence. Like a long lost friend enveloping you in an almighty etheric hug. And then it dawns. I encountered this presence sometime ago. About two years ago, when a rapid, expansive stream of awareness had swept me up, for a brief moment, out of the doldrums of my life, before the matrix had sunk its relentless teeth into me once more.

Yes, I remember now. The system had deemed this incredible lucidity was somehow psychotic, and forcibly administered debilitating drugs, which seemed to contract me down, like swallowing the genie once more into a dark and dusty bottle. It's you again isn't it?…my thoughts reached out into the canyon. *Yes, it is. I told you I'd come back for you.* Warmth fills my heart. A long-lost friend has returned. I didn't know who he was, or where he came from. I just knew him, better than I'd known anyone. And I knew he knew me. It was as though he could pass through the very fibre of me, and resonate something I could truly feel. Yet he was never invasive. It was like he'd appear, and suddenly disappear. I yearned to know more. What was he all about? Where had he come from? Why was he here? Why did it feel so good when he was around? *Be patient, my dear friend,* I felt the resonance, *for in its time, all will be revealed.*

The presence seemed to drift off as my attention was drawn back to Maria. Our time at the canyon drew to a regrettable close, and on the flight back, I continued the review of my life with her. She was simply an angel, genuinely happy to hear the challenges of my life. Maybe it resonated something in her too?

I was going more and more deeply into my feelings. It was like peeling off the layers of an onion. I realised how unhappy I was at home, that my life was not serving me. The love that had once existed between my wife and I had expired aeons before. I felt constrained and imprisoned and I was desperately missing the feelings of joy, love, excitement, anticipation and passion - the magical chemistry I was now feeling.

I had been starving myself of the very essence of life itself. My life had become dull, grey and boring. Yet again the tears flowed, at the feeling of entrapment, but also they were tears of joy, at the realisation there was actually nothing wrong with me. No, I was not dead to love, I could still feel it. Hallelujah! Love was very much alive within me, I had just buried it deep within. This miraculous, primordial truth had been masked by a web of illusionary needs and wants, yes, but it was still very much there. It had been heaped upon by expectation, yes, and disillusionment, together with the machismo of 'boys don't cry'. Boys aren't sensual, caring, loving, gentle, peaceful. They are strong, determined, exploitative, tough. When the going gets tough, the tough don't break down and explore their deep inner feelings, they get going.

In the pauses, realisations began to flow about love, and what it truly meant to me. I realised that just as for everyone else, the material world causes us to objectify feelings we have on the inside for a person (or something) on the outside. So we may fall in love and the deep feelings of joy and passion on the inside, become associated with that person. Soon, an expectation of them takes root, that they should fulfill our need for love. It actually becomes our purpose for them in our life. We become attached and needy, in a way that the other can never quite fulfill. We squeeze a little harder, wondering why it continually feels less good, until, if we're not careful, as had happened to me, we've squeezed all the juice out of the relationship, like some dried up fruit.

Through my encounter with Maria, my relationship with love was changing. Although I was deeply attracted to her, the experience in the canyon had shifted something in me, perhaps irrevocably. I was realising that by accessing my true feelings inside, and not projecting them into neediness of someone or something else, that love would activate within me and touch all life around me, not just one form of life. So the neediness began to diminish. In those precious moments, I discovered love once more. Not just for Maria, but *for the whole of life*.

We arranged to go out to dinner that evening. I changed in my room quickly, in case I should bump into John, and risk him having the bright idea of joining us. Romance was now on the menu; two would be company, but three would definitely be a crowd. I wait for Maria in one of the hotel bars playing great contemporary music on large overhead TV screens. The air of anticipation heightens within me, and also some feelings of guilt. I had not yet been unfaithful physically, but in my mind and feelings, I was already well past the point of acceptable friendliness. Should I go on with it? What would happen between me and my wife? Would I tell her? At that moment a video song by a band called Creed begins to play, on the large overhead screen, which seems to speak into the depths of my soul:

"Please come love
I think I'm falling
Holding on to all I think is safe
It seems I've found the road to nowhere
And I'm trying to escape
I yelled back when I heard thunder
But I'm down to one last breath
And with it let me say
Let me say...
Hold me now
I'm 6 feet from the edge
And I'm thinkin
Maybe 6 feet ain't so far down"

(lyrics by Creed)

So poignant is the song, so emotive the feelings, it feels like it is being sung just for me. And as the song ends, Maria arrives.

We dine at a luxurious, rotating restaurant, at the top of a high tower, overlooking practically the whole of Las Vegas. The restaurant is circular, with enormous glass windows, the tables looking outwards, so your eyes can feast on the spectacular panorama. The twinkling street lights, and the bustle of life far below, contrasts with the softly smooth ambience of the restaurant. We sit next to one another, so that we can admire the view, intensifying the chemistry. Occasionally we gently and lightly touch one another, the atmosphere is electric.

Maria was provocatively dressed with plunging neckline and floating, silky dress. The recurring dream that had begun months previous, was now becoming reality.

On the way up to her room, the chemistry is already beginning to bubble over in the elevator. Dampened lips and fumbling fingers heighten an electric air of expectancy. It feels like there is no time to waste. If the world were to end that night, it would have to wait for what was about to transpire. Even as the door to Maria's room clicks shut, so her silky dress is rustling to the floor. And there she is, the divine feminine, in all her magnificence, only very lightly veiled in see-through laciness. But it was me who would surrender that night. A light push from Maria was all that was needed, as I fell backwards onto the bed. Now, she softly strokes and kisses me, which electrifies my senses, building an energy, which quickly wants to explode through every pore of me. Part of me wonders why it is so intense, why so alive? The rest of me just doesn't care! Later I realised it was the divine feminine that had come alive in me – a sensual intimacy, which had long since been subjugated under a mountain of forced masculinity.

Maria sensually pleasures me, such that I so much want to melt into her. In teenage times, there would have been a rapid explosion. But this time is different. A new sense causes me to focus more within, to manage my feelings by being more attentive with them. The electricity builds and builds, seemingly into every cell of my being. And it takes time to build, initiating a depth of feeling I've never before experienced. It feels like I'm being connected up to the electricity mains, like being plugged back into life itself. So that when I eventually do orgasm, my whole body begins to shake and vibrate, as though electric currents are coursing up and down through me. There was no doubt about it, I was experiencing orgasm *in every fibre of my being.* It was literally mind-blowing. I could sense Maria was quite shocked by it. Although clearly sexually liberated and experienced, I don't believe she'd witnessed anything like this intensity before. I know I certainly hadn't!

Finally, after what seemed like hours of sweet sensuality, we fell into each other's arms and into bed. Maria fell asleep quickly, but there was simply no way my eyes would close – I remember thinking perhaps they'd never close again!

I lay awake most of the night, eyes glued to some imaginary movie screen on the ceiling; there was no imagery, but that didn't diminish the sense of inexplicable expectation and excitement. Suddenly it was simply thrilling to be alive, even if all I could see was a blank canvas. Maria, on the other hand, was now in deep slumber, somewhere else in the Universe.

At 5am I could contain the energy no longer, it needed some kind of outlet, some flow, before I exploded. Where to now? I thought. An answer seemed to effortlessly materialise in the form of an inner vision – I should go to the roof gym. It was situated on one of the upper floors and there was an outside patio, which looked out onto the streets below. At that time, the gym was closed, so I wandered around outside. I had come to love early mornings from my Army days. Just before it gets light, there is a stillness in the air, which is quite unlike any other time of the day. I guess it's the expectation of the sun returning, to bring light, soothing warmth and vibrant energy back to the earth. I began to practice some martial arts - routines known as 'katas'. A kata is a pre-planned sequence of moves passed down through the ages. It is essentially meditation in movement, the mind becoming one with the body.

Because the moves are so practiced and trained, the mind does not need to think about what comes next. Awareness surrenders ever-deeper inside, quite effortlessly. As you connect with inner feelings, you begin to release any tension that you might be holding – because identity no longer needs to justify itself in the outer world, it has no position to hold. As Bruce Lee once said, "the key to good martial arts is to be able to flow like water and then freeze like ice." You can't flow as water if you are tense within the movement.

Tension builds hand-in-hand with identity. The more there is someone inside trying to move quickly, the more slowly you move. When there is no one trying to do anything, tension eases and you move instantaneously at full speed. That's why Bruce Lee was able to throw a one inch punch and knock an opponent clean across the room. I had come to know this as mastery of 'biomagnetic energy' - 'chi' as the Chinese know it (although I have to say, I'd never related it to other areas of my life prior to this, like sexual intimacy for example!). It has many other names. The Japanese call it 'ki', the Indian yogis call it 'prana', the Tibetans 'ihund', the Egyptians (and Mary Magdalen) called it 'ka'. I believe it's what Einstein referred to as 'Quantum Energy'.

Performing the ancient kata was sheer joy. I couldn't fully understand why. It just seemed to take me into a place which was beyond this world with all its meaningless trials and tribulations. This was an expression of 'me', and it seemed to ignite that feeling, like blowing on sparks in an open fire, suddenly igniting wildly dancing flames. It's like I became the flames, with heat and power, a sense of ancient connection, right back to something primordial, beyond space and time.

Then suddenly the presence is there again, like he's dived off the fence, swirling back into my experience, flowing effortlessly with me. I joyfully welcome him. He's always activated an intensity within me – it's like he was helping me come home to a deeper sense of self. Somehow, he doesn't need to be told what I am now exploring. An exchange begins, again not with words, it feels more like knowing is activated within me...

Ki is the absence of efforting. Ki is consciousness that is released when we give up internal questioning and struggle. Ki is the opposite of trying. If you wish to have the entirety of the power of the Universe at your fingertips, the key is to surrender all effort, all wanting, all trying. To experience the maximum ki in your life is to completely surrender to the flow of consciousness within you. The False Self - your ego - must yield on the altar of life's experiences to the True Self – the pure flow of consciousness. This is the mistake most people make. When they discover ki, they want to do something with it: to heal themselves or others or to 'save the world'. But the True Self, that which they are seeking to harness, needs or wants nothing. It loves the perfection in all outcomes. 'Good' and 'bad' events are merely judgments of the ego. To the True Self, all outcomes offer the opportunity of an experience, and no experience is more preferable than another, as long as alignment with the pure core of being is happening. Desire for an outcome, even a perceived honourable and selfless desire, diminishes the power of the True Self within you.

These realisations that were landing within me – *each divine revelation* - were as manna from heaven, expanding and opening me up, to an ever greater flow of unconditional love.

Suddenly, I became both the movement and the moved, dissolving into a new effortlessness, where flow happened spontaneously. There is no longer anyone inside saying "go" or "stop", "turn" or "block". Crystal clear clarity is arising from within, as the inner and outer worlds unfold into one. Then, on the horizon, attention (at this point I cannot even say 'my' attention) is drawn to the sky beginning to lighten, the blackness becoming purple and indigo, as dawn gently kisses the distant panorama. At the sun's first appearance, I'm compelled to stop. Frozen in time, I notice the early morning chatter of traffic far below me receding further and further into seemingly distant galaxies, until there is no sound at all. Nothing is worthy of this stillness, of this beauty, of this peace.

Time had ground to a halt, and yet simultaneously accelerated. Within the apparent blink of an eye, the sun was fully up and radiating golden warmth. Suddenly, I am being washed through with wave upon wave of unconditional love, seemingly from a source of infinite benevolence. Release after release, unfolding upon unfolding, surrender into surrender. I was being loved completely and wholly just for me. There was no judgment in the love and no need for anything to be reciprocated. It seems to penetrate every fibre of my being, seeing me with complete openness, honesty and clarity. It sees my darkness and loves me unconditionally; not in spite of it, like another human might, no, it loves me **because** of it. For the first time in all the forty years of my life, I feel totally accepted and worthy. Being 'me' in that moment was entirely and completely right. No one was criticising, questioning, abusing or judging. There was not even the requirement for a payback, no need for me to reciprocate. I was allowed to swim in it, to sink in it, to breathe it into every pore. This was my initiation to the magical, universal flow of divine love I have since come to know as the "Awakening".

Aided by the ancient and timeless presence, my very own soul had begun to infuse into me, and I just simply knew that this sense would no longer evaporate, as it had done in the past. I'd made a deep connection with my soul and it was here to stay. I was beyond overjoyed.

You'd broken through: you'd finally penetrated permanently, the dense inner layers that had built a wall of resistance and separation from the true, interconnective, deeper meaning of life. Unknowingly, you'd applied something I call "Breakthrough"...

Breakthrough is a direct confrontation of the moment, by embracing and expressing your inner pain, penetrating deep into the tightness, unwinding it, and breaking through with the lightness of your soul.

Breakthrough can only happen from the place of complete inner surrender – a giving up of the need to shape and control the outcome of events in the external world. This surrender enables you to feel into, and become as one with, your pain. In which case, the barriers of internal separation from reality – those that create the polarity of separated identity (the pain of the ego) – dissolve. Now the soul can flow freely through you, washing away the pain, and delivering you onto the shore of absolute truth – the Void of Presence, which rests at the heart of all life; it is the beginning and the end, the question and the answer, the mystical Shambhala, which, whether knowingly or not, all are looking for, within every experience they have.

I'm not sure how long I spent basking in this unfathomable beauty. Time was irrelevant. I just knew that from that moment onwards everything changed. I knew that nothing in my life would ever be the same again. I realised that, perhaps like everyone, I'd had plenty of previous tasters of this experience in other events and circumstances, but each time, the feeling had dissolved again. Now was different. I simply knew – I had broken through into my deeper, Cosmic Self, and nothing was going to drag me back. I was simply ecstatic.

2

Romancing the Flame

*"...it's going to crack you up, melt you down,
then fill your heart at the simplest of things..."*

I'm now floating through the gambling arcade in the basement of the Las Vegas Hilton as if on a cloud. It is day 2 – the second day of my life's restart. I'm drinking in the juice of life through every pore. "Please don't switch this off", I'm thinking. "Just don't EVER switch this off!" And the presence is with me immediately to answer...

That's entirely up to you. It's a choice of where you put your attention now. Do you need some kind of outcome from the moment? Do you need to fix or control life? Because all such efforting closes you down. However, if you can just keep opening to the flow you're now feeling, then the flow will keep strengthening through you.

In the gambling arcade, the air is thick and heavy, the ringing and buzzing of slot machines seems to perfectly reflect the intensity of the minds they're sucking in. All the while, thoughts are popping in as I survey 'life'. Somehow I'm effortlessly tapping into the deeper meaning...

Every moment has this 'deeper meaning'. What is that? Everyone is immensely creative, their very inner beingness shapes the world around them. It creates a mirror by which to see yourself. You can ignore the mirror as most do. Or, you can witness the reflection of yourself that you're seeing, and connect into the flow that's working tirelessly to reveal the authentic you – your very soul. And the moment you do this, you plug into the Source of Life, which is an infinite power source. It's like plugging into the mains electricity and having it permanently running through you.

"So that's what's happening – now it makes sense!"

Not only had my experience of the world changed, but it appeared that everyone's experience of me changed too. Now I seem to be drawing eye contact with complete strangers, everywhere I go. Even here in the gambling hall occasionally someone looks up, away from the flashing lights, and somehow connects with a light in me. People are more friendly than previously and conversations begin spontaneously: someone sharing the same lift, the lady at the hotel reception, a janitor sweeping up in the lobby. I begin to notice synchronicities –

circumstances just clicking into place. A question would come into my mind only to be answered immediately by the sign on a wall, the chance comments of the person standing next to me, the number plates on a passing car.

Yes, thrilling isn't it? This language of synchronicity is the mother tongue of the Universe. It is your rightful language – one which, in the depths of our soul, we all know. It's what connects us together into a greater cosmic brother/sisterhood.

I realised that everything had this hidden meaning, each communication was a divine message of love: "I am here, I am all around, I love you." With each divine 'coincidence' the inner feeling of connection strengthened, and I would frequently break down into tears. The realisation of true unconditional love was just so overwhelming.

Like so many, you've been divorced from this energy for so long. When you finally recognise it, when you surrender to it, it's going to crack you up, melt you down, then fill your heart at the simplest of things. You reclaim the sweet innocence of life. It's the very opposite of control and manipulation, and there's an enormous sense of relief that comes with it.

I was passing through the gambling arcade to meet up with Maria. I felt like I'd fallen in love with her. But somehow, I kind of already knew that what I'd really fallen in love with, was life itself. And there she is again, standing before me, a vision of loveliness, the perfect reflection of the love I am feeling inside. "I love you!" I announce as our eyes connect once more. But then instantly something in her shifts - I recognise a sudden closing down in her eyes, a falling of her expression, a wilting of the smile. She'd obviously misunderstood me. Intuitively I could feel what was going on within her, an incredible miracle in itself, but now I was too intrigued by the outer interplay, rather than simply embracing the magnificence of the fact that I could actually feel what she was feeling and know what she was thinking: 'being in-love' means deeper connection – *a relationship*. I sensed that's something she definitely didn't want – a holiday fling yes, but nothing beyond…

When you break through, and open into the flow of your soul, you connect with people on multiple levels. Most people are trying to manipulate the moment to get what they want, what they feel they really need, or else to avoid what they're resistant to. The result is that their minds are so full, they never hear this higher language. But as you lose the need to control the moment, you start to pick up on the divine dance between souls – what someone is really saying beyond what they'd like you to think of them.

I made a brief attempt to explain to Maria the magical experience I'd had the previous day, in the early morning light, way above the hubbub of life. Unfortunately it went straight over her head...

Something you'll just have to get used to!

I try to explain that the love I am feeling is unconditional, just as it had been given to me. It has no expectation, it isn't even romantic - at least not only and always! It isn't looking for something in return. It's 'just' a feeling, coursing through me, that needs no ownership of anyone else. It doesn't even need to be owned by me. It is just flowing. But as I quickly came to realise, unless you've tasted this internal superhighway of unconditional love for yourself, it's practically impossible to properly understand.

So the chemistry between Maria and I changed pretty much instantly. She'd quickly moved on, which I was saddened by. It touched on something deep within – a sense of loss. The magic between us had evaporated, almost as quickly as it had begun, like some vanishing desert mirage. But my sadness was comforted by the seeming omnipresence of the presence. He seemed to travel everywhere with me by now, always on hand to help in making those deeper revelations. I couldn't put words to them at the time, although that didn't even seem necessary. It was that his energy catalysed in me a shift, which led to a deeper sense of knowing about life and the situations in which I found myself involved.

It was clear that in searching for love through the external world, I'd lost something precious that I was now reclaiming...

There's a connection people can make internally to a phenomenon, which is the manna of life itself - their own Twin Flame. It's the other part of their soul, which doesn't incarnate, stays close to the Source inside, and acts as a powerful polarity or 'pull', drawing you onto the inner journey. This Twin Flame loves you like no one else can. She knows every intricate part of you; she knows what makes you tick and come alive. She knows your darkness yet loves you because of it. She manifests as reflections into the outer world – it could be in the sweet song of a bird, the passing of expansive cloud formations, the glint in the eye of a person serving you, and sometimes, your Twin Flame will manifest a very close reflection in physical form, what some call a 'soulmate'.

Now when a soulmate does appear, it's all too easy to project onto them the sense of this eternal flame, this eternal love. You're blinded by your own neediness for them to be real. It convinces you they ARE real, and for a brief tantalising moment, that is indeed, in a way, true. They are such a close reflection, that they're almost – not completely, but almost - the same thing.

What tends to happen, is the person is then so blinded by this apparition, that they project all of their love onto the physical manifestation – onto the person. And in that moment, although they gain a beautiful experience, they lose something on the inside. In bottling up the fleeting essence of their Twin Flame, they've diminished its ability to manifest anywhere, anytime, in anything. Increasingly, they now need it to be in one particular thing, and so if you're not careful, your soulmate gets heaped upon with expectation and subtle, subconscious neediness.

"So how do you overcome that? How do you not do that?"

*It is by realising that everything you encounter on the outside, no matter how beautiful, no matter how perfect, is actually experienced on the inside. And you couldn't recognise that beauty if you didn't resonate with it. In other words, you can only appreciate it because **it's already an integral part of you.** You're simply witnessing a deeper* *aspect of yourself - which for most people is unconscious, they're not aware of it. That's why when something reflecting that consciousness appears before them, they're literally drawn like a magnet - they're drawn to the lost aspect of themselves.*

Even these beautiful experiences you need to break through, by directly confronting the moment, your feelings in it, where you would get owned by what's happening, defined and limited by it. If you can unwind and expand through these owning contractions, you'll unleash the soul with a phenomenal sense of rightness and fulfilment. In that very moment, you will be manifesting your destiny.

"Wow. I get that. It means whenever I see or appreciate something truly beautiful, I don't have to own it, because I already have it. It's already in me, waiting to get out."

Bingo!

Just at that moment a gambler hits the jackpot and their slot machine is now spewing out coinage.

Perhaps the most difficult thing in the Universe to master, is to be able to embrace the reflections of the Twin Flame you're witnessing, enjoy them to the fullest, in every moment, but then as the reflections dissolve, let the manifestation of your love dissolve too. Then it's waiting inside of you, as incredible potential energy, ready to rise again.

When you can live like this, the energy inside of you is constantly creating and reflecting, everywhere you go, no matter where you go. It's like riding a wave of pure magic in your life.

This is the phenomenal power of Breakthrough.

Yes please. I'll have some more of that!

3

Nothingman

"Your soul is meant to be liberated,
a flowing experience from the presence of The One."

The passenger jet bumps down hard on the tarmac at Heathrow International Airport; it was landing through the dense, damp and cold fog, which was hanging in the air like thick veils, obscuring reality. Maybe it's been like this since I left? I was wondering, but with a wry inner smile. Nothing was going to dampen my heightened mood, no matter how hard it tried.

That said, on the way home, a nauseous knot began to gather, grow and tighten in my gut, with every mile closer. I knew I had to face the music. There was simply no avoiding it. How unfair is this! I thought. It seemed totally right in Las Vegas that I should feel the liberation of my soul, basking in the ever-present sunshine of the divine. We deserve this, it is our birthright, our destiny, how we're supposed to live. But why do I have to pay for that? I found myself thinking.

It's not that you have to pay for it. You've willingly disconnected from it, to some degree. Your soul was tempted into identification with the drama – thinking it really needs something out there to make it whole and complete. But then you realise that's not necessary, that if you just let go of the need for it to be a certain way, then your awesome freedom will create ever-new experiences to taste that bounteous divine union - the sense of rightness within. But you have to keep choosing that; you have to keep choosing the freedom, the natural flow of the moment; you have to keep finding and expressing yourself as you really are - then trust that the Universe will organise the rest.

"How do I trust? How do I let go?"

Confront and embrace the moment you've now created, exactly as it is, without needing to change it. Totally honour it.

"What do you mean by honour?"

I mean you have to willingly step in the direction that seems to cause the pain, and to fully express what you feel.

"Really?"

It's the only way. Your soul is meant to be liberated, a flowing experience from the presence of The One – the Source. It yearns for it. So if allowed to – if you don't resist – it will willingly take you into the places where you identify with the illusion of reality, so you can learn to let go and be awesomely okay in it. The soul is forged in this crucible, to always stay liberated and free. It's called 'self-realisation' – but it's not given on a plate. You have to work for it!

"How do I work?"

Honour the pain by stepping willingly into that course of action which seems to create the pain and is clearly drawing you toward it – like going home now. Feel the tightness, wherever it is (like in your gut), then become as one with it by exploring intimately into every nuance of it. These are exactly the touch-points where the soul is identifying. Ask: "What do I think I need from this situation? What am I afraid will happen?" Imagine the worst possible outcome – feel deep into any tightness. Because The One in you isn't afraid of anything.

"What happens then?"

In becoming as one with the pain, without needing it to go away, you become awesomely okay with it to be there and remain. You express it out into your world. Maybe shout or scream about it, move, adopt an expressive position. When you do this, you break through and unleash the soul. From that place, you're touching the infinite potential of the Source, because it's where the soul originates from. And so now anything can happen. You'll create miracles because you unleash through you a flow of universal rightness. You manifest destiny.

I pull the car over into a lay-by. The pain is wanting to double me up, so I let it. I want to bang on the steering wheel, so I don't stop myself. After a while, with my face red and flustered, my attention is guided to the CD folder. I quickly flick through it, but without really thinking, an obvious CD just jumps out. I instantly know the track I'm supposed to play…"In the air tonight" by Phil Collins:

> *I can feel it coming in the air tonight, oh Lord*
> *And I've been waiting for this moment for all my life, oh Lord*
> *Can you feel it coming in the air tonight, oh Lord, oh Lord.*
> (Lyrics by Phil Collins)

The sound, the feeling, the sense of the way the words are sung, seem to speak directly into the heart of the pain and animate it. Within moments, it becomes so easy to forget that I'm in a car, pulled over in a lay-by, with the lights of other cars whizzing by. The windows are now all steamed up with my explosive animation, the headlights flickering in, as if I'm in some translucent haze. And it's becoming deeply transcendent. To the extent that I almost begin to enjoy it.

You're beginning to accept the purpose of it, why you created it, that perhaps it is not such a bad thing after all. At least your pain lets you know you're really alive again!

Suddenly something clicks inside – like someone in there has thrown a switch. I realise I am completely okay with this - with the potential breakdown of my family and what that might cause. I've found myself naturally letting go, expanding out inside. It feels liberating. I can do this, I can take that course of action - the one I can literally feel wanting to happen.

You've come home to the abode of The One again.

"I thought I'd done that. Why do I have to **keep** doing it?"

There will be many touch-points of the soul where it identifies in particular situations and circumstances. These events touch your karma – past life attachments in particular experiences, for example a tragic and painful passing on. Or the painful breakdown of a relationship - maybe your partner got hurt? Your soul still contains these hooks into the illusion of reality. And so these internal eddy currents of consciousness will keep manifesting reflective circumstances in your outer world until you've worked through by integrating soul through them all.

Your consciousness creates, and whatever you have in there, will manifest into the outer. You can avoid it temporarily, as most do, by trying to focus on something more 'desirable', but it's only ever temporary. It will always come back to haunt you, unless you look square into its eyes, and work through it. There is no ultimate avoidance – the only way out is to keep breaking through.

I'm now standing in the doorway, about to press the bell. My gut has tightened again – this is the moment of truth, this is really real, I'm balanced on the blade edge of life. I feel love and compassion for my wife, but at the same time, I simply know what my soul is calling me to do - how to be. I know there is no viable alternative. I have to confront the moment and honour the pain by stepping directly into the path of it. With that, I press the doorbell.

Amanda, my wife, opens the door with what you'd usually expect, your dear partner having been away for a week – a huge smile and a generous hug. Even though in truth our marriage was on the rocks, like so many people, it was still held together by heaps of cement called 'denial'. For many, it's just far too difficult to even begin to contemplate the stark-staringly obvious. Or else you "do it for the kids" – you bury your true heart-felt feelings because of the trauma you imagine others will suffer if you actually did summon enough courage to walk the path of truth...

*Lying to one another actually does not serve anyone in the end, not even the innocent, such as children. What needs to be understood, is that the universal Law of Attraction draws people and circumstances together to act as mirrors, causing them to see their deepest inner feelings – the real truth – then to express that out into the world, no matter what the apparent personal cost. Because it's the apparent personal cost **that is your identification.** It is where you attach to the illusion of physicality - either you need for it to be a certain way, or you're resisting what clearly wants to now happen.*

At the highest levels, each soul, no matter how old or young, is demanding of you the truth, and fears not the consequences of that. Even a child can discover how to be whole and complete – without mother or father – if helped to do so in a compassionate, loving, empathic, but above all, truthful way.

I absolutely knew I had no choice but to tell my wife the truth about what had happened. That it had 'only been a fling' yes, but nevertheless, I'd felt a chemistry that I'd long missed in our relationship - that I'd actually fallen in love.

I couldn't wait any longer. I couldn't hear any more TV soap opera dramas, eat any more half-hearted candle-lit dinners, share any more half-truths. So practically as soon as I'd put my bags away, I told her that I had something to say, and without hesitation, before dinner was on the table, I 'spilled the beans'.

It felt so good to share - well not good, but 'right'. I wasn't happy in it, but despite the pain, it was just so wonderfully liberating to share the truth. It was like chains were being cast off me, chains that had held me down for so long. I could feel myself dissolving on the welcome shores of The One inside of me. Pain was all around, but how could this be wrong? How could being in truth be wrong?

For Amanda it comes as a total shock, you can see in her eyes her reality collapsing in on itself like a high-rise demolition – floor collapsing upon floor, collapsing upon floor, until all that's left are tears, falling on dust covered dreams.

That's unfortunately what happens when you've built illusionary realities; when you live a lie and are not being honest, either with yourself or your partner. Each then builds illusionary realities around what they expect or want. They are false, and at some point they're bound to collapse. It's necessary, but definitely not pretty.

In fact, despite the initial shock, Amanda handled the aftermath remarkably well. I think there was still some dim inner light of hope that this might just be some 'mid-life crisis' (I was 40!) and that it would all pass. Indeed we did get back together for a short while further down the path, but for now, there was only one choice to be made – I had to leave the matrimonial home in order to create space for reflection, to explore deep-seated emotion, and most important of all, so that each of us could rediscover something about who we truly were.

Make no mistake, it's hard when you have the sense this is 'being done to you', as in the case of your wife. But in truth, nothing is being done to you at all. It's just that people have allowed the wool of their own neediness and expectation to be pulled down over their eyes. Most would rather live in the illusion, because the truth often looks too tough or too cold.

When you come into the abode of The One – the Void – it mercilessly strips away any false constructs you've built up as the idea of who you are. It's not that The One doesn't experience life in a material way, of course it does, through souls like you and me. But The One is formless, shapeless, beyond containment. The soul flows from The One as a spontaneous streaming consciousness, which is meant to be liberated and free, beyond prediction and limitation. It may walk side-by-side with another, but it is definitely not bound to them. The ego builds its constructs around life, and as you come into The One, those fixed constructs will be deeply challenged until they are inevitably broken apart. It's like you've become nothing, and everything, simultaneously, all rolled into one. The paradox is, you can enjoy relationship more, not less. Because you're able to give wholly and completely of yourself, in truth, as you truly are. There are no false promises or expectations.

As I'm leaving the next morning, in the cold light of day, I pause to look up at the matrimonial home we've lived in, and, in many ways cherished. I reflect on some of the good times we've spent together, and the great ones – like our lovely children. In some ways I'm feeling deeply saddened of course, but in others, I can feel the unfolding wings of my liberated soul. It's a bitter-sweet experience, that just feels 'right'. Nothing can now stop the burning inside to truly discover myself, to truly know me, to uncover my destiny. Whatever in the Universe can be wrong with that?

Nothing. Absolutely nothing!

I could have known all of this previously. If I'd been truly honest with myself, the tell-tale signs were there a thousand times. Like the fact that we'd split up before getting married, after a holiday – the only time we'd spent some real time together. Like the fact that we bought into the seriously questionable truth that 'having kids brings you together'. Whoever said that? Whoever considered that a justifiable reason to stay together, or even have kids in the first place? Wow, how f***ed up society really is!

But now truth was speaking to me, through the effortless flow of life. I'd opened myself to the dialogue.

You see that's the problem. Many speculate about the nature of God – the divine – but when God begins to speak through their thoughts and feelings, when God tells them something inconvenient or just too contradictory to their hopes, aspirations and fixed constructs, they drown out the music. They'd rather switch it off.

That morning, as I leave the house, I am awake. I am listening. I am positively alive to the Universe all around me. I am tuned in and watching, and so as I get into the car, the fact that my trousers snag on a bunch of CDs in the door pocket, the fact that 'Vitalogy' by Pearl Jam just falls conveniently onto the ground beside me, is no longer just a coincidence. I can literally feel the interplay in it, the magic hanging in the air like angel dust. I can feel the synchronicity.

Because for the first time, you're not trying to get something from the moment - you're confronting and breaking through into the truth of it. Your mind is therefore empty. You're responding to the natural organising energy of life.

I pick up the CD. What do you want to tell me? I'm thinking. The CD had been a gift, which I'd only listened to once and generally found it was not my kind of music – a bit too thrash bang. But now, something in it intrigues me. What should I do? It would have been too easy to let egoic mind have its way – just put the CD back and get on with your usual day. But the soul in me has now emerged just enough, so as not to let that happen. So something new transpires for me, ***the narrative changes.***

I pause, open, and hold the space to see what might happen.

Wow. Yes that is a major shift for you. Just something as simple as holding the space without knowing where it will lead. An empty space with nothing in it. Something the ego seriously struggles with.

Somehow, from somewhere (thank you presence!), the number 5 pops into mind. I could have easily overridden it. Perhaps these little pearls are landing for people all the time, yet in busy and over active lives, just as soon as they land, the mind has already buried them in an avalanche of other thoughts.

This morning is different. Something has shifted irrevocably inside. And I resolve, in that moment, that if I am going to break up the matrimonial home, then I really owe it to my family to be in truth, to really explore the truth, no matter what may come. Because they deserve that all-in commitment of me.

So I slip the CD into the player and punch number 5. As soon as the first bars start playing, they tug on something deep inside me, something that I can now feel. The song is 'nothingman'...

Once divided...nothing left to subtract...
some words when spoken...can't be taken back...
walks on his own...with thoughts he can't help thinking...
future's above...but in the past he's slow and sinking...
caught a bolt 'a lightnin'...cursed the day he let it go...
nothingman...
nothingman...
isn't it something?
nothingman...
she once believed...in every story he had to tell...
one day she stiffened...took the other side...
empty stares...from each corner of a shared prison cell...
one just escapes...one's left inside the well...
and he who forgets...will be destined to remember...
nothingman...
nothingman...
isn't it something?
nothingman...
oh, she don't want him...
oh, she won't feed him...after he's flown away...
oh, into the sun...ah, into the sun...

(lyrics by Pearl Jam)

Within seconds, tears are streaming down my face. It's like a force of benevolence all around me is speaking directly into my heart - something that recognises my pain and my truth. Something that loves me absolutely unconditionally. Something that would move heaven and earth for me. Something that yearns for me to be me. And what's more, it clearly has no personal investment. The feeling is totally incredible.

You're breaking through now, time and again, into the deeper meaning, the deeper purpose. You're having the courage to directly confront the moment, to pause long enough, to open the internal space past the expectation and neediness that would contract you. Then you're listening to what arises – the sense of rightness that flows from that. You're putting this into action, you're fulfilling your destiny, which is now connecting creative feedback loops with the Universe. And so the entirety of the Universe is beginning to speak to you. This is how you can now live. This is how you were always meant to live. This is Breakthrough!

4

The Journey Begins

"By regressing into your past, you can reclaim those lost nuggets of soul gold buried there."

That morning I tell my fellow directors what has happened. Married themselves, they listen, wide-eyed and ashen-faced, unable to imagine the collapse of my world that has only just begun to unfold – it is like they're watching the collapse of the Twin Towers, all over again, right before their very eyes.

With that, they were sympathetic, and suggested that for the time being at least, I should move into the offices and stay there. It was great, absolutely wonderful - the 'office' being a lovely farmhouse, in the rolling Hampshire countryside, providing a liberating sense of space, and invigorating fresh air. A fold-out bed appeared as if by magic, and without even trying, I now had somewhere comfortable to stay. It seemed to fall into my lap.

It's always the way when you're not controlling life. The soul is immensely creative when you unleash it, and allow it to flow out into the world. All manner of miracles and magic happen.

It was totally awesome. It meant I had oodles of time to reflect, and to begin to meditate. This space and aloneness seemed to bring me ever deeper into the connection with the presence. It was like a constant dialogue was unfolding between us, from which ordinary life was becoming a distinct distraction. This was totally amazing. Every question, every thought, seemed to be instantly answered in the synchronicity all around me: the lyrics of a song, the swirling of clouds out in the fields, and even reading between the lines of what my colleagues were saying and expressing through their body language. It was like their souls were speaking to me – partaking of the dialogue – even without them being conscious of it. Wow!

In the evening hours especially, when all had left, and quietness descended its peaceful veil upon the building, that's when the presence came really close. That's when we began to journey, deep into my past, deep into all the experiences that had brought me here. But this was unlike any journey I'd previously experienced. It was like being at the movies with the presence – I was watching the movie unfold, having countless realisations about it, like being in conversation, but then also, at times, feeling myself right there in it, in the movie as well!

This is what 'regression' is all about. You're allowing yourself to feel into the energy that you've created. A part of you is still there, hooked in by subconscious ties – judgments and resistances to what actually took place. This is how karma builds. You're not able to be truly and awesomely okay in the circumstances. So fragments of the soul 'break off' and get lost within those experiences. That's why, when you animate them again, it feels like you're actually in them. And here's the incredible opportunity: by journeying this way into your past, by regressing into the situations and the feelings associated with them, you can reclaim those lost nuggets of soul gold that have gotten buried in the compacted sediment in the riverbed of life.

As the opening scenes of my life's movie roll, I recognise myself as a young boy of seven. Tears well in my eyes at the instant recognition of innocence and open vulnerability. I feel like I'm being reacquainted with a stranger, someone that had long been buried in the psyche's shadowy darkness. A tender young boy, full of bright-eyed wonder, that life has steadily wrung out, like a limp rag. A deep empathy with the youngster washes through me, stirring energies that have long lain dormant. I want him to live again, for this innocent lamb to rise from the darkness and be reborn. As the consciousness of my inner child activated inside, I found myself spiralling into the movie. Suddenly I had reached the bottom of the rabbit hole. Christopher had come back to life and I was he.

Within me is burning an unquenchable excitement about the world, with an inner yearning to delve into its wondrous mysteries. Eyes are brightened with inner expectation; ears acute to the finest frequencies; bushy-tailed at the prospect of infinite possibility. There is an extraordinary interest, captivated by the ordinary. There is practically no sense of time at all. It is simply swirling all around in this one moment.

Almost incredible isn't it? You knew more about the truth then, than in all your grown adult life!

And as I look back, at the same time, I can clearly feel there is already a growing reticence about the dangers, fears and limitations of a world, which sadly cannot match the place I have incarnated from. The inner warning bell is already sounding, signalling the conflict between the unconditional love I had once known and a seemingly unforgiving, uncaring world of cold harshness.

Why is the world like this? What have I done for people to behave as they do? Is it all my fault? From the vantage point of Chris the movie-goer, a deep sadness washes over me as I recognise the plight of the youngster - another of God's lambs was being fed to the wolves. They were tears of recognition, of sympathy, empathy and of deep realisation. I was right there with him. This was the journey I had taken many times before, a journey that all souls take from light into darkness and then back again. This time – as the movie-goer – it would be different though. I would make this journey in full awareness, forgetting nothing. Despite the realisation that I would confront times not only of joy, but of great pain, fear and sadness too, I revelled in the prospect of what the unfolding movie was about to reveal. How ever it turned out, this was going to be the ride of my life.

All souls experience this when they pass on. The bodymind falls away and you ascend into the angelic realms, where you're held and nurtured, empathically supported as you relive the journey of your life.

"How does that actually happen?"

The energy – the consciousness – of your life's experiences is contained within your Fourth Density 'causal body'. Fragments of soul that were not self-realised (realising of the One Self), break off and create eddy currents of consciousness – memories and your reactions to them. Most of the time, people have no access to these, because they're so engrossed in the density of the lower, physical realm. But when the bodymind falls away, your consciousness is no longer limited from 'rising' and expanding into them. Your soul now reanimates them.

"So why is this happening to me now? I'm not dead!"

In Las Vegas you had a powerful letting go, which is very similar. It just unfolds over more time. Anyone who is truly committed to uncovering their soul, can relax, soften and regress in this way.

Images of my father now flash onto the movie screen. A powerful personality, who has shaped my early experiences as much by what he left out, as by what he gave. The hard work ethic, generosity and commitment to purpose in him, ensured I wanted for nothing materially. There was just one vital ingredient absent, the one thing that had been missing from his own childhood - unfettered, unconditional, fully-expressed love. Not that he didn't possess it within him, not that he didn't love me dearly. I came to experience it in later years, but as the child, my heart yearned for the expression of it, to be wrapped up in a warm, totally accepting hug. Alas it never came and my soul thirsted for it, just as the seemingly abandoned Christ on the Cross.

Unconditional love. Priceless and irreplaceable. And when it's not given, especially in the formative years, the youngster takes on all manner of self-doubt, a sense of worthlessness or even self-loathing.

My Dad had taught himself Yoga to counteract his long-standing addiction to smoking, and had become very skilled at it. I would often hear him early at sunrise practising his "lion breath" before an open window. I looked on, as he explained to Christopher the technique of letting go of tension within the physical body and feeling the light, subtle vibrations around it - the energy body.

It is through the energy body that you feel the natural flow of the Universe unfolding through all events. You intuitively know what is "Right Action" in the moment. When you can let go of those things you desire or want, and instead, allow the heart to guide you, then you really begin to fly.

At precisely that moment, I find myself as Christopher again, floating on the ceiling of my bedroom looking down on myself, lying on the bed - I'm having an out-of-body experience...

Although you didn't realise it at the time, this was your first introduction to the release of attachment to body and mind, the identification with what we call the "ego". When you, as the soul, release yourself from ego's enveloping grasp, you expand immeasurably. When it happens, it is so liberating, it can feel just like flying, as if you're floating down the street, walking on air. This was your first experience of Breakthrough.

"Why me? Why so early?"

You were just ready. You'd travelled enough (in past lives) to actually internalise the true meaning of letting go. You were able to feel deeply enough inside your physical cells, that the idea of releasing, precipitated a rapid surrender. In some people, the experience can be so strong, the soul momentarily leaves the body altogether. However, the real key to life, is to feel that way all the time, whilst still in the body.

Unfortunately, like many who experience such 'paranormal activity' at an early age, the experience freaked me out somewhat, and my initial exploration into meditation came to an untimely and abrupt halt.

Never fear. Spirit will always find a way of waking you up eventually and if one doorway remains closed, another will surely present itself.

As if by magic, a new opening via the martial arts appears, and through it, images of a young boy in a Judo suit take form. Suddenly, I'm being tossed around a Judo mat like a rag doll, by a boy much older and bigger than me, who seems to take great pleasure in wringing every last ounce of energy from my helpless, immature body. Why am I doing this to myself? I'm wondering as the movie-goer. Ah yes, because my Dad thought it would be good to learn to defend myself, and to 'toughen up'.

I am now right there in it, tasting the sweat, the smell of fear filling my nostrils. I'm thrown, tossed in the air, like laundry on a windy day. Then down, fast and hard, till I hit the canvas, face first. Blood instantly spurts from my nose, covering the front of my suit. It makes me cry, to which the instructor says... "don't be wet, get a grip, toughen up."

Looking back, how did that make you feel?

I'm angry. It pisses me off - that life can be so unforgiving and uncaring, so unjust. I feel like I literally want to explode and lash out.

How best might you do that? How might you express the anger, but without projecting at anyone (which is counterproductive).

As the movie-goer I confront the feeling and go deep into it. The anger is now welling up and bubbling over. I can't contain it, I don't want to. Suddenly I'm thrashing around the room, kicking and punching furniture, beating cushions on the sofa.

How does that feel?

"It's releasing, letting go. It feels good!"

Now how can you apply that energy in a positive way, with rightness?

I slip into a martial arts kata, moving with strength, kicking, blocking and punching, but with grace and focus. There's a great sense of purpose and clarity, and of pure presence. A timeless here and now.

Brilliant. You're breaking through the density and unleashing soul.

As I now pause, I can feel a warmth building, a glowing heat rising up from the very base of my spine.

This is it - the great benefit in regressing into your pain, expressing it, then unleashing Right Action through it. You harness and focus soul.

After some while of breathing, feeling and integrating the incredible warmth of soul, I'm projected back into the movie once more. It's now the late 70s, and I'm transfixed by a remarkable film, "Enter the Dragon". The low-budget production and limited plot seemed of little relevance. What impacted most was the amazing physical presence of Bruce Lee. He pranced and danced like a cat, as if every fibre of his being was packed with high explosive, which he nevertheless controlled with effortless grace. It seemed to me at the time, this was what it meant to be truly alive. As a young boy, like so many others, I could see how I had been crushed and constrained by other people's fears and limitations.

You'd done it to yourself - something inside of you had accepted it.

"Yes, I'm beginning to see that now."

Bruce Lee became one of my early heroes. It was as though he gave permission to find something more. He'd set a bench mark, which even if it wasn't achievable, showed many of us the direction in which to travel; and most of all, to expect the seemingly impossible. Looking back, I could feel this as a deep and poignant moment for Chris...He didn't feel to be the sacrificial lamb anymore. It was time to let this cat out of the bag!

Whenever anyone is impressed by something they see in the outer world, then it calls on something deep within their soul. Actually what's happening, is that something you're seeing outside, is already being activated inside. You couldn't recognise it, or be inspired by it, if you didn't already possess some of those qualities in yourself.

It was this that inspired me to take up Karate, a passion that was to stay with me for over 25 years. I was taught by five outstanding Black Belts. They were humble and unassuming people - bread delivery men, machinists, factory workers. In the uniforms of daily life, they looked ordinary. Yet underneath, in the evenings and early mornings before sun-up, they honed muscle fibre to blue twisted steel, conditioned skin like elephant hide, and sharpened split-second reflexes. I often wondered what Mrs Jones felt as she received her daily bread from Neil, our senior sensei, who to me, was like God and the father I so badly craved. Six foot four, long black hair, stomach muscles ribbed like corrugated iron, "Don't be a wimp," I could hear him saying now, as he punched press-up after press-up, on granite-hard knuckles. I believed in Neil. And from that moment on, every time I put on my suit and belt, I could feel his energy in me. I felt totally invincible.

He was simply mirroring something deep within yourself. A soul that is liberated in some way, through some art, will always break through the moment and prosper. It could be in the martial arts, yoga, music, painting or any other vehicle of expression you choose to mention.

What is the purpose of training to such extremes one might ask? Looking on as the movie-goer, it quickly became obvious. I'm now in the Sixth Form, preparing for A levels. I've discovered beer, girls, punk rock, striped mohair jumpers and black leather jackets, loud cars and nights on the town, no doubt a heady cocktail of hormones and other distorting chemicals. As Chris the movie-goer, I watch a collage of swirling images unfold: the experiences of many being sucked up into a whirlwind of external distraction, generating internal uncertainty and confusion. In some, it leads to depression and anxiety, as the world contracts them, victimises and intimidates them. In others, it unleashes hyper-activity, that at times becomes uncontrollable, leading to aggression, frustration, anger and violence. I was one of the fortunate ones. Karate - the way of the empty hand - had extended me an open hand of friendship. It gave me a chance to stand square and centred in the eye of an emotional storm...

The soul begins to yearn for full expression in the teenage years: the inner warrior, a courageous fire of purpose and truth; the divine feminine, sublimely surrendered, vulnerable to all, yet in its purest form, inviolable. These powerful qualities within, can easily be distorted by the misshaping hands of a society, keen to exploit wayward emotions for material gain. It is so beneficial therefore, to engage in something that centres oneself deep within, in the core of your being. One that becomes inviolable to external tantalisations.

Suddenly I find myself in the dojo, in white lined Karate suits with a visiting national sensei, Bob Poynton, instructing us. He is demonstrating how movement must precede intention. "It needs to be instantaneous". Suddenly he unleashes a punch, his clenched fist a visual blur, closely followed by the flash and crack of his suit, like thunder after lightening. But Bob has slightly misjudged the distance to his target (an understandable mistake at warp speed, I was thinking!). He 'engages' unintentionally with Pete, one of our club's Black Belt instructors. The punch breaks away a part of one of Pete's front incisors, which he then spits out onto the floor without drama. The class watches on, aghast at the awesome control Pete seems to have over his emotions, not to mention the searing pain he must now be suffering. How does one stay so centred and calm, so free from emotion? I wondered.

Suffering is a choice. It is a decision made about the experience we know internally as pain. We can either identify with the drama and create a false reality, which becomes true for us, or alternatively, we can transcend it by experiencing the feeling in truth – by breaking through into the expansive feeling of soul. In other words, by a process of continual practice, we go deep into the heart of it, let the pain wash through and accept it without judging. That way pain becomes just another experience and we're no longer limited by it.

I could already appreciate how this aspect of "Enlightenment" (of which I now seemed to have an intrinsic understanding) would be a continual theme in the events that follow - being fully in the event, thoughts, feelings and emotions; definitely not denying them or pushing them away, but not identifying with them either.

As with life, to truly master the martial arts is to master one's fears, by confronting them full-on, all-in, without shirking back. In which case, you become as one with them – The One in them. This is a truly enlightened state.

In free sparring, the best senseis would encourage intuitive action from a place of no-thought, because clearly, at those speeds, the process of thinking is just too slow. Looking on as the movie-goer, it dawned on me that it is possible, indeed desirable, to live completely 'empty-minded' and be successfully guided in life by the inner pull (the one I'd been feeling). To live from the heart, the place where The Absolute and our unique expression of The Absolute - our soul - meet...

The inner pull comes from the heart - the heavenly meeting place where the wave of higher consciousness enters this plane of existence as the soul. The heart guides us on a path of self-realisation and spiritual evolution, leading to Enlightenment, and after that, on a pathway of ever higher vibrational harmony. What gets in the way of divine guidance is the ego - identification with the bodymind - shaped, conditioned and contorted by the constraints of daily life. If however, you can surrender the ego's doubt, fear and disbelief, you feel the inner pull of the heart guiding you on a pathway, which yields everything in life. Specifically, you get what you need, in order to be who you truly are. It won't necessarily give you what you want, or more accurately, perhaps what you think you want, but it will give you what you need.

The realisation immediately projected me back, to an experience revealing the ego to me at the age of 15, whilst working on a building site in the summer holidays. The images were now flashing before me and materialising into form.

Our senior sensei, Neil, was an expert in breaking techniques and had quite recently explained the philosophy behind it. One might quite reasonably ask why anyone would want to break a masonry tile, piece of wood, block of ice or a house brick? I guess the answer is the same as for many things, when you have trained and developed in a particular practice or art, you wish to explore, test and express your fullest potential. Looking on as the movie-goer, I wondered, that if there is one hundred percent belief in yourself and what you are doing, is there a need to test at all?

The act of intentionally testing your beliefs means you don't truly believe at the deepest level. If you don't believe, you send that vibration out into the Universe which then manifests and limits your delivery of Right Action. You interrupt the flow and limit your fullest potential. However, 'testing your beliefs' is not to be confused with authentic expression of the soul, which is the purpose of life itself. Expressing yourself, in its purest form, without needing to prove anything, leads to complete self-belief, complete belief in The One.

Suddenly I find myself on the building site again, as the teenager, stacking bricks in a secluded corner, when the flash of inspiration lands to try to break one. I feel very confident *(the kind of confidence that goes with naivety!)*. I support the brick on two others, and then begin to concentrate the mind. I am sure I can do it. I'm just so convinced in the teaching and leadership of the senseis. Inspired by them, I completely believe anything is possible.

Using the 'hammer blow' technique I'd been shown, I clench my fist and focus on a point just below the bottom surface of the brick. Now I imagine the brick isn't there (looking on, I'm amazed at how literally the brick has disappeared!). There's crystal clear clarity in my mind that I will deliver a perfect technique to that particular point in space. I breathe deeply, background noise quietens into silence - you could have heard a pin drop. I raise my fist a few feet above the now empty space. I steady myself, and then unleash instantaneous downward motion. That's all I'm focusing on: immediate, explosive action. In the next instant, I feel my hand kissing the surface of the brick, and a strong sensation of heat ripples from the surface, back through skin and bone, but incredulously, there's something missing - there's no feeling of striking anything hard. It's as if the brick has literally disappeared.

Now, as the movie-goer, I watch Chris' hand passing through the brick as in some illusionist's trick, until it falls in two halves on the ground. I look on with smiling eyes at the teenager, whooping and pounding the air, exhilarated by an endorphin-induced adrenaline rush. Chris the teenager had conquered fear *(at least he thought so!)* and the shadow of doubt, no inconsequential achievement at such a young age. However, this newly acquired self-belief was about to be severely tested.

Unknown to Chris, a fellow builder had seen the event and was completely bowled over by it. This was the 1970s and martial arts were not commonly known in the west. You simply didn't break house bricks with your bare hand! The colleague looked on with an expression of curiosity and utter amazement. Back in the drama again, I feel him enthusiastically clapping me on the back. He drags me over to the site office to demonstrate this amazing feat to our fellow builders. Soon word had spread around the site, and within ten minutes, I have an audience of about 30 people. As the movie-goer watching the incident from a far, I wondered why did I subject myself to such a display?

At this point in your life, like many, your "inner child" contained a reasonable degree of self-doubt caused by the perception of too little unconditional love in your childhood (in this case from your father). This manifested in your actions as approval-seeking from peers and elders, often causing you to seek centre stage, even if it didn't feel right.

Looking on as the movie-goer, I could literally feel the sense of lack as a tightness just below my belly button *(your sacral chakra)*. And now, back in the movie, a brick is chosen and propped up between two oil drums. In looking on, I see that although I felt uneasy, inner personality distortions dictated that I couldn't disappoint the crowd and resolved in my mind that if I'd done this once, I could surely do it again.

From the movie-goer's perspective, I knew a tough lesson needed to be learned, and as the naive youth, I was now about to learn it.

As I hit the second brick, the experience is now vastly different. As flesh impacts the surface, inwardly I instantly acknowledge its hardness - unmovable and unflinching. A searing heat is unleashed though my hand as the bones and ligaments compress against each other. As the movie-goer, watching now in slow motion, I notice the striking hand take on a strangely fluid dynamic - like blancmange - and I wince inwardly, my face contorting as if I'd tasted a bunch of sour grapes.

Back in the movie, the brick on the other hand, is completely unmoved by the experience! Needless to say, the onlooking crowd take the side of the brick, bursting into raucous laughter and wailing wildly, whilst Chris crumples inwards, looking desperately for a quiet corner into which to crawl. As bad as it is, the pain from my bloodied and battered hand is unable to drown out the suffering internal chatter of a badly bruised ego.

Miraculously, nothing was broken, except my sense of self-esteem and pride. I could clearly see how it served to cement an element of self-doubt, deep within my psyche, for many years to come, that would always rear its ugly head when on the verge of some great success. As for my continued time on the building site, I was instantly christened "Grasshopper", after the student Caine, in the hit TV series "Kung Fu". I became the butt of everyone's jokes for the rest of my time there. I saw how this was a great introduction to the importance of humility!

As I now reflected on the incident, I wondered what had been the key difference in trying to break a brick the second time? As I had come to discover, with the benevolent help of the presence, no question ever arises without its corresponding answer...

My dear friend, in trying to impress the crowd, your spirit was identifying with the material phenomenon of matter itself. You were wanting to shape the brick, their attitude to you, and your attitude to yourself. In this space, before you'd even raised your hand, you'd identified with the mass consciousness that knows bricks are harder than hands. Also, more importantly, your inner need to impress was identifying yourself with the idea that somehow, you are incomplete and less than who you really are - the inviolable One. As your hand struck the surface of the brick therefore, the initial feeling of its hardness was relayed along your nerves to your brain whereupon, in your mind, the doubting aspect of your soul accepted your material reality rather than your spiritual one. Your consciousness was diverted into the condition that knows bricks are harder than hands, and you manifested that as your truth.

Although I as "Grasshopper" deeply regretted the incident, I as the movie-goer did not, for I had received important guidance on something of deep relevance, which can both help and hinder us all – self-doubt. And what's more, I could actually locate the centre of it, inside me.

How does your intuition tell you to work with that now?

I feel into it - the sense of self-doubt. I realise I haven't fully accepted myself, which is why I've needed the acceptance - approval - of others. But now I know my inviolable connection to Source. So I focus on that, and feel it, like a still lake, with unfathomable depth, in my sacrum. Wow.

Is that not amazing?

In my early years, self-doubt ensured that I became ultra competitive, and on the surface quite successful – it's what spurred me on, after many had fallen by the wayside. I featured in the school football, rugby, rowing, swimming and athletics teams and was chosen as House Captain and Head Boy. However, through all this, I was so keyed up with winning, or trying to win, that I never actually enjoyed the experiences themselves. During the events, although raging passion and commitment ensured I was generally successful, in actual fact, I rarely performed as well as I knew I could have done – as I came later to understand, the growing burden of tightness mostly prevented free flowing fluidity of action.

This is what lack of self-esteem can do. Even though in this case it was compensated by the all-in, raging passion of commitment, nevertheless, self-doubt was what prevented the greatness in you from breaking through. It consigns many people to mediocrity.

Eventually I overcame sufficient self-doubt to attain the coveted Black Belt in Karate. As the movie-goer, the award ceremony was now taking form in front of me. A beaming, Black-Belted student receiving the accolade from another of my early childhood heroes - the Karate Union of Great Britain's top sensei - the lion known as "Keinosuke Eneoda". He was an 8th dan Black Belt and everyone both loved and feared him.

He was austere, disciplined and tremendously powerful. Despite his austerity, he had a ready smile and a great warmth to him, all of which made him extremely popular and respected. He died suddenly at his peak, from cancer. The world of Karate was shocked. Despite his 68 years, he was in such great shape. As I now reflected on it, I realised all thought is powerful, and if we live our lives expecting an enemy to be around the corner, then somehow, we will manifest what we expect, but perhaps in the way we least expect it - the enemy within. It occurred to me that his death had many parallels with that of Bruce Lee...

It was his constant striving for self-perfection that inadvertently caused him to identify with perceived non-perfection. It is right and aligned to work for continual self growth. However, this is meant to unfold naturally, from the place of completeness, where the soul originates from. If, on the other hand, you are efforting to achieve this sense of completeness by something you achieve in the outer world, or something you gain mastery over, you form an identity around your own internal darkness – your own sense of lack. In the end, for both men, it was these inner demons that delivered the killer blows.

An image of Gichin Funakoshi, the founder of modern Shotokan Karate, now floated into my awareness. Somehow, he allowed inner perfection simply to unfold, rather than striving for it. He ended his life much as he had begun it - a humble peasant. It was not until afterwards that his efforts truly flourished into the global phenomenon that Karate has become. Funakoshi applied his philosophy to all aspects of his life - it is tremendously liberating not to be affected by what others think or say about you. It is tremendously liberating not to judge yourself, or need to be more than you really are, right now in this moment...

You've got to find a harmony and balance with effortless commitment. You're looking for perfected expression, something that just feels 'right' in the moment. Yet even though you're continually improving, or working to improve, there's still the sense of completeness from where that expression arises. The true winning is unleashing the perfected expression itself. This leads to joy and harmony as you move into perfect balance with yourself and life.

As if to prove the point, I'm now flashed forward to a Karate Dojo, standing face to face with "Mo", another menacing Black Belt. The kumite (fight) is about to begin, and I have assumed one of the lead roles. A class of 30 looks on with keen interest. The atmosphere is electric. Something is distinctly wrong though, because everything is blurry. I can only just make out Mo's black, heavily-muscled form, in his ghosting white Karate suit. As the movie-goer, I wonder what's going on? Why can I not make him out properly? How am I going to fight if I cannot see? How can I have any possibility of even defending myself, let alone winning? I search my memory bank. Ah yes, this is that amazing evening where the Universe in its infinite wisdom has decided I should leave my contact lenses out. I found myself now becoming the young, keen, and partially blind, martial artist.

Blind in more ways than one!

One of my contact lenses had fallen out, and broken, right before the session and yes, I am now facing one of my worst nightmares, unable even to see the whites of his eyes.

Although at the time, I didn't hear words from higher consciousness, looking back, I could see that my energy was sufficiently heightened that I could feel their vibration, which somehow, then found their way into my inner knowing.

In a time of heightened tension, awareness greatly increases. But this can only happen where you actually overcome fear and identification with the moment - where it's not owning you. You then break through by softening internally into connection with your soul, and its flow 'downwards' from the infinite potential of the Source.

So I realise the vibration of the word "surrender", which the Universe has provided, but not as a thought, rather as an inner feeling. I also understand that the feeling means that I should surrender my fear, but not to surrender to fear. Besides, short of high tailing it out of the door, I didn't feel I had a choice!

You were in total surrender, with no choice but to follow the flow.

I'm now in the body of the warrior again, gloves off, as "Ajime" (commence) is called. I notice the instant the 'A' of the word Ajime begins, time slows way down, and a subtle movement of energy wells up from my dantien (pelvic region), with which mind engages. I could easily ignore the feeling, as I'm sure most so often do. From the place of internal surrender however, it is sufficient to initiate movement forward and sideways to the left. Effortlessly, without thought, I turn back through 180 degree toward the centre, as Mo's flying sidekick shoots straight past my nose, missing by a whisker. Now Mo lands in front of me, his back completely exposed. My body and being already know what to do, they're already moving, as if this dance between us has been already written in the annals of history. My body moves, hips initiating the first impulse, and now the fist places itself, where it's meant to be, a controlled blow to the base of his spine. It's an "Ipon" - a "knock out". The bout is over, seemingly before it has even begun. Both me and the audience are now frozen in stunned silence: no one has ever scored a full point against Mo.

The true lesson here is that you surrendered all ideas about what you should do because you had no other choice. You couldn't fight your way out. You couldn't control the moment. You directly confronted the truth of the moment, softened into it, and became absolutely vulnerable to the natural flow - what the universe wants to happen. You're breaking through the physicality of the moment, and thus begin to feel the subtle vibrations of Right Action internally, flowing down from the Source. Most are too engaged in thought and efforting to notice - they're too tight inside to feel it.

I would like to think I took no pride in the victory (*yeah sure!*), but that didn't stop me turning up to the next Karate session full of eager anticipation, seeking to build on my new-found skills, and of course, minus my contact lenses. As a keen Black Belt, I had never been grounded by a Yellow Belt (beginner) before, but as I completely missed the sweeping leg kick of my opponent, I remembered there was a first for everything! I was dispatched unceremoniously onto my backside, to the sound of raucous laughter from onlooking colleagues.

Bemused, I wondered why my new-found intuition had so easily eluded me? I didn't get it at the time. But now, as the onlooking movie-goer, watching together with the presence, clarity was emerging through ego's misty veils...

Intuition is much misunderstood, which is why people so often think it has failed them. Crucially, it is not something you apply with the mind in order to get the outcome you want. You're connecting up to the natural flow, the one that embraces all, from the tallest mountain to the lowest grain of sand. And it wants the same for all – a chance to realise and express something deeper about yourself.

"So intuition leads not to the outcome we would necessarily want, but one that is in keeping with our destiny of self realisation...?"

Yes, exactly. It is a common misunderstanding when people read of so-called 'miracles' and the abilities of 'masters' to seemingly shape the Universe through the power of their own will. In truth, they were simply being a vehicle for the Right Action of the Universe to unfold.

In this case, with all your new-found power, you needed to learn about humility – that in your highest truth, you are a servant to the divine, and the whole of life. As for the other guy, just like you many years before, he needed to overcome fear, and know that with such Breakthrough, literally anything becomes possible.

Later, I would study quantum mechanics at university, and I realised how it offers perhaps the best scientific explanation of how such 'miracles' are possible. It has taught us that there is no such thing as matter as we might conceive it. The concept of solid matter is an illusion, consisting instead of packets of energy called 'quanta'. Each string of quanta is linked to every other in the Universe. The human body consists of quantum energy vibrating at a particular frequency. It can be likened to a wave moving on a universal sea of energy. According to the 'Heisenberg's uncertainty principle', these quanta only exist as matter when they are observed by something. The very act of observation brings them into being from the surrounding universal energy field; our minds are continually creating our physicality in every moment.

It is as if we are living in a hologram of light, a dream, and when we walk through the dream, the light is crystallised as matter by our thoughts and beliefs. In other words, we make the dream real. The problem we face in trying to purposefully manifest miracles, is that every movement, touch, sound, taste that we experience, reconfirms in our subconscious minds, the erroneous view that we consist of solid matter, that everything around us is separate and cannot be shaped by our consciousness alone. Unconscious awareness recreates the reality we have come to expect.

You're making subconscious judgments about how you have come to expect reality to be. And those judgments make it real for you.

An image of myself as a baby cradled in the comforting arms of my mother suddenly flashes onto the 'cinema screen'. I can clearly feel how I am making no distinction between myself and my mother. All is experienced as one. And as I grow, "I" - as the soul - become increasingly conscious of my body, learning how to influence the mind to cause movement to happen...

This is no easy skill to acquire, especially as the mind itself is only just beginning to develop.

Looking on, I notice how I receive great help (and also much hindrance) from the people around me. In witnessing the way others move, I acquire a model of what is possible. I learn that what one person can do, I too can do, and so I acquire all the motor skills of those around me. Gradually, over time, my evolving mind takes control, which my soul acquiesces to.

With the acquiescence, I can see how, like most people, I lose the ability to create without limitation. My mind steadily becomes a prison, created from other people's fears and limitations. Of course my parents are only seeking to protect me from accident and harm. So, as with every other baby, I learn how to move the body in particular ways. I then relate to this limitation, learning what I can and can't (supposedly) do (like breaking house bricks!). This belief is reinforced over countless limiting experiences, and thus begins our descent into a matrix of ideas, restrictions, control dramas, limitations and taboos, which prevent many of us expressing our full creative and divine potential in life. Initially the soul doesn't override what the ego wants, because it identifies itself with those desires. As the soul progressively breaks through this illusion however, it acquires, over time, the ability to project itself completely into all cells of the body and all aspects of the mind...

As this happens, you're progressively infusing the moment, through your physicality, with the unswerving belief and knowing of The One – the soul being a flowing expression of The One, a place of infinite potential, where literally anything is possible.

Many people question and doubt the miracles of awakened masters such as Jesus, and yet there are hundreds, perhaps thousands, of people on the planet today, capable of performing miracles like some he is reported to have accomplished. Orthodox religion would have you believe that such masters are somehow apart from the ordinary and are 'special'. Indeed Jesus was special, but no more special than you are.

Just like you, he was ordinary - awesomely ordinary! He didn't come to take your sins away; he came to show you that through the process of spiritual breakthrough, a path on which you are all embarked (whether you know it or not), you can all shake off the shackles of limited physical experience and become the expanded divine beings that you are. You no longer accept the limitation thrust upon you. It then becomes possible to create a new narrative.

These realisations were just too enthralling for words. Reflecting back, I could see how I'd become ready to challenge life's apparently obvious limitations. And as the movie-goer, I'm just brimming with excitement of the journey to come. It's now landed within me... literally anything becomes possible - Yeehah!

Pay attention to that feeling. Harness it inside. It's immensely creative.

Shaking off the shackles of limited experience accelerated for me as I left school and entered university. The movie rolled on next to the dreaming spires of Oxford, the university of countless aspiring dreams.

5

Black and White... and Shades of Grey

"ALL experiences, the good, the bad and even the seemingly ugly, are reflections, pathways to divine inner stillness, which in truth, is the ultimate experience of them all."

Images of an 18 year old now materialise at home, standing nervously by the front door, like a cat on a hot tin roof. In my sweating palms, a letter of monumental importance has just arrived. In my truth, at this moment, it offers either the doorway to my hopes and dreams or alternatively, a sudden plunge into hell. Initially, it didn't even cross my mind that I would be good enough to go to Oxford, one of the most prestigious universities in the world. If my two closest friends hadn't already been accepted, I probably never would have applied. In my interview however, the Gods were once more smiling and somehow, the right answers to the right questions just appeared, as if out of the blue.

When you're doing the right thing, that which is aligned with your soul and the flow, although the path is not at all easy, at the right time, things will click magically into place for you.

There were many times I reflected on such 'miraculous events' in my life, and even though I may not have been awake at the time, I somehow knew in my heart, that there were forces much greater than my own mind that had opened doorways for me. This was one of those supreme sequences in one's life, where everything clicked magically into place. God or no God, you just knew it was meant to be.

Divine synchronicity however, is quickly buried under the avalanche of daily thoughts that go on within a sceptical mind, so even though I just know in my heart a place at the university is mine, nerves are still jangling as I fumble clumsily with the letter. My mind instantly focusses in on the word 'congratulations' - sufficient kindling to ignite a spontaneous combustion of wild, uncontrollable dancing and shouting, which, like a raging fire, ravages everyone else in the house too! It might have read, "congratulations, you've been accepted to serve in the college bar." What a let down that would have been!

When you look back, when you regress into the feeling, what do you notice?

I can feel the excitement, the uncontrollable energy. Which feels great. But I can also see I'm blind in it. There's no sense of presence.

What had you lost?

"My intuition tells me in one word - oversight."

Yes, a crucial aspect of the soul, which keeps you connected to the here and now, is that sense of oversight. You're in the experience, but you're also watching yourself in it. You need that oversight to continually align yourself with the right expression - the rightness - of the soul.

Now looking back as the movie-goer, at my pride and pleasure having being accepted into Oxford, I marvel at how I'd been just as much a prisoner of good fortune, as of bad. I'd been searching all my life for external experiences of wholeness and harmony, when the true flavour of these could only ever be tasted inside...

ALL experiences, the good, the bad and even the seemingly ugly, are essential to gain the fullest taste of life. Yet at the same time, they are still only reflections, to the state of divine inner stillness, which in truth, is the ultimate experience of them all.

A moving collage of early 'successes' and 'failures' now flashes through my mind's eye in quick succession. I see how easily I'd been seduced and then identified by them. The inner revelation landed, that along with everyone else, my being had purposefully created every experience of my life, in order to realise that the only thing of true and lasting value is the divine inner state of grace. Looking on, tears of joy are now welling up inside me again. I'm sure I've found the key to the prison of my mind, the door is being unlocked, I'm breaking through into the light. Even feelings of regret at my years spent in the wilderness dissolve as the lyrics of a favourite song comes to mind:

"You have to go there to come back!"

Time now advances a little, to the moment I announce my success to my two dear friends. The three of us are sharing a car to college, and I, as the movie-goer, now watch on, as the good news precipitates a surprising, deathly hush. Although only a few moments in duration, it seems like an eternity, until they're able to summon a half-hearted attempt at congratulations.

In my heart of hearts I know of course that my success has, in their eyes, devalued their own, but if I had acknowledged and accepted that at the time, what would it have meant for our friendship? At that stage, it was an avenue down which I had no desire to travel. I was still living in bliss, what need had I of the painfully obvious truth to spoil it?

Many people's self-esteem is gained only at the expense of others. Yours was a classic archetype accounting for countless so-called 'friendships'. Many people live in relationships, not of mutual empowerment, but mutual dependency and limitation. Energy is all too frequently gained at the expense of others. And so often, it is with those who are seemingly closest, where it happens most of all.

In looking back, I readily saw how I wanted them to like me and accept me. I couldn't see that for this to truly happen, I had to love myself, be accepting of myself *(warts and all)* and be totally comfortable in my own skin...

It's only when you can truly believe in, and accept yourself, that you can give unconditionally and be a true friend to another.

Once more I feel to focus on the point below my belly button, on the spine - the sacral chakra. Again I feel an unwinding warmth of self-acceptance through it, which eases it a little, but this time, disappointingly, it won't fully go.

Put your attention in it and work with it. What happens?

Suddenly, glimpses of different characters flash before my eyes, each morphing quickly into the next, like a movie in fast forward, so I can't immediately recognise their faces. There's a school boy winning acclaim for some sporting success, a playground bully impressing his will on others, a smart-suited businessman manipulating other people for his own ends, a guy chatting up a girl in a bar in front of his friends. Now the presence is helping me see the flow of energy as light. In each case, the personalities are draining the energies of others and of their surroundings. They are like energy vampires.

We've all experienced such people. They are seldom genuinely interested in you or your story. They turn conversations in the direction of subjects that interest them, not you. They cannot empathise with you because in truth, they cannot really feel you. If they offer love, it is frequently conditional - they want something in return. If you allow them to, they will drain you of energy very quickly and leave you feeling cold, hollow and tired. It's not their fault of course, they, like you, need help to fully realise the completeness already inside of them.

Then, suddenly, in that moment, the faces all focus into view, condensing down into one face, just one person. It's shocking - they were all me!

I wonder how I'd succumbed to taking other people's energy away from them? I wasn't a bad guy, just a regular one really.

It's because you were not fully accepting of yourself and generally, the society you live in is the cause. From the newspapers, TV soap operas and best-selling titles, to politicians, teachers, priests and police, society has made a virtue of inter-dependency, which in truth, is not mutually supporting, but mutually disempowering. If we are completely content to be who we are, we wouldn't need anyone to accept us, to support us, to be friends with us or to love us. It is only identity, or rather our identification with identity, that needs these things. Without such identification, we don't need anyone to accept our point of view. This brings with it breathtaking freedom. And most important of all, it means you can truly be friends with another and truly love them unconditionally.

I was saddened at how I'd been. How I'd let myself and others down.

Do you realise you were only behaving that way because of the conditioning of your past and upbringing? Can you forgive yourself?

"Yes - I get that - it's not my fault, but it is my responsibility to put it right."

And it can only begin with self-forgiveness.

So I go deep into the sacral chakra, reflect upon some of those places where I'd controlled others for my own ends, realising it only happened because of the sense of lack. "It's not my fault!" I yell out with deep soulful passion..."I forgive myself!" And now there's that unwinding sensation again, and a deepening sense of coming back to me, of coming home.

The presence was opening my internal floodgates as deeper realisations continued. It's because we've taken other people's energies ourselves that we can ultimately know how and why it happens to us...

The way to perceive whether someone is stealing your energy, is to always to be in complete internal awareness - to have oversight - always watching if inner peace is beginning to dissipate. Each time it happens, it's because someone or something has pushed your internal buttons. In other words, an attachment for a desired outcome within your personality has activated: a conditioned mental, emotional or physical reaction, over which, you have no governance. You are no longer behaving authentically - your alignment with the soul has been lost. This is what is de-energising. And in truth, no one does it to you. You do it to yourself. No one takes your energy, you give it away.

As the movie-goer, I could now see how vitally important it is to have this 'oversight' - to be continually aware of one's thoughts, feelings and energy, always watching which internal buttons are being pressed, whilst at the same time, being consciously engaged in the interplay:

Tightness will get activated, but oversight is the key. It provides the possibility to unwind and break through into the expansiveness of the soul. For only then, can action arise authentically from the Source.

In that moment, I simply knew there was nothing to fear from accepting and surrendering to the truth of the moment. As I now look on, accepting this, I'm connected deeply inside with my feelings. I can feel the acceptance opening me up, and like some great gordian knot, steadily unwinding itself. Suddenly the simple trust to accept, has landed within me.

The sense of relief is indescribable.

You could call it "Breakthrough!"

6

Stepping out of the Looking Glass

"It's that unmistakable energy that brings people together and unites them as one. It's called 'love'."

The renowned Oxford professor has now just made a grand entrance. In his inimitable, flamboyant style, he strides purposefully through the audience of spotty northern chemists (as we were affectionately known) and draws a large artistic 'G' on the blackboard. "What does that stand for?" asks the professor as the audience descends into a reverent hush. At first no one dares break the silence until a bright spark from the back chirps up, "Gibbs free energy, Sir." "NO Sir!" bellows back the professor "It stands for the garbage people write about it!" The lecture theatre explodes into raucous laughter. It was one of the lighter moments in a discipline that, could at times, get a touch boring and intense.

Back then I was much less concerned with Physical Chemistry in the labs and much more interested in practical chemistry with the 'fairer sex', which Oxford seemed to possess in abundance. Right back in it again, as a young man, pumped full of hormones, I'm finding it seriously hard to concentrate: how can you do that, when your dream vision is sitting on the row just in front of you?

How amusing! Free energy is the natural underlying pull to increasing harmony within the Universe - or as you were discovering, particular aspects of it! It's that unmistakable energy that brings people together and unites them as one. It's called "love". Not surprisingly, you'd rather experience it at first hand than hear about it from some dusty old professor!

Suddenly I found myself swirling into a ballroom dancing class, landing there with a heavenly angel in my arms called Nicki. My friends and I had quickly tired of the college bar with its near constant drunken rugby raucousness. We'd gone on a quest for a more divine nectar. What we needed was an environment with the feminine touch.

So between embarrassed smiles, bruised toes, rose-tinted cheeks and cheap Chanel perfume, love poured between the spaces of the instructor's staccato guidance: "forwards two three, left two three, feet together two three." Smoothly harmonious it may not have been, but through the awkwardness, there was no denying the imperishable flow of sweet scented softness...

Ah Yes! What a beautiful introduction to universal chemistry. No matter how barren, hard or infertile the environment, love flows unceasingly. It matters not if the surroundings are constricted, nervous or tentative, the soft and forgiving rhythm of life will break apart any awkward resistance. Just take a look at the softness of water, how it moulds, shapes and shatters even the hardest granite.

Abstract concepts of ordered flexibility and formless form begin to swirl through my mind. On the one hand, there is the orderedness of lectures, tutorials and laboratories; on the other, sweaty freshmen's discos, champagne and strawberries on a sunny afternoon punting down the river Isis. As fumbling fingers grasp at frustrating buttons and stocking tops, the rising tide of testosterone sweeps any attempt at centredness mercilessly away. As the feminine veil drops tantalisingly before my eyes, it seems internally, another veil is being added...

Trying to remember it's all just an illusion? At that stage, it's practically hopeless! And why not dive right in and let the current sweep you away? It's only after you've been completely swallowed up in physicality's fervent rip tide, that you may one day, find yourself again, washed ashore on some inner desert island, abandoned, all alone...all-one.

The problem I could see, was that at the time, it was all over far too quickly. The sense of expectation, the burning need to dive right in, to be swallowed up and fulfilled. It meant I literally couldn't contain myself. And as the movie-goer, I could sense the lack of satisfaction for my surrendering partners too.

The paradox is, that if you can stay centred, already in the completeness of which sexual climax gives you a physical sensation, then sexual intimacy lasts much longer and you enjoy it more. In this way, it's one of the most enchanting evolutionary practices.

"How do you make that a reality?"

Breakthrough of course! You have to realise that The One inside of you is the solution to everything. It is the question and the answer, the beginning and the end. If you start there, then experience flows from you. Within intimacy, it builds as a sense of energy, with which, by attention, you can fill all of your bodily cells. It's like dancing on the blade edge of life: you're in it, but not lost in it. It means sexual release becomes a choice. You're no longer owned by it.

"I only wish I'd known that earlier!"

It's never to late to begin.

But then, I'm wondering what's the point? If you've reached that inner state of perfection, what need of sexual intimacy at all?

Who's here to deny the experience? Only an ego resists the life that unfolds before them. Tasting of the physical is not the problem. Being lost in it is. And sexual intimacy is one of the most powerful ways of evolving spiritually - at least as much as formal meditation. Because you're constantly dancing on the edge of identification, and as you release, if you stay focussed, powerful flows of kundalini energy are unleashed through your being and that of your partner, which you can channel into higher dimensions of awareness. When processed correctly, loving sex is like riding a rocket into the heavens. And it can last for hours.

Fortunately, despite the alluring distractions, I did attend enough chemistry lectures to discover quantum theory and a universal life energy known as the "Zero Point Field (ZPF)". I learned that it is so-called because the energy exists even at the absolute zero of temperature (-273 celsius), where previously all life was thought to cease. The energy even exists in a vacuum. It is thought that matter exists as a kind of energetic 'soup' formed of 'quanta' - little packets of energy. Quanta manifest as matter from the ZPF when observed by conscious awareness *(you and I for example)*. When not being 'watched', the matter dissolves once more back into the ZPF, then existing everywhere and nowhere...

You're held in place mostly by your conditioned beliefs, which create a matrix of thought, emotion and feeling. You walk on the floor and it feels hard and solid. You hear footsteps, feel the weight of your body, touch someone's hand, feel the wind on your face, it seems real. But what is real? All these things are not really things at all. They are simply vibrating energy that your brain interprets in a particular way.

As the floodgates of truth began to burst wide open, the question arose *"how do we see objects?"* Well that is simple, I thought - light illuminates something, which is then reflected into our eyes. The images are focussed by the lens and cornea onto a 'photographic plate' at the back of the eye called the iris. From there, the images are converted to electrical impulses, which then travel along the optic nerve to the brain...

And then what happens?

"A good question!"

We don't see objects in our separate minds at all. In other words, they are not recreated separately from the external world somewhere inside of ourselves. That's the mistake traditional science has been making. Rather, we are existing in a unified hologram of light - a dream of the one Seer, through which we, as apparent individuals, then walk. As we proceed through the dream, we encounter apparent objects; in essence, they are nothing more than translucent images in the dream. However, our collective experiences, conditioned from the very moment we were born, tell us the objects are real. Since the experience of matter shapes from awareness, the illusion is manifested in our brains and bodies as what we perceive to be 'solid' and 'hard'. And so the dream becomes 'reality'.

The penny was dropping. Thought connected to feeling is now rushing through me. Finally, I'm beginning to understand in an experiential way, the earth-shattering implications of what my Oxford professors had been trying to convey. Now I'm looking all around me at the objects in the office: the ceiling, the walls and the floor, the desk in front of me and the seat I'm sitting on. They're not really objects at all, but characteristics of life. Each characteristic, hardness for example, gets cemented in our consciousness creating a virtual prison cell as real as iron bars and concrete. But it becomes possible to break through all that.

"Eureka...!"

You are bombarded with billions of snippets of information about your reality every second, but you can only process a small proportion of these. To deal with the overload, the brain superimposes a map of the reality it has come to expect over the incoming information and then filters out the rest. In other words, it discards the vast majority of the incoming information. In this way, you make the reality you expect, real. However, in truth, you are only experiencing a wafer-thin slice of reality. That is until you delve more deeply. The Universe is just a mirror by which to know yourselves. You spend your lives efforting and manifesting material goods and experiences, or failing to, when not one jot of it matters at all. You have to step out of this looking glass to discover what is really real.

The words *"just let go"* now flash into my mind as the movie-goer. That's exactly what I'm doing: unfolding from within myself - by regressing into the experiences, I'm steadily discarding the belief system that has been programmed within me. My soul is literally yearning to expand out into the infinite possibility that I can become.

You are now beginning to experience yourself as the "Seer", existing in and through all things. When you don't identify with the 'little you' inside, the 'limitless you' breaks through and arises effortlessly outside to fill the Universe. You are no longer someone 'in here' looking 'out there'; you are 'out there' experiencing everything 'in here'. It feels like crystal clear clarity. Eventually, you are so beyond identity, it feels as if no one is here at all. The pain will still feel real within the 'little you', and you cannot escape it. However, suffering due to the pain, is entirely your own personal choice, depending on the degree to which you identify with it.

I was becoming increasingly enthralled with my trip down the rabbit hole of reality. It took me deeper and deeper into age-old questions about our absolute authentic reality such as the nature of the big bang, supposedly from where it all began...

It is not easy to see the truth through the filters of life's conditioning. Contemplating nothing for example, is not straightforward, especially since the mind has ALWAYS known something.

I wondered if there was a point in contemplating the beginning at all?

If we continually challenge what we believe to be real, then eventually we break through ideas and concepts into The Absolute - a miraculous taste of the supreme being. That is worthwhile!

So looking on, I now open myself up, to allow in a new understanding of how it all began...

Before there was something, nothing was everything. This condition is what Science calls "Singularity", but we can also call it "Unity". According to probability, there were two possibilities for what might happen to Unity: it could either stay as it was or subdivide into parts of itself. Because at this point, time and space were limitless, there was an infinite probability that both possibilities would happen. Therefore it is certain that Unity would divide up. This condition we can then call the "Separation".

The instant Unity divided, awareness emerged - awareness is the divide. Consciousness then happened, which is simply the awareness of a difference between one thing and another, where in this case, 'thing' is simply a flow. It is also known as "spirit" - it is an experience of something going on. So, at this point, what you really had was not Unity and Separation, but "Unity Consciousness" and "Separation Consciousness".

Once Unity had thus separated, there was now nothing to prevent it from further subdivision. According to probability, an unstoppable chain reaction was sure to ensue, resulting in the "big bang", although a more appropriate description might be the "big flow outwards". What we can still see of the big bang is merely what is going on in 'positive time space'. In other words, what we witness in the physical Universe.

Now since the flow outwards came from nothing, it must also be balanced by an equal and opposite flow back inwards. This happens in 'negative time space' what you might refer to as 'quantum space'. It is as if The One is both breathing outwards and inwards simultaneously.

To better understand this, you could envisage the Universe as a pond. If you, as The Absolute (The One), cast a pebble into the centre, then ripples will flow outwards. Or at least they appear to flow outwards. In fact the water is not moving outwards at all, it is only the disturbance that is moving. The water particles are simply moving up and down. They don't move anywhere because there is an undertow pulling them back to the centre. The two forces are balanced. So in the material sense, that which is above the surface of the pond we observe as a flow outwards to ever-increasing separation - what science calls 'disorder'. We witness the effect in the physical as the 'every man for himself' syndrome. Beneath the surface of all events is the opposite - the organising draw back to Unity. Science calls it 'increasing negative entropy', although as you discovered in the irresistible pull guiding you through ballroom lessons, 'love' is probably a much better definition!

Now back to the big bang, where the return pull to the centre caused the separate parts to gather in clusters. In other words, Separation Consciousness got denser - it condensed. Over billions of what you have come to know as 'years', gases formed, which then condensed as liquids and solids. Planets took shape and then life on the planets. Thus we witness what Darwin referred to as evolution. All the while, there was, and is, a driving force pulling the parts back to Unity. This Unity Consciousness evolved into an intelligent life force, now shining a light through the entire Universe, guiding us all back home. Our souls are each a unique vibrational harmonic of that light.

Some scientists would argue that no such intelligence exists, but Darwin himself said that for his theory of random evolution to be completely accurate, there would have to be evidence of one form of life slowly evolving into another over generations, but nowhere in the fossil records do we see any evidence for this. There is, for example, no record of something approximating to a horse gradually forming a longer and longer neck over successive generations until it became a giraffe. You either have a horse or a giraffe, but nothing in between! When you consider the billions of different species on the planet and their corresponding fossil legacies, isn't it strange that there hasn't been ONE DISCOVERY of a missing link? Quite apart from that, mathematics confounds those who lack the trust in a guiding consciousness. There simply hasn't been enough time, enough generations, of random step changes to form something as complex as a human brain, for example.

WOW! Practically all my grown life I had wondered how to explain the creation of the Universe. Was it created by God or not? Now I found myself just sitting there, staring at my hands. Finally, I know the answer... I am God! God is in me. Just like God is in You!

Hallelujah!

My mind was now unravelling at a speed of knots. In this realm of infinite possibility another question quickly arose in the form of a quote from the Matrix: "everything that has a beginning must have an end", which led me to ask, "if God began in this way, then surely it must also end?"

And herein lies yet another paradox. Our problem in contemplating the beginning and end of God, happens because we are considering The Absolute from something that is only relative - the mind. In other words, we are contemplating something which is even beyond the limitation of space and time, within a mind that knows ONLY the limitation of space and time. That's why all words and thoughts merely point to doorways through the mind. We have to step through the doorway to direct experience. We cannot postulate absolute truth, we can only experience it. Once we provide a definition of what God is, we are simultaneously creating what God is not - I can only have 'this' in the presence of 'that'. That's why as The Absolute, God has neither a beginning nor an end. However, the relative, which arises from The Absolute, has both a beginning and an end.

"So if God has neither a beginning nor an end and is everything/ nothing simultaneously, then surely God cannot be experienced...?"

Yes.......and no! You have to work to hold two apparently contradictory truths simultaneously in your mind.

"I'm not sure I can do that!"

It's not easy in the beginning. The ego likes and depends on a singular truth - in this way it justifies its very existence. Holding two contradictory truths simultaneously is very destabilising for the mind.

"It sure is!" As I contemplate it, it feels like the foundation stones upon which I have built my reality are being steadily stripped away. It feels like my mind is turning to blancmange.

When there is experience at all, that which we are experiencing is not The Absolute. It is an experience which ARISES from The Absolute - either Unity Consciousness or Separation Consciousness or a combination of both. At the same time, the divine paradox means The Absolute CAN BE EXPERIENCED, within and throughout the dynamic equilibrium, as a total LACK OF EXPERIENCE.

With this revelation, distinct unease and tightness wash through my head. My mind wants to realise, and hold onto, a concept. I have not yet fully integrated the idea of me as infinite potential; I still need some form of identity to relate to. I find myself fast-falling over a cliff-edge, and each time I think I have something solid on which to grasp, it turns out to be just another flimsy straw...

For there to be experience at all, there has to be relativity - I know 'this' only in the presence of 'that', but The Absolute is the all of it, therefore it is neither 'this' nor 'that'. So The Absolute can best be considered as infinite potential before experience even arises. It is like trying to grasp a helium-filled balloon. The more we grasp, the more we push the balloon away until one day, we stop grasping and the balloon gently comes to us and with that, the full beauty of our awesome magnitude.

"Can it really be that simple?"

Just consider the experiences of your life. As a soul, you begin by believing you are separate from all things, that everything happens by chance. People try to shape the circumstances of their lives to be more happy and content. The more you chase, the deeper into the Separation you fall. You become more and more attached to experiences, the need for love, joy, fulfilment, success etc. All these circumstances have just one purpose: they are divinely configured each with an underlying pattern, a hidden code, inviting you to surrender the attachment, release inner tension, feel once more the Unity Consciousness flowing through you, and thereby you're brought back home, as a wave, within yourself, onto the welcome shores of The One - The Absolute.

Exactly as revealed, I could see the patterns in my life continually reoccurring. I had been continually repeating the same mistakes to show me precisely to what I had become attached - where I was getting tight, where the ego was taking ownership of the soul. However, because I previously had no awareness of the mirroring phenomenon of the Universe, I had simply no idea this was going on. I only subscribed to a reality of chance events to which I should react. I had never at all contemplated that I was shaping my own reality according to the attachments I held inside...

It is when you notice this, that you have the possibility to transcend your attachments and let go of them. How many people get divorced blaming the other for their problems in the first place? How many get remarried just to repeat the same mistakes? The underlying truth through all circumstances is that you fail BECAUSE you are trying to capture an experience which cannot be captured. It can only be experienced as the total letting go inside. That's why people get addicted to things like alcohol, drugs, food and sex, because within each is hidden that easily missed experience of completeness. Since completeness is also nothingness (because nothing is everything), you struggle to accept nothing as the cause of your experience, attributing it instead to the object of your desire.

This was making superlative sense to me. The apparently separate pieces from the jigsaw representing my earlier life were now clicking magically into place and I was increasingly able to let go of self-identification. I could see that in truth, I was The Absolute, and that all experiences in my life, had arisen in patterns inviting me to relinquish an attachment – to *break through* perceived needs causing me to identify with the flow towards increasing separation rather than increasing unity. Then the question arose, if I do let go, will there still be an experience that is uniquely me...?

Consider it this way. A sailor is lost at sea in a small sailing boat. He's run out of food and water, there is no land in sight and apparently not even the slightest breeze to propel him. He is alone facing his certain death. With the realisation of his imminent demise, he gives up efforting and struggling inside. He notices the sun beating down on his face and then the faintest of breezes gently kissing his cheek. The breeze was always there, but he was too engaged with internal thoughts, needs and fears to notice. He had become too desensitised to feel it. Something within him - his very soul - urges him to align the boat with this faintest of breezes. His mind rejects the notion - "it's not strong enough to carry me anywhere." The soul however is very persistent, especially now that it can finally be heard above the din of daily internal chatter. Eventually, even though the sailor is dying, he surrenders to the pull of the soul and aligns the boat as best he can with the direction of the breeze. Sometimes he misses the breeze by a fraction and the boat stops once more. But he keeps working to pick it up again. He becomes completely engaged in the process of steering the boat on the right course, so much so, that he forgets his problems.

Correspondingly his sensitivity increases, and he finds that he can align the boat with increasing accuracy. With each new increase in sensitivity, he notices that the breeze grows in strength. It is almost as if the breeze is responding to his awareness of it. The breeze gets stronger and stronger until it becomes a wind, blowing the little vessel along at a tremendous pace. The wind becomes so strong, that he can hardly feel where it ends and he begins, so drowned out are the ideas and troubles he was previously dealing with. Then something truly miraculous happens. He notices he is no longer the sailor inside the wind, but he is the wind with the sailor inside.

And then, not even that. Finally, he realises he is the sky, with the wind blowing through it.

WOW! I could see it fully. It made absolute sense; everything clicked into place. There was no question - I wanted to become the sky with the wind blowing through it.

For the first time in my life, I felt truly free.

7

Walking down the
Blade Edge of Life

*"It is the very key to a life of complete fulfilment:
being totally present in the moment,
but not at all lost in it."*

Suddenly I found myself in the stroke seat of a fast racing eight. It's early morning on the river Isis, the sun is rising gloriously over the meadows; dew is still clinging precariously to bending grass, and the river is lightly shrouded in cloaking mist. I'm leading the crew, all eight perfectly in time, as one with each other, the blades echoing a crisp 'chunk' in the quiet hush, as they slice into the water and a 'whoosh' as they leave, the crew floating deftly forwards across the finely balanced shell, readying for the next stroke. One of the great benefits of leading the crew, is that you get to see past the cox, to the glass-like water and the ripples gently bubbling from the stern, as, like a deep morning breath, the boat rises and falls with each majestic stroke. At Oxford, I had discovered a renewed passion for rowing, a sport I'd been deeply seduced by in my earlier years.

This was pure heaven. To be able to relive such breathtaking power and harmony, but now as the movie-goer, in full consciousness.

How does it feel to be experiencing that?

"There's just such a sense of rightness to it. It's like destiny expressing itself here and now - like I'm being what I was always meant to be."

Get to know that feeling in your life. It's where you're touching the soul, fulfilling the purpose of your life. It's sheer ecstasy.

We were preparing for the "Oxford Bumps" races. So called because crews start one behind the other, the challenge being to literally bump the boat in front. In so doing, your crew ascends one place in that particular division. My college was "Head of the River", meaning we were top of the first division, a position the college had successfully defended for seventeen consecutive years. We were doing some full pressure work across the course, readying ourselves for what we hoped would be another victorious conclusion.

Reflecting back upon it now, I saw how achieving success in rowing had become a burning ambition, because I could taste the excellence in it. I could feel the intense exploration of a deeper meaning, a deeper purpose of life. This was a powerful step, yet still, back then, excellence was associated with some material outcome – some big 'win' to affirm the feeling.

There's the snag. Authentic feeling, experienced truly as The One, needs no particular affirmation, no victory or 'big win'. It just is.

The glamour of the Oxford Bumps attracted many thousands of people to the riverbanks, which greatly added to the sense of occasion. It was a party-like atmosphere; we felt like movie stars. Champagne and strawberries, bustle and chatter, waving and cheering from the river banks, heroes and heroines. To anyone seeking peer acceptance, it was pure nectar. And yet as I looked back now, on race day, it was the darkened stillness of the boathouse we sought - a quietly focussed atmosphere to unwind rapidly knotting stomachs, dissolve bubbling emotions and to calm increasingly jangling nerves.

As the movie-goer, I could clearly feel why the quietness most appealed. It was the unvocalised camaraderie of the crew that meant most to me... *people who empathised with you - who recognised your pain.* Before the race, we shared in each other's unspoken fears, away from the bustling madness, like soldiers preparing for battle. Spiritual or not, you just knew we had been here like this, many times before...

My dear heart, when you engage yourself in life's deepest passions, you seldom realise you're reactivating the karma of past life experiences, recreated in an entirely new environment. The purpose is the same though: to delve deeply into those moments where you lose yourself, where you allow the external illusion to dictate your absolute, aligned expression of truth. It is only by reliving your nightmares, that you can truly realise it was all just a dream!

Suddenly there's an explosion of light and noise as we emerge from the boat house, heads bowed, desperately avoiding the crowd's deeply questioning gaze, fearful of what the inner inquiry might unfold. As we step up to the water's edge, expectation and the crowd's crazy desire is heaped on top of already pumping and yielding hearts. Like the Light Brigade before us, to me, it felt like riding into the valley of death...

That's your karma for you. It's a filter, through which you uniquely perceive reality. It makes events like these take on a much greater personal significance.

I found myself sitting at the start, cradled in the river Isis, the cox holding a 'bung line', keeping us positioned close to the bank, 30 or so other crews stretching out into the distance behind us. We were the head crew and it was their job to catch us - if they could.

So as to increase the sense of occasion, the Bumps Races are started by a cannon *(charge of the Light Brigade indeed!)*. The final countdown has now just begun. I can hear the chasing crews' coaches calling time from the bank, but now, my focus is centering in our boat. The time has come… "30 seconds," our coach quietly sounds. I notice the over-accentuated calm in his voice - he's been here before too. "Come forward," calls the cox. Everyone slides forward together, adjusting their final positions, relaxing sweating palms. "20 seconds," "Touch her bow," the cox straightens us in the stream. "10 seconds," "Square your blades," it's the last we'll hear from the cox as we engage the swelling tide of the water. "5 seconds," all goes quiet, everything moves into slow motion, you could have heard a pin drop. "Three," eternity has a limit, "Two," the moment has finally arrived, "One," a deep intake of breath…

"Boom!!!"

Muscle and fibre take the strain, the boat begins to lift, gently at first, like an Apollo rocket, packed with high octane energy, and yet ever-so-slowly lifting from the gantry. We surge forwards for the next stroke, gulping in air as the boat accelerates. It's a good clean start, we're pulling together as one, the nerves have dissipated; we already feel like we're riding a wave of invincibility.

Wow - now you're sending the shivers of God up my spine!

After only a couple of minutes into a race, legs are burning as lactic acid builds and the lungs are screaming for more air. Somehow, one has to learn to deal with the pain in order to continue to be effective, both as an oarsman, and as a member of a finely-balanced and integrated team. I had, by now, become intimately acquainted with pain and I had so far, discovered two distinct ways of dealing with it: you can either try to ignore it completely and hope that it goes away *(but it never completely does)* or, you can bring your attention right into the heart of it and focus on it intently. It's like you learn to revel in it, until you can even begin to like it…

There is of course a third way. That is to be present with the pain, to go deeply into it, so it becomes your experience, whereupon, you cease to define it. It's like you're finding it extremely hot, yet rather than seeking cool, you become the heat, with no separation from it. That way it stops owning you – there's no 'you' to be owned.

"I'd never considered it that way - becoming as one with the pain, so you make no definition of it. It just 'is'..."

When you stop defining it inside yourself as something undesirable, you become The One in it - pure, unadulterated presence.

As if to prove the point, I found myself back in the race, passing the Boat Houses, well clear of the opposition, the boat flowing like poetry. The crowds are cheering wildly, and the Oriel supporters are chanting their customary support - "Ooorrrieeelllll." Despite the pain and the noise, the sense of stillness is overwhelming. The chanting of the crowds is quietened by the crisp 'chunk, whoosh' of the blades entering and leaving the water, my eyes are glued to the ripples flowing out from the hull. There's no escaping the burning fire in my lungs and the aching tightness in my legs, but something is eclipsing all of that now. No, it is not the sweet scent of victory, it is something indefinable, something much deeper than that. Although I was not ready to understand it at the time, nevertheless, I had discovered how to touch this blurring edge of reality...

Finding yourself on the blade edge of life is, without doubt, one of the most exhilarating experiences possible. It is the very key to a life of complete fulfilment: being totally present in the moment, but not at all lost. I put it to you, this is the experience that is the quest of every soul's journey. And more, everything that one might seek in the external mirror of life, is but a dim reflection of this true light – this Breakthrough - that which souls are really seeking.

"Wind down" calls the cox, deliriously happy, whooping as he punches the air. We've won! Any need to manage the pain is suddenly cast aside, the mission has been accomplished. Now you're floundering, lungs are burning, like a fish flopping around on an uncomfortable bank.

From the movie-goer's vantage point, I notice the energy of my soul being sucked right back into identification with the illusionary reality once more. Firstly, there's the burning pain, which intensifies as the need to manage it ceases. Then, as the worst of this subsides, it's quickly followed by the great joy of victory...

How easily the God within you falls from grace! The serenity of non-attachment is so readily drowned out by your experiences, both the painful AND the joyous.

Looking on, the sense of revelation was stunning. I'd experienced nothing like this. I realised it had been the finely balanced sense of stillness, inner peace, and absolute serenity, which I'd been really seeking my entire life - walking down the blade edge of experience - drinking it fully in, but without ever being drunk. I had been gifted some tantalising moments, only to have them disappear frustratingly from my grasp. Clearly, I had associated the serenity with the joy of winning and therefore sought to win more often. Yet the more I tried to win, the further from the truth I receded....

Whoever said, "It's not the winning that counts, but the taking part?" He was a very wise person indeed!

I now understood wholeheartedly, that to take part in the realisation of who we are, is winning indeed. As I looked on the now jubilant victory scene, from the movie-goers vantage point, I simply knew, in every cell of my being, that self-realisation was the ONLY victory worth having...

Always work to penetrate your experience into the abode of The One - of pure presence. This is always the real victory to be won.

Our success on the river set a new record and the Oriel Boat Club had a traditional ceremony for celebration. As soon as the crew crossed the finishing line, bottles of champagne were tossed out to us whilst still afloat. As I downed the fizzing bubbly, I could still feel my heart pounding at around 200 beats per minute, whilst at the same time, gulping in huge quantities of air. Needless to say, the mix is an explosive one. Any possibility of revisiting the curious experience of serenity and calm, on the blade edge of life, quickly vanishes, like the disappearing spot on a switched off TV screen. I was right back in the matrix once more. Sadly, the next few hours pass in an alcohol-induced blurry haze, with little real connection to true experience. As the movie-goer, tears of sadness begin to well up.

Don't worry – you've got to go there to come back!

Now I'm witnessing a collage of hazy images: the crew, accompanied by our rowdy supporters, collecting an old boat and marching it along the towpath onto the High Street and back to college, jubilantly blocking most of Oxford town centre in the process; then I'm witnessing a carnival, flags waving, Oriel supporters cheering and somewhat bemused shoppers wondering what on earth was going on; now the boat is being carried into college and smashed to pieces on the central pathway inside the first quad; next, as evening falls, I'm seeing a raucous "bump supper", the boat then set aflame; and, after the fire has taken a furious hold, the first crew linking arms, jumping joyously through the flames, this being the climax of the ceremony...

What a shame this heartfelt 'joie de vivre' was drowned out by alcohol!

It took me a long while and many races to realise that like any drug, alcohol disturbs the fine inner balance of consciousness. It may open you up at first, but as you come off it, the after-effect makes it ever more difficult to connect with the subtle feelings of the soul, and thereby completely missing the delicate beauty of the moment - *the real moment.*

As the movie-goer, I found myself flashed forwards, lying helplessly drunk on the ground, just as one of the crew loses his balance and falls on top of me. I have just enough remaining presence to reach up and put my hand out to stop him. However, as he falls, my elbow hits the ground, my hand bends backward, past the point of no return, until there is a loud "Crack!" as my wrist snaps. There's no pain though, I am completely anaesthetised by the alcohol. That is until morning time, where now the dull throbbing seems to fill my entire Universe.

Sometimes you just have to learn the hard way!

I was deeply upset, because it seemed like I would be out of rowing for some considerable time. The doctors in Oxford advised me that it could be up to eight weeks before the plaster would come off. This was devastating because I was fully intending to do Boat Race trials for the University later that year and a good performance in the summer bumps races would be essential. Selection for the crew commenced in just four weeks!

Yet again, the Universe was kind though *(it's always kind when we care to follow it's guidance)*. 'Coincidentally,' before the accident, I had watched a TV program encouraging continued use of broken limbs to stimulate more rapid healing. So contrary to the doctor's advice of extended rest, I spent many hours squeezing a squash ball and still used the broken arm in my daily life, as if nothing was really wrong. From deep within, I found the inner resolve to dispel the idea that I would not recover in time...

Within the cellular memory of your body lies the consciousness to heal quickly. It is only uncontrolled minds that create dramas around injury, locking yourself into a new illusion, which then becomes reality. However, if you choose not to identify with this illusion by not giving in to it, you ultimately settle into a state of being that is awesomely okay with it, and then the mind no longer interferes with the body's miraculous healing processes.

It's another wonderful example of Breakthrough - you're confronting the truth of the moment. Becoming awesomely okay with it. Not letting it define you as something lesser. So you bring the light of your soul into the drama, a light that knows the inviolable completeness of The One that you are. This, you then manifest, as your healed - aligned - reality.

"Wow, that touches something deep inside. I can feel the incredible majesty of The One in me - it's immense, creative potential. I feel humbled by it."

That's often the response - a quiet, reverent humility.

There was some considerable pause to bask in this eternal sense of everythingness - a quiet completion, the answer to all questions.

When you're there, it feels like everything is fulfilled!

Some while later, back in the movie again, I had gone home for the Easter holidays, still carrying my broken arm. But a quiet determination was working to overcome it *(actually you were already learning to transcend it - to penetrate through the injury)*. So I kept on training, running every day, and even working out with weights, although being very careful. As I looked back on it, I perceived how open-mindedness and acceptance, coupled with determination, were positively affecting the healing rate. Three weeks after the accident, I was advised to visit my local hospital to see if the break was setting properly. I'd been given a new type of plaster, through which, it was possible to x-ray, so at the hospital, a couple of shots were taken. To the utter astonishment of the nurses, the break had completely healed, in a mere fraction of the usual time...

In your endeavours, you'd diminished your fears, doubt and disbelief by becoming as one with the experience - not allowing it to define you. Unknowingly, you were touching the abode of The One - inside yourself - and thereby unleashing its incredible reordering, healing power.

The plaster was removed, and the next day, I went out rowing. Although the tendons and ligaments were sore at first, I persevered, and within a week, I was back to full power. In my eagerness to get on with training, the miraculous truth of the body's incredible self-healing power, brought on by my connection to the infinite potential of the Universe, was quickly lost, as other priorities took precedence. Once again, like so many of us, I had been gifted a miraculous taste of the divine – *an incredible Breakthrough* - but had failed to see it.

However, as I looked back with the movie-goer's eyes, with tears welling up and heart near bursting, this divine revelation of God was no longer lost on me.

8

Turning Victory into Defeat

"It is not about 'winning' or 'losing'.
If we see life as a continual process of self-realisation,
we can all win all of the time."

As the journey down memory lane rolled on, I found myself once more in the stroke seat of a racing eight, the heavy green Thames water rippling under my blade as I nervously await the call of the starter, "Are you ready?" I glance across to my right, the 'enemy' in light blue, eight sharpened blades glinting in the sunlight. This was the start of the Oxford Cambridge Boat Race in March 1985, the culmination of many months arduous training. A fellow crewman once calculated that for every stroke completed in the race itself, more than 3000 are taken in preparation. I was beginning to relive some of those moments now.

Two years earlier, where the venue was the icy-cold Putney in London, Boat Race training had begun in earnest, a commitment of Olympian proportions. The selection program was the brainchild of head coach Daniel Topolski, a tough but likeable man of Polish descent, who had won silver for Great Britain in the World Lightweight Rowing Championships. His humorous and cocky demeanour concealed the will of a wolf, who'd just scented the kill. He enforced a gruelling regime of five or six hours per day, seven days a week. When we were not on the river, we were either thrashing tired limbs around the running track or pumping iron in the gym. Most of the rest of our lives were spent recovering from the previous training session. Needless to say, studies mostly went by the wayside. At first I felt guilty, until I realised I was not there for a degree in chemistry at all, rather I had come to find the truth about myself in the crucible of high-intensity sport.

Well at least by that stage you'd discovered more than most. There is nothing – ever – going on but self-realisation. Degrees come and go, relationships come and go, careers and even lifetimes, but one thing lingers throughout: what you have, or have not, realised at a soul level.

Fifty or so bushy-tailed hopefuls show up for trials, but initial enthusiasm is pounded into dust by the onslaught of near constant physical, emotional and psychological stress. International and novice oarsmen alike are reduced to tears as the punishing regime takes its backbreaking toll. Within a few weeks, the number is axed to form two equally matched eights and a crew of reserves. Clinging on by the skin of my teeth, I had escaped the first cut and rowed with the 'also-rans'. The problem for me was one of size and power. At only six feet and eleven stones I was quite diminutive for an oarsman, and could have easily rowed lightweight. Despite Topolski's own lightweight background, he was sold on the doctrine of size and strength. To him, the best way to achieve boat speed was by way of long limb levers combined with muscle mass. Consequently, most of the important selection tests favoured the big guys. What seemed less important was the skill with which their power was applied. Despite our differences, I saw Toploski as a great coach, and since he had presided over an Oxford winning streak of 10 years, it was definitely not my place to argue with him. As I now reflected back on the dynamic between my own physical limitations and Topolski's preference for size and strength, I see that the seeds of my own undoing were sown at an early stage...

All too easily, people let others' judgments form an illusionary reality and thereby limit their capability. Everyone is unique, with unique capacity applied in a unique way. If you allow others to put you in some kind of box, you risk never finding your greatness.

As I looked on as the movie-goer, with the benefit of higher perspective, I could see my biggest mistake was the one which so many of us seem to make in life - trying to be something we are not; allowing the truth of who we are to be influenced by mass opinion and dogma. In my self-imposed mission to be a heavyweight, I piled on the pounds to increase body mass and strength. Although this worked to a degree, I came to realise too late, that my power to weight ratio, and thereby my effectiveness in the boat, was quite drastically reduced as a result. Many motivational gurus today would say that you can be whatever you want to be, and there was a time when I might have believed this, but as I looked back, I realised how delusional the idea really is. It creates a world of the False Self, a bubble, which at any moment is likely to burst...

Better to discover and unfold the dream you were meant to live, rather than that of someone else you want to be or by whom you've been influenced. See the reflection yes, but embody you, not them.

It was now mid-winter, shortly before the December trials fortnight on the London Tideway. I'd picked up a dose of food poisoning and was off sick for several days, during which time, I'd lost nearly a stone in weight. Upon my return, although I had expected to be quite weak, it turns out the reverse is true. To my great surprise, my run times are several minutes faster, and most importantly, I feel much sharper, both in the boat and the gym. Looking on as the movie-goer though, I can still feel the conditioning, like a ball of knotted knitting in my head - neural pathways that have conditioned me to seek bulk and power. And so, lack of self-belief and self-acceptance ensured I returned to the false path of weight and strength...

The Universe uses its awesome creative will to shape events, revealing what the best pathway for each of us is. It is conditioned behaviour patterns however, that often divert people down the side-roads of life. It is then that we give in to fate, rather than embrace our true destiny. Become who you really are. Then the Universe will always provide you with a vehicle through which to express.

Despite my ignorance of the Universe's guiding hand, brute determination ensured that by the beginning of December, I'd edged up the rankings and squeezed into the top twenty.

You can sometimes successfully override the true purpose of the moment... but only for a while!

'Success' in rebuilding weight and strength granted me the dubious pleasure of attending the infamous December and January fortnights. These were selection training camps, spent on the Thames at Putney, during the Christmas holidays and were what can only be described as 'ball-breaking', with training lasting from early morning before sunup, to the darkness of evening twilight. Once more I'm back there in the boat, muscles aching, body stiffening in the wintry coldness, just as a wave of chilling water swells up over the bow and washes shockingly down the back of my neck, literally freezing the shirt on my back.

It is especially when you put yourself out, when you're prepared to explore to the extreme, that the possibility of incredible Breakthrough can occur. Spiritual mastery is not a building up process at all. It is a ball-breaking, shattering, breaking down process. Which is only a problem when there's still 'someone' inside resisting, trying to hang on and 'win' something.

This shattering process yielded a pecking order, from which, the Blue Boat and Reserve Crew (Isis) were eventually chosen. The climax of the training was a duel over the Boat Race course itself between two equally matched crews formed from the top sixteen. The race is a fiercely contested trial of courage and commitment, four and a quarter miles of gritty hell. Each oarsman gives their all, keen to impress the gang of selectors and pressmen, following in their wake in a flotilla of small boats, like an unruly gaggle of geese.

It is now the night before the race, and I am in my hotel room chatting to Mike who will be stroking one of the eights. Mike is a superlative athlete, at the very pinnacle of International Rowing. He consistently comes near or top of all the Boat Race tests. He is sharing some friendly advice on rowing stroke, when suddenly the door bursts wide open, and in walks Graham, the Oxford President.

Graham is an engaging but humble Aussie, with a ready sense of humour. With a broad smile, and big slap on the back, he announces one of the key guys has food poisoning and, "Chris, it's your lucky day - you'll be stroking one of the eights tomorrow." At first I thought he was kidding, except despite the laughing smile, he was deadly serious. Yet another amazing synchronicity (which I didn't get at the time), ensured that two guys, who barely knew each other, had shared a room - one, perhaps the best stroke on the planet, advising the other, an aspiring hopeful, when the next day, they would be duelling it out, head-to-head, in one of the most gruelling competitions on Earth.

Nothing happens by chance! You too are a great stroke - that's what the mirror is telling you. But if you truly want to express your own greatness, give up copying others. Witness the reflection, yes, but then do it your own way.

The Universe had presented me a golden opportunity: in one moment I was not even in the race, in the next, I was stroking one of the eights. The stroke seat is a thrilling place to row, and yet is probably the most technically difficult. You cannot hide in the stroke seat, you cannot slacken for a moment since this would be clearly conveyed down through the crew. In Mike, I sensed an amusement with the news, like a cat playing with a mouse before the kill.

For the rest of the evening he continued to advise me, with an ever-so-slightly patronising air. To him, the race was already in the bag. In looking back as the movie-goer, I was somewhat irked by it.

That's totally understandable - greatness lies in everyone, not just the Olympians of life. Find your way, what feels right, and express that.

This touched me deeply, knowing that in their own way, everyone is special. It eased my irritation.

Back in the 'race', I don't think anyone that day considered the unthinkable was at all possible - that I could lead my crew to victory...

To the Universe, it is not about 'winning' or 'losing'. If we see life as a continual process of self-realisation, we can all win all of the time. That isn't to say we shouldn't care about the outcome. It isn't to say that we shouldn't give of our best, for it is only in the absolute commitment to caring that we discover it ultimately doesn't matter.

The moment of truth had arrived with both crews lining up next to one another on the cold, blustery Thames, 18 minutes of pain the daunting prospect. Finding myself once more in the boat, I'm curiously relaxed in the feeling that we don't stand much of a chance. Therefore, what have I got to lose?

The truth is, if you're not competing with another, there is nothing to lose and with that, there is no tightness to spoil the performance.

The event turned out to be a real corker. Geoffrey Page writing in The Telegraph, described it as a "bonecrusher of a race". Actually, although it was close and keenly contested, for me, it was a beautiful experience - one of pure poetry.

As the movie-goer, I found myself now back in the race, occupying the familiar stroke seat. Predictably Mike attacks really hard off the start and so his crew take an early advantage. Conversely, an inner voice keeps telling me to ignore the opposition and find a consistent rhythm that can carry us through. With no expectation, nothing to win or lose, I settle into a rock steady rhythm, which, like carriages behind a locomotive, the crew clicks in with me.

The boat is literally humming. There's the crisp 'chunk, whoosh' of the blades echoing cleanly across the water, as all eight enter and leave perfectly in time. Swinging together, attention is keenly focussed within our own boat. We're relaxed, doing our own thing, expressing ourselves, come what may. Mike, on the other hand, launches attack after attack, like a bulldog with a bone, desperate to cling to his slender lead, frantically raising and lowering the pace. It seems the more we can hear their struggle, the deeper we sink into our own effortlessly sweeping rhythm. As I find myself looking back down the stern of the boat, to the gaggle of reporters following in our wake, all I can now see - what stands out a mile - is the open-mouthed face of Dan Topolski. Normally a vociferous man, he is deathly silent. I find myself thinking... Yes, even he can witness pure poetry when confronted with it!

Ah yes. So it is. The perfection of the Universe. Totally unpredictable, and yet recognisable to all, even through the thickest rhinoceros hide!

Coming into the home straight, Mike's crew still holds a slight lead, but we still have a resounding rhythm. Internally, disbelief and self-doubt have long since dissolved into quiet inner confidence. Anything is now possible. I can feel that timeless place once more, that hallowed void, that respects no champion or previous history.

It's a place where literally anything can happen.

And in my mind I know, I simply know, that Mike and his crew are there for the picking. I know in my bones the race is already ours. From the place of complete stillness, I feel the words "turn up the pressure" gently, but very positively, float into my awareness, which I convey to the steering cox. There was no need for drama, "Right Action" is about to happen - an ordained event, just as natural as the sun coming up in the morning...

If you can confront the trials and tribulations of your life, those that make you really tight in some way, perhaps because of fear or anxiety, then you open a doorway through the experience. Whatever is going on, how ever ego is owning the moment, beneath it all, 'rightness' just wants to happen. It is positively bursting to break through.

My crew could scent the 'kill'. As crude as that feels to me now, nevertheless, that's how it felt at the time - it seemed to have some sense of rightness to it. I looked across at Mike and he looked back at me. In the moment our eyes met, we both knew it was all over - a done deal. Fixing my gaze back down the stern of the boat, I called our first and final push - it would be all that was necessary. With that, the boat rises majestically out of the water like a swan taking to flight, surging on the unquenchable wave of absolute self-knowing. The pain of burning lungs and aching muscles vanishes as some distant desert mirage. This is our moment of truth. This is our destiny waiting to be expressed. We literally power past Mike, whose crew are by now at our mercy. We romp home comfortable winners. And as we cross the finishing line, exhaustion quickly gives way to jubilation, but quietly and with respect - they are, after all, our brothers.

Internally I was ecstatic. It felt like I'd proved something. Since arriving at Oxford I'd longed for a victory like this. News would quickly reverberate around my college and others across the university would take note - "this guy was someone to be reckoned with". It was clear - peer acceptance was still very much on my inner menu. But at least, looking back, I could clearly now see, the incredible dynamic of soul Breakthrough, which happens to many, before getting quickly swallowed up in the ego again.

Consider it this way: throughout the Universe, light is infusing the darkness. And right on the edge, in the twilight, are many grey areas. Now the macrocosm manifests through the microcosm as individual souls. Some are born to work within the twilight zone, as are many on Earth right now. And breaking through is the forging of the soul. You have to get lost, in order to truly find yourself. But fear not, one day you will not only Breakthrough... but stay that way.

"That may well be the case, but when you're in it, it sucks!"

That it does!

9

Dreaming Spires,
Aspiring Dreams

*"The paradox is, that in this profoundly unattached state,
you'll create miracles and magic beyond your wildest dreams."*

Indeed my rowing success did make an impact with those at my college. I suddenly become quite popular and a bit of a celebrity - *a legend in your own lunch time!* chipped in the presence, as we both laughed out loud. Previously, at my college, I'd been very much of a loner - no surprise really, with the rowing, I was hardly ever there. So I had just one good friend, a charming Scotsman called Bobby. He was a great guy, full of friendly banter and witty repartee - he could keep you entertained for hours on end. Consequently, he was a popular guy at Oriel and his room was often buzzing with all kinds of interesting people and social antics. It was during one of these days, in his room, that I was to meet another person that would have a big impact on my Oxford life, an extraordinary lady called Cassandra. Suddenly, I found myself once more on a journey into the fantastical and ancient, the staid and the revolutionary, the old and the modern, for Oxford was a place of superlative contradictions. It was like a portal of paradoxes.

Just like all of us, you were being shown time and again the mirror. Who are you really, this or that? What serves you? What is your highest truth? It's all about exploring the black and white choices in life and finding your own uniqueness in the grey areas in between.

As the movie-goer, a streaming photo album of images passed before my eyes as the inspiring, exciting and thoroughly intriguing chemistry of Oxford began to course once more through my blood stream. I may have spent a good deal of time looking down the stern of a boat, but the sheer majesty and wonder of Oxford certainly did not escape my attention. Suddenly, together with the presence, I was floating ghost-like around cobble-stoned streets, walled by gothic cathedral sandstone, peering through leaded and stained glass windows, spying on high with carved stone gargoyles. There was the stiff-collar formality of oak-panelled dining halls, adorned by dusty portraits of fellows gone by. Mortar boarded and black-gowned students revelled through college quadrangles, the formality being well and truly pierced by young-blooded joie de vivre...

How wonderful contrast is. The serious with the sublime, the superlative with the diminutive. It lets us know that to give life true purpose, we must really give it energy; we must really care. And yet if we care too much, we get attached and drain the very juice out of it.

Yes, Oxford was a place for living. A place of self-consciousness for some and self-mastery for others. A place of exquisite finery, frequently drowned out by boorish drunkenness. Evening dinner began sedately and religiously with the latin grace "Benedictus Benedicat..."

Bless, O Lord, us and your gifts,
which from your bounty we are about to receive,
and grant that, healthily nourished by them,
we may render you due obedience!

I found myself back there again as a handful of roast potatoes winged past my head and splattered on the wall behind. Someone else was striding up the middle of the table, tipping over dinner plates and wine glasses. But it was all okay, all was in order, because we were wearing dinner jackets and black-tie! It was as if Bacchus and the Angels were locked head to head, permanently poised on the knife-edge of battle, and God only knows who would win.

It was in this heady cocktail of charged energy that I met Cassandra ("Cass" as everyone knew her). It happened late one morning, after lectures and just before the afternoon's rowing session. I'd taken a detour to Bobby's room on the way to lunch. He was there with his roommate, who we affectionately knew as "Boiledcake" or "Cake" for short, after the packaged gifts his doting mum frequently posted to him *(if only she knew!)*. Standing with them is Cass, an attractive blonde with a razor-sharp wit and wall-to-wall smile. Bobby introduces me... "This is Chris, the man who strokes Isis", "Really?" smirks Cass, "and what do I have to do to stroke Isis?" Cake and Bobby cackle in unison, I just smile inwardly. Somehow, I can pick something up that isn't immediately obvious. Confident, and at times almost crushing, but what is it I can feel behind those eyes?

It's like anyone who comes out fighting, there's always something that provokes them, pushing them on.

"Vulnerability. That's it. In this case, a carefully concealed insecurity."

You should know that well. You can always pick up those resonances, because when you do, they're reflections of you.

Despite distinctly different backgrounds, with greatly contrasting social status, there was something that united us. Looking back on it as the movie-goer I could feel it once more in my sacrum (my sacral chakra).

Insecurity mostly comes from a lack of unconditional love in the formative years. Perhaps a parent who didn't quite fulfil on unspoken expectations? Over time, you learn no one can replace the requirement to find unconditional love for yourself.

Tears welled up, with a sense of loss and deprivation - some sense of tragedy that I'd missed out on something essential.

How do you feel to fully honour and express that pain of deprivation?

Immediately the question curls up into a ball on the floor, into the foetal position. It intensifies the feeling, causing the sense of loss to flood through me and out into the room. I'm there for some time, before I can once more feel the presence breaking through the emotional mist.

Never forget, love is always there my friend. It never went away. Look inside your heart.

So I go into the heart, and feel the sense of love for the Universe, for the incredible sense of benevolent presence I'm now beginning to feel again. The light once more ignites, and the healing warmth spreads through me. I can feel my sacral chakra unwinding and opening.

After some while, although tentative, I'm ready once more to re-immerse myself in the movie.

Cass and I were set to become very close friends indeed - allied by the mutual sense of loss, of something missing. Only three days later, I was lamenting to Bobby how I had no girlfriend to take to lady's evening the following night (Oriel was an all male college), when low and behold, just a couple of hours later, in my college post box I find an invitation. It's in the shape of a greeting card, a woman arm-wrestling a man and winning. Inside is an invitation from Cass... to my own college guest dinner! The presence and I looked at each other, thinking exactly the same thing: Yes, she had balls!

So began a beautiful relationship that was to last through the rest of my Oxford time. She was the daughter of an aristocratic mum, and famous author father. And she had two highly charismatic and humorous sisters. As a family, I had never met anything to compare with them in all my life. They were highly educated and erudite - warm, charming and friendly; silver-spoon with top-notch table manners. It would be easy for anyone harbouring self-doubt (like me for instance) to be self-conscious in their presence. When they occupied a room, they filled it, and everyone loved them; we became their theatre audience, watching respectfully from the 'cheap seats', while they hilariously engaged us with their witty repartee.

Cass' parents separated when she was a young teenager and although they stayed connected, nevertheless the pain of loss was clearly evident. We may have been from wildly different backgrounds, but this we had in common: the burning desire to prove oneself, caused by perceived lack of love from a father-figure...

It's what inspires so many people to so-called 'achievement' and success. It's the perceived sense of lack that spurs people on.

From time to time, we would go to stay with her mum and dine with her two sisters and socialite friends. In the beginning, I felt like a fish out of water. This was a place of code and etiquette, a social minefield, with faux pas exploding frequently twixt knife and fork... was I holding them properly? In an atmosphere of educated and humorous banter, I found myself with little to say, so out of place I seemed. As I regressed back into the situation once more, I could feel all manner of tightness in my bodily field – especially my throat – it was as though someone had a stranglehold on me.

That's what self-consciousness does. It causes the soul to attach to a needed outcome, becoming stuck in consciousness exchange points called "chakras" - what are they thinking of me? This makes people tight on the inside, unable to be relaxed and respond authentically.

Somehow though, I learn to surrender. It seems I have so little to offer, I'm not witty and humorous for example, so why bother? Steadily I let go within. Steadily I unwind, shedding the self-consciousness.

Looking back on it, I can literally feel my throat chakra beginning to expand through the experience. It deepens the tone of my voice, harmonises the resonance. And when I speak, it seems I have much more time, and with that, confidence.

Yet again, in an entirely different 'arena', you were breaking through. You were learning to confront your feelings in the moment and unwind through them. At times, it was coming naturally to you.

And so, overtime, the social dynamic changed for me. It appeared Cass' family friends became somewhat intrigued by me too. As I looked back, I could see they longed for the straightforwardness that I presented. With no airs or graces, and unable to prove anything to this socially skilled group, I discovered bit by bit, from pure surrender, how to sit back and just be. What was the point of projecting anything and trying to be clever? With their educated minds and witty repartee, they reminded me of fencing duelists, who, with their pinpoint accurate foils, would score ten points before you even had time to pick up your fork. The warrior in me knew when to surrender...

You were learning the greatest gift of all: to become awesomely comfortable in your own skin, which arises from the discovery that you have nothing whatsoever to hide or prove. When you can do this, then you can sit quietly in silence and your 'words' will speak so loudly, everyone will be fascinated to listen.

My education at the hands of Cass and her family unlocked many important keys for me at Oxford. Up until then I had felt quite insecure about my standing in the world. About seventy percent of Oxford's students in those days were from rich, public school backgrounds. They seemed so confident and accomplished. Yet with Cass' help, I could see how many of them were every bit as vulnerable and insecure as I had been; it was just that in the schools of Eton and Harrow, they'd been taught to cover it up well...

Yes, you can learn how to put on the mantle of self-confidence, but in truth, it is only ever really paper thin. True self-belief on the other hand, comes from becoming totally vulnerable to the moment –

breaking through the need for it to be any particular way or even to be accepted. When you can be prepared not to conceal all, but to expose all, then you will soon discover there is nothing to win and nothing to lose. Then, there is nothing that can be above you or below you, better or worse. Nothing that can be taken away.

Looking back as the movie-goer, the feeling was wonderful. It was like sitting in a bath tub of soothing self-acceptance!

After a welcome pause, back in the movie, my growing romance with Cass became an emotive force for me in the years that followed. We were lovers and the best of buddies. She showed me how to confront public school small-mindedness. Everyone had a weak spot and she knew exactly how to find it. She seemed to know instantly how to burst someone's illusionary bubble of self-importance. We fought the Oxford class war and became utterly invincible. We laughed in the face of the system and turned the upper class upside down. I was rapidly stripping away many insecurities and loving every minute. We were like revolutionaries ready to take on the world. Steadily, but surely, the skies were opening up. How big was my dream for life?

Ambition is often misunderstood. It is no bad thing, providing it wells up from deep within and we don't become identified with the object of our yearning. Ambition only becomes negative when it's other people's dreams we're taking on board or we're trying to score at the expense of another. When it rises from your core however, ambition is destiny, and by embracing it, you can ride its surging waves of passion to ultimate fulfilment.

As the movie-goer, I could clearly witness, that with this unleashed energy, my soul was breaking through. There was many a time when I felt utterly invincible. And at others, I'd crumble again. But the reason was becoming increasingly clear...

Unleashed, wilful soul, is pure energy, with direction and purpose, which is easy to attach to material outcome. On the journey to spiritual mastery – mastery of the soul - you must learn that the flow itself is sufficient. It doesn't have to create, or not create, any particular thing.

The paradox is, that in this profoundly unattached state, you'll create miracles and magic beyond your wildest dreams.

During those particular years, for me, the expression of these surging waves of passion was rowing. It was never far from my consciousness. It had become the forge through which to test the metal: to burn away the dross and smelt the folded blade. Rowing was my Excalibur, it pierced armour and steeled the soul. If there was some destiny on my distant horizon, I could not see it now, but I was certainly being well prepared for it. Victory or defeat, I was learning to be successful with either.

My journey down memory lane returned next to the river, where I was going to learn all about what it really means to be truly victorious in life, even and especially, during 'defeat'.

10

Wearing Defeat as your Suit of Victory

"You never lose from an experience in which you evolve and grow."

Yet again, in Boat Race training, I was to struggle in competition against much larger rowers. A number of the previous years Blue Boat (first crew) had left, and Dan had been recruiting American talent at the World Rowing Championships that summer. Apparently it was not that hard to win a place at Oxford if you were tall, blond and Californian, with big muscles and big money!

Once more, although I didn't have the strength to compete one on one, I was able to create a rhythm that lifted a crew, rendering the whole much greater than the sum of the parts. Once again, the winter trials race on The London Tideway was, for me, another great success. This time the boat I was stroking went behind by over a length and a half, normally an unrecoverable margin, before hauling back the deficit to win by the same distance. After the race, the national press was pretty much convinced - I would be stroking the Blue Boat. It seemed the coveted prize was within my grasp. I wanted it more than anything I could ever remember. It was an all-consuming passion, I dreamt about it, thirsted after it, hungered for it. I did not study or party, I did very little but train, eat and sleep...

Yes, you've got to follow your passion. But be careful not to bury yourself in it!

"It seems to me that's not an easy thing to do?"

No. It requires a lot of mastery. But your passion is a great teacher. The only thing to do is to follow it, but always remember, it's your self realisation - the revelation of you - within it that counts.

"How do you do that... be in it, but not lost in it?"

You have to become the Observer of yourself, all the time - watch your thoughts and feelings. Become that which is witnessing.

Clearly, at the time, I was still missing the point. What was it about pulling a carved piece of wood, 34 times a minute, 6 hours a day, 7 days a week until lungs gasped, hearts burst and limbs ached?

And then, as the movie-goer, it landed for me. It wasn't the rowing at all, that was merely the vehicle. It was self-mastery that had so bound me up - even back then. Getting to know the intricacies of self. Constantly improving, constantly growing. There was something majestic about this. Something beyond confine – beyond the judgment or measuring stick of others. No one could tell me what was right or wrong. No one could determine this but me. I was realising the importance of mastering my own life, my own destiny...

Awesome! Yes, you were getting it underneath. As with everyone at this point on the path, there are still many distorting veils to this truth to be peeled off, that it may bask naked in universal sunlight. But you were getting it – you were breaking through!

I was flashed forward to 'judgment day', when the final crew selections for the Boat Race are announced. We were waiting with nervous trepidation in the Leander Club Room, at Henley-on-Thames. It was the day of reckoning we had all been waiting for. For those of us whose places in the final eight were uncertain, every stroke pulled with tired and aching muscles had but one agenda: to get through this final selection process and win a coveted seat in the prestigious Blue Boat.

The usual camaraderie and witty repartee has vanished into the eerie silence. It's my turn to go in. To get my news. I know that on the individual tests such as weight lifting and the rowing machine I would be way behind. I'd even performed badly on the running, but was able to put that down to shin splints (hairline bone fractures) - probably caused by being too heavy for my build (yet another sign that I would have fared better had I been lighter). Somehow though, I feel sure that my skill in the boat, which had been well noted by the press in trials race performances, would win over. Surely success in race conditions would count most?

Dan is smiling quietly as I enter the room, but his face takes on a much more serious tone as he begins to speak. I did not hear most of what he had to say, after the earth shattering news **that I had not** made the final cut. It felt like receiving a short, hard punch to the solar plexus, leaving me nauseous and weak. With just one quietly spoken sentence, as strong as I had become, I was pole-axed. I couldn't even splutter a reply, because there was no wind in my lungs to carry the words...

When you allow yourself to build dreams founded on expectation, hopes and desires about some particular outcome, you always make yourself hostage to fate, and in particular, other people's judgments of you. Of course you have no control over either, only over how you respond – how you choose to be in the moment. This is your true destiny. This is always your true victory.

In looking back, I realised that had I looked at reality the way it really was, instead of interpreting it how I wanted it to be, I could have easily predicted this outcome. Had I listened all along, it was in truth, the only possibility likely to happen. Dan had his particular requirements and I did not meet those. If I'd dared to accept and see the truth building before me, I'd have been prepared for this moment - *you'd have been more present in it.* Reliving the event now, I could feel a sharp pain in the middle of my forehead.

It's your Third Eye chakra, some call it the "soul centre", it's where you manifest core beingness. The Third Eye recognises authentic reflections of you, in the mirroring circumstances around you.

"Clearly my Third Eye is not functioning properly!"

Put your attention on it, feel into the tightness, reflect on the sense of rightness of being, unwind and shine through it, like the sun.

So I feel deep into it, and reflect on how I am being when all feels right with me and the world. In no time, I can feel it unwinding and the light of my soul shining through. How awesome!

After some time bathing in this unfathomable sunlight, I found myself back in the drama, drowning in self-pity - a strong contrast. I was wondering what was the point of trying to accomplish things at all?

The only point of doing anything, is to express in every moment, who you really are. If you find a particular way of living brings out the very best of qualities in you, then you should keep living that way, no matter what; constantly uncovering new facets of that beingness, regardless of what is happening in the outer world. Your purpose here is to unleash and glorify your soul - what greater victory can there be?

I overreacted to the disappointment, which left me feeling cold, defeated and desperately deflated. In the misery that swept over me, I was unable to see the positive side of rowing in the reserve boat, Isis; the chance to continue doing what I really loved, together with the opportunity to improve on last year's performance. Having lost all perspective, I quit rowing that afternoon. I simply could not accept having to face my shattered dreams day in, day out. Through the desperate haze of disappointment, I could no longer appreciate the joy and upliftment of the sport I loved so dearly and the camaraderie of my team mates...

When you are continually living for those things you think you want, you are in fact living in thoughts and ideas rather than authentic reality. You are therefore removed from the true beauty of the moment. In this way, it is so easy to take for granted those things you truly love most, the passions that stir your blood. It is in this place that you so often make decisions that shape your life in a way which doesn't serve who you really are.

I went back to work in the Chemistry labs the next day, but if somehow I was harbouring the illusion that chemistry would pacify my longing for the self-realisation that the crucible of high-intensity sport had provided, that bubble was not to endure long. On the surface, training for a sport like rowing may appear dull and repetitive, but the continual measuring of oneself against perfection, offered the invitation to find ever more supreme levels of self-expression. Even without realising the underlying driving force, it becomes like a drug. I didn't know it at the time, but in truth, I was totally addicted...

You'd discovered the quintessence of life's purpose. Bared of complexity, distortion and confusion, sport is an art form, which continually challenges the participant to discover and unfold ever deeper realms of their true nature. It is addictive because this self-realisation is the ONLY thing happening in our Universe. When you accept this and surrender to it, even the addiction itself dissolves into complete self-acceptance and continual expression.

I soon realised I'd made a big mistake. At that time, rowing connected me to the essence of my True Self and I was really missing that. From the movie-goers perspective, I could also appreciate how it activated the 'warrior' energy within me...

Warrior energy is vital to us all. It is that energy that drives us to break apart the status quo of a lower level of harmony and understanding - to break through into an even higher and more complete version of the truth.

Another less favourable trait, which the sport revealed in me, was attachment to glamour. The Boat Race is televised to many countries and many millions of people. Although I would have denied it at the time, I could now see in truth, how secretly I revelled at the prospect of my 15 minutes of glory. Of course glamour and fame is just another illusionary storm in a tea cup...

The need for acceptance by others for your achievement is merely a substitute for lack of self-acceptance. In any case, the accolades that may be received from others, simply stimulate within, a feeling that was already always present. And when you keep looking within, you will find the keys to unlock that door without the need for anyone else's clapping approval.

Together with the presence, the image of Britain's most famous Olympian Steve Redgrave manifested before us. During his rowing career, he went on to win five Olympic golds, a Herculean feat. Yet for each of those precious moments of victory, thousands of hours would have been spent quietly training, away from the hubbub of life. It was abundantly obvious: there was so much more to it, for one to constantly apply oneself in that way. And surely, no amount of TV interviews and adoring fans, could replace the absolute feeling of completeness, in finding perfect right expression of one's true purpose for being?

Here is the real prize. It doesn't matter if it's an athlete winning a gold medal or a housewife dropping the kids off at school. Authentic sense of achievement is a private matter, achieved when we find perfect 'right expression' of an innate longing to fulfil our destiny. Whether experienced alone or in the glare of the public eye, in truth, it is a personal thing, experienced on the inside.

As I took a while to reflect on these revelations, the warm glow in my Third Eye was positively beaming through me. It felt like sitting on a deckchair on the beach, basking in warm sun.

I had to work a fair bit to pull myself back to the movie, but it continued to be a gripping ride, so it once more compelled me - a lost soul calling from the past. Sitting now in the chemistry labs, twiddling my thumbs, it was clear I desperately missed rowing. It didn't take long to figure out I'd made a monumental mistake.

Whatever you do, don't stop, don't rest, until you find your passion. And then keep expressing it!

I would soon have another bitter pill to swallow however. When I called Dan to ask if I could return to take up my Isis stroke seat, he welcomed me with open arms, but also told me that if I'd been around that week, I'd have been trialled at stroke in the Blue Boat, because it had not been flowing too well. Holy Shit!

You'd accepted "No" for an answer - given in too easily. NO ONE knows what the future may bring and how the twist and turns in the river of life may reveal unexpected opportunities. But in order to take full advantage, you must stay open, with trust, belief and enthusiasm in your heart. In which case, an infinite array of possibilities open. 'Miracles' do happen, but only when you hold the space for them.

In the Boat Race that year, Isis, with me in the stroke seat, went on to win against Cambridge in record time. Although I derived much motivation and benefit from it through my life, I had never truly gotten over the sense of having missed out on the Blue Boat stroke seat. Until now.

With the help of the presence, I felt like I was finally ready to let go. So I took myself right into the very heart of it - regressing into the sense of loss and tragedy, of having given my all to something I truly believed in, only to watch it apparently come to nought.

You've got to feel deeply into these regressions, feel into the contractions they cause. This is where you identify with the illusion of reality. This is where your soul is being owned and your sense of presence lost. So feel into the tightness, fully honour it, until it no longer defines you. Then you become 'as one' in it. You become The One through it.

A great gordian knot inside my gut - like a thick black serpent - began to unwind itself. And with that, a huge sense of relief and warmth filled my body. My soul moved beyond the notion of defeat. Upon which, I settled into that curious state of nothing/everythingness, that had popped up in my life a number of times before. Like I was totally free, with nothing owning me. It was an amazing feeling of total invincibility. The words, *"I wear Defeat as my Shirt of Victory"*, popped into my mind.

Once more, my cheeks were dampened with the joy of realisation. It was as if in its infinite love, the benevolent open hand of the Universe was shaping reality just for me - to awaken me, to uplift, rejuvenate, to enlighten and above all, to unconditionally love me. There was seemingly nothing that it would not do to help. For me in that moment, I had broken through the polarity that judges 'victory' and 'defeat' by the outcome of some event. I felt like I had inherited not just the Earth, but the whole Universe!

11

All in a Day's Work

*"To surrender is not to give in,
it is to recognise the truth of the moment
and apply yourself wholeheartedly to that."*

As I sat with the presence, again my eyes began to well up. They're tears of knowing - finally getting to know who I really am. All my life I'd been pulled in various directions, seduced by the hopes and desires of others, taking on their goals and ambitions and then thinking they were mine. My True Self doesn't need to win, it doesn't need the love and approval of others, I am good enough, absolutely perfect in fact, just being me. I can now see how the soul in each of us gets 'hijacked' in this way, and it begins at a very early age. Right now, I feel liberated; washed through with wave upon wave of unconditional love...

The waves of love are being generated in yourself, by yourself and for yourself. This is what happens when you completely let go of the need to be something you are not. It has a simple name, which belies its great significance - "Self-Acceptance".

After some considerable pause to steady my emotions and feelings, to integrate what I'd experienced, images began to appear on my inner movie-screen once more. It was time for another thrilling instalment of this epic rollercoaster ride.

It's now toward the end of my time at Oxford and I am studiously working at my desk in Chemical Crystallography, trying to catch up on all the days, weeks and months I've missed ('squandered' according to my professor) whilst out on the river. I'm wondering what to do next in life when, as if by magic, someone drops a flyer on my desk advertising a sales job with an American corporation called The Dow Chemical Company. In the previous weeks, I'd been training for Henley Royal Regatta, and so had invested no time in job hunting at all. Most of my friends and colleagues, on the other hand, were consumed within frantic corporate 'milk round' applications and interviews. The sales job with Dow was the only one I decided to apply for, because somehow, something felt right about it. As if it was meant to be...

You'd only really been interested in rowing. You'd invested no effort in what should happen next - which is actually a great place to be. Therefore, you weren't struggling internally to manifest a reality you might have wanted. This is incredibly significant. Because without knowing it, you were completely surrendered to the future.

It is only in this place of surrendered openness, that you can truly feel what is the best pathway in life; that which is flowing with the energy of higher consciousness. And in this state, rightness simply happens, things effortlessly click into place.

At the time, I still didn't believe in divine synchronicity. To me, all action was random with no guiding purpose. The fact that everything to do with my application just clicked perfectly into place, was just good luck. I'd had my share of bad times, the mathematical law of probability dictated that at least some of the time, I was bound to pick a hand of aces. On the interview day, my vehicle, the Boat Race minibus, broke down on the way to the interview. I exploded the engine whilst revving it too hard! But something propelled me onwards anyway. Leaving the van on a nearby verge, I manage to hail a taxi. In London, there is traffic gridlock, causing many interviewees to arrive late. For me however, despite the exploding engine, every connection works perfectly, and I arrive at the venue with a couple of minutes to spare.

As I looked back, I could feel the crown of my head, around the fontanelle tingling - a curious sensation, as if someone was tickling my head.

It's the crown chakra activating, that which initiates spontaneous synchronistic magic in your life.

I wondered what the 'exploding engine' synchronicity was all about? It was only later I discovered that Dow had been responsible for the infamous Agent Orange used in the war on Vietnam. Maybe there was some intuitive resistance to me going there?

No situation is ever black and white. There's never absolute 'right' and 'wrong'. The flow reflects this. Some things will click perfectly into place because you manifested them – there's a perfect 'fit' for the exploration you're now meant to have. But that doesn't make it all 'right' in a perfectly aligned sense. It means there'll also be some distortions to work through. That's why you create less than perfect realities.

"I see. That synchronicity went straight over my head at the time!"

For most it does. But fortunately, the Universe never tires of sending the messages.

"Fortunately!"

I laughed at myself as I now watched the drama unfolding. I could feel the hand of the Universe shaping the events to ensure that I got that job, it was clearly meant to happen – I was meant to get it, and to see something *(about yourself)*. The words of a popular TV commercial at the time popped into my mind: *"for the man who doesn't have to try too hard."* I found myself laughing and could feel the presence laughing along with me.

Certainly you don't have to try too hard when the crown chakra is fully functioning - things just click rightly into place.

As we looked on, it was suddenly abundantly obvious – *a revelation* – how our society strangles the very life energy from us. We spend our days efforting, trying to shape circumstances, experiences and time to get the outcome we want. Most people spend their whole lives engaged in control dramas this way. We plan our work, play, relationships, security, retirement, even our funerals. Few, if any, consider the Universe conspires a pathway, configuring all events and circumstances with just one purpose - to reveal ourselves to ourselves, and all we have to do is be open to it. Even many who are spiritually aware try to use the spiritual laws to manifest the outcome they desire. I was truly beginning to understand the meaning of the word 'surrender'...

To many, the word 'surrender' has a negative connotation. Centuries of struggle and conflict have created a virtue of fighting, struggling, and controlling. However, to surrender is not to give in. It is to recognise the truth of the moment and apply yourself wholeheartedly to that. If that means doing nothing, then do nothing as if your whole beingness depends upon it. It takes great courage to stand in stillness whilst everyone else is busily flapping around you.

It was the deepest revelation of all: to surrender to the natural energetic flow of the Universe. One that reveals itself through synchronicity and a deep inner yearning of what should be done, irrespective of our hopes or fears of what the outcome might be. If we stay open to the flow, then express the highest truth we hold about ourselves in the moment, "Right Action" will naturally happen:

It will flow as a consequence of authentic beingness.

I contemplated all the people I had known and couldn't think of any who had been ready to surrender to the Universe in this way. My friends had all been very talented people, who went on to be leaders in industry and finance, shaping not only their lives, but those of many millions of others. I reflected on how corporations were shaping the planet with no regard whatsoever for the natural order of things. I could see we were systematically raping Mother Earth to get the things we think we want, making ourselves miserable and unhappy in the process, kidding ourselves that the toys and distractions we create can somehow replace the feeling of unconditional love of pure existence within. For a moment, even in the state of bliss, I experienced great sadness too.

Out of my sadness, I was flashed forwards once more to another moment in my life's review. I find myself now in Dow Chemical's London Sales Office, sitting behind a fake wooden desk, with a fake wooden smile, telephone in hand and glued to a computer screen, trying with all my skill and carefully chosen words, to close an order for an industrial cleaning compound.

There is something unnatural and sterile about corporate life - like a cheap fitting, starched and shiny suit. It was a million miles away from the searching simplicity of Mother Thames.

This is what you came to see. Something that isn't you, so you could unwind the identification, let it go, and move on. It's the distorted aspect of yourself - your shadow side - which draws it. The trouble is, many people get stuck in it, and don't change, they don't unravel and fully break through, even though the opportunity is always there, even though the synchronistic messages keep coming thick and fast.

Put simply, truthfully, my job was to manipulate people to buy things from us. Like many corporations, Dow invested heavily in our training. We learnt how to identify the personal goals and fears of potential buyers and then push their buttons for our own ends. We learned how to fuel and prey on artificial desires with skilful subliminal marketing. We discovered how to project our power through carefully controlled body language and neuro-linguistic-programming. I was learning how to manipulate what I thought to be 'reality'.

It's very close to the whole manifesting agenda within spirituality these days. It's just wrapped up in another suit.

As I reflected upon the events now, I could see in truth, it was not only the customers who were being manipulated, but myself also...

Trying to control reality, identifies you with that which you are trying to control, because you build fixed relationships - 'tightness' - to the circumstances you're trying to manipulate. At times you may appear to 'win', but the persona you become is so much smaller than the infinite potential that you are. You make yourself much less, and live a lesser lifestyle as a result.

As we looked on together, it was clear that in the beginning, I was quite easily seduced by the money and the expenses that went with the corporate lifestyle – I changed my car three times in the first year!

And alas, like sand slipping through grasping fingers, no matter how much the bank account filled up, it just as easily ran out – there was no holding on to it. Like so many people in society, as my pay regularly increased (the sweetener to maintain motivation), the more false needs I acquired and the more money I 'needed' to spend. And whatever happened to humour? Friendliness flew out the window as stress devoured us, in the endless effort for year-end targets.

Personal integrity was a sad casualty on this 'battlefield' too. In April 1984, Britain broke off diplomatic relationships with Libya, following the murder of the police officer Yvonne Fletcher outside the Libyan embassy in London. An act of Parliament banned the shipment of many types of chemicals that might be used for military purposes, including some of Dow's products. Like spies on high, myself and the presence were now witnessing a hushed conversation, concealed behind closed doors, which I'd overheard at the time. A boss and their employee were calculating how best to avoid the embargo… "We've done this before, it's easy, you dispatch the goods to somewhere nearby, then switch papers mid-channel. The chemicals are diverted to where you need them to go. It's a done deal."

As we looked on, my heart felt heavy, like a sinking ship. It wasn't because the embargo was being broken, it was more about watching conniving colleagues, their souls submerged under a wave of never-ending sales targets. And my sadness deepened, as I realised this was happening all over the world, from drugs companies to food, weapons to water. Precious few give a damn about the consequences. Whatever branch of industry, it is all just a numbers game.

The deeper you dig, the more you uncover the basic truth about society – that unrestrained, unbridled capitalism, makes a virtue out of profit. But when one profits, somewhere down the chain, another must lose. It's a basic truth of living on a planet of finite resources – there's only so much that Gaia can give.

The Fletcher affair rapidly soured my taste for the corporate gravy train. But as I looked back, the revelation landed, that we must all go through such experiences to learn, evolve and grow.

This is the natural order of life – what some call "The Law of Attraction". What you hold within, manifests its mirror in the outer. Some stay stuck in the reflections they create. Like dealing cards, most live a life of shuffling circumstances - they always get the same hand, until they change the dealer. But if you can work through, if you can unravel the tightness and find your truth in it, then this is true alchemy, this is true Breakthrough. And with each one, now the hand you're holding really can turn up Aces.

Life now dealt me a completely different hand - worlds apart in fact. Having broken through my need for corporate success, I discovered a new-found interest in global politics, and I became an avid current affairs reader, even whilst at work during the day.

When you find a new interest, give energy to it, express it out into the world. Begin now. Where you are. And it will change your reality most positively to reflect the new passion.

At the time, according to popular press, Communism seemed to be spreading a dark shroud over democratic freedom. This stirred my blood – injustice and oppression were for me, even greater motivators than capitalistic inequity. The more I read, the stronger the inner flame of this passionate altruism was kindled. This was a vital issue of our times, the iron fulcrum, upon which, the very nature of humanity was being defined. As JFK so eloquently and passionately expressed at the Berlin wall... "Ich bin ein Berliner," we are all Berliners now!

The picture painted in western media was that Communism, bent on globally furthering its 'Big Brother' indoctrination, threatened our very existence. Of course the same might equally be said of the western superpowers - an alternative truth that I readily overlooked. After all, was it not us furthering the cause of freedom?

Never forget, whatever '-ism' you call it, one man's freedom fighter is another man's terrorist.

In those times we lived constantly under the threat of all-out nuclear war, and the only thing that seemed to stand in the way of oblivion, was something called "MAD" - Mutually Assured Destruction *(how appropriate!)*. If we could convince the Warsaw Pact of our unwavering resolve to defend ourselves (by launching all-out nuclear war in retaliation), then there might still be a meaningful future for us and our children. Mad, it may well have been, but western governments and the world's media had drip-fed us the propaganda of fear, and many, including myself, believed it to be the only realistic means of self-preservation. It was so much a part of our culture, that even pop stars like Sting were singing about it...

In Europe and America, there's a growing feeling of hysteria
Conditioned to respond to all the threats
In the rhetorical speeches of the Soviets
Mr. Krushchev said we will bury you
I don't subscribe to this point of view
It would be such an ignorant thing to do
If the Russians love their children too.

How can I save my little boy from Oppenheimer's deadly toy
There is no monopoly in common sense
On either side of the political fence
We share the same biology
Regardless of ideology
Believe me when I say to you
I hope the Russians love their children too
There is no historical precedent
To put the words in the mouth of the President
There's no such thing as a winnable war
It's a lie we don't believe anymore
Mr. Reagan says we will protect you
I don't subscribe to this point of view
Believe me when I say to you
I hope the Russians love their children too

We share the same biology
Regardless of ideology
What might save us, me, and you
Is if the Russians love their children too.

(lyrics by Sting)

It was this heady cocktail of passionate idealism that drew me toward service in the military – something I'd never even considered a remote possibility up to that point. But I was deeply disillusioned. There needed to be meaning in my life, way beyond the corporate skyscraper of nine-to-five. I needed to make a positive difference in the world. This was all about upholding democratic freedom – a chance to protect the innocent, to right injustice and overthrow oppression…

All 'good' and 'just' reasons quoted at the outset of countless wars. At these levels of consciousness, they're unfortunately unavoidable – people simply manifest in the outer their own inequity, injustice and judgment that they hold on the inner. Consider the Second World War for example, and the level of nationalism, in so many countries, which manifested as unconscionable barbarism.

It's hard to imagine, but very true, that many people – the majority - were holding this level of angst within themselves.

I thought long and hard about whether or not I could bring myself to harm another if ever required to. I reached the conclusion, (frighteningly easily), that I could trust my government to make the right decisions, and that if I was called on to defend our freedom against someone threatening the life of our loved ones and children, then that could be acceptable. We had stood in our truth against Hitler, was this not a similar situation?

There is no greater service than helping others to be free from injustice, oppression and barbarity. Sadly, this inner pull is frequently manipulated and abused by those who would control you for their own ends.

As I looked back, there was a sense of uneasiness in my heart.

It's the Heart Chakra, where you discern non-judgmental Right Action - you're being invited to discern the truth from the illusion.

Suddenly, visions of the winged horse "Pegasus" appear on the 'cinema screen'. The presence and I are descending - floating down into Browning Barracks in Aldershot, the home of the historic Parachute Regiment. My soul had been drawn to an elite force that trained its soldiers to the peak of physical and mental endurance - what I considered to be the ultimate deterrent.

You never did things by halves!

There were resistances to overcome before the selection process though, especially since The Paras have a reputation for being so gung-ho. But no, I was never one to do things by halves. For me, it was never about dipping one's toes in. It had to be all or nothing. I rationalised that in a time of great crisis, the Paras are the kind of people you can rely on to perform in the confusion and chaos. Strength, courage, bravery, unswervable inner will, psychological stamina and determination are key characteristics they look for in their soldiers and build on in the training...

Let's face it, there's no 'nice side' to any conflict. You were always one to get right into the deep-end of truth. In the confusion of kill or be killed, which is what all conflict boils down to, The Paras and those like them, are the crystal clear expression of government policy beyond spin, hype and fuzzy edges. In your culture, war and violence are invariably sanitised to create neatly packaged and acceptable truths, the illusions which make going to war more readily palatable; they are that from which best-selling movies are made. The reality of course is never, ever, glitzy.

Having taken three days holiday from Dow, I was now glued intently at an introductory briefing, given by a serving Corporal of 2 Para - a veteran of the Falklands War in 1982, his face horribly disfigured, having taken a bullet in the lower jaw. I can hear him now; clearly the bullet has done little to dent his resolve, as his rasping and rakish tone fills the hall like machine gun fire: "I've no problem dying for my country, I'm just here to make sure the other fucker dies for his country before I die for mine."

Wow. How I winced at it, looking back. The callousness tightened my solar plexus and sickened my gut.

Yet this is authentic. This is real. How many armchair heroes out there condone conflict, by their thinly veiled denial of the reality of war? Or sanitise and gloss over, or glibly accept the 'collateral damage'? There are no soft, woolly edges when you unleash such action.

Actually I wasn't afraid of the truth. There was something distinctly refreshing in it. When you see the truth, you can deal with it. Even if you don't like it, there's great honesty. At the time, I admired that. And as I looked back on it, I could appreciate why this (unrepentant truth) had appealed to me. But now, with a more compassionate alignment, feeling much more connected to the whole of life, I also winced at the dispassionate inhumanity of it. And it also occurs to me, that the Para is simply the physical manifestation of what we tolerate and allow within society. He is not to blame – responsible, but not to blame. He, like many others, has been conditioned by society.

What was it the tabloid press reported, as the battleship Belgrano was sunk off Argentina by a British torpedo, killing hundreds of soldiers - the children of mothers, the fathers of children, the husbands of wives?

"Gotcha!"

And this – the reporting - was seen as no outrage. It didn't bring people out in the streets by the millions. For too many, it was acceptable nationalism, acceptable judgmentalism, acceptable barbarism.

In that moment, the "Gotcha" revelation came clearly into view for me, bringing tears once more, to deeply saddened eyes…

Thank you tabloids for the mirrors you present!

I was able to see through the hypocrisy of a society that washes its hands of individual responsibility, and instead, projects its own judgments onto others, thus producing a soldier with a loaded weapon in his hands. We support governments and media that dehumanise others, or we too easily turn a blind eye, whilst we get on with the day job. A Para with a fixed bayonet, is simply the outcome of that ignorance...

When you subscribe through the ballot box to a regime that supports the gun, no matter how neatly you package it, you are at some level, each responsible for pulling the trigger.

Back then, I was fully accepting of the threat posed by the Warsaw Pact, and despite reservations, my overriding belief in the need for a strong deterrent ensured that I was ready to take on personal responsibility. As I looked on as the movie-goer, I was saddened I'd felt the need to take that route, but also understanding and accepting of why I'd done it. I could find peace with it – no self-judgment.

It's only by exploring these controversial situations, and ourselves in them, that we can find true alignment in the heart, and with that, inner peace. Yet another Breakthrough.

Yes, looking back, the uneasiness was unwinding for me. I'd made a choice in truth. And I'd committed to the full exploration of it.

How ever you consider the rights or wrongs of armed conflict, there are no grey areas when you're jumping out of an aircraft into a war zone. It requires focussed, unfathomable courage and the Paras can't afford for anyone to freeze whilst jumping. Selection involves ball-breaking tests of physical stamina, courage and confidence. The pinnacle of which is the "Tranazium" - an aerial scaffolding, that at its highest place, is around the height of a three storey building. It has a very simple aim - to test if you have the bottle. Suddenly, I find myself standing in line on the training field, staring nervously at the cold hard steel in front of us, the gurgling of my tightened stomach clearly audible to those left and right of me – assuming they had any spare attention to listen. The Colour Sergeant instructor begins explaining: "And why aren't there any safety nets gentlemen? Simple. So you won't be tempted to fall into them!" To heighten the sense of unforgiving coldness, the sky is grey and the voluminous clouds are just beginning to dump snow on us. "And what happens if you do fall gentlemen?" the Sergeant continues, his timing impeccable, as a green military ambulance, with a large red cross on the side, chugs its way onto the field in front of us. The Sergeant smirks, "Anyone needing a ride home?" It is crystal clear, the Paras (through necessity) have developed a fatalistic sense of humour...

What else might a soldier do but learn to laugh in the face of death?

The withering cold, the ambulance and the unforgiving Sergeant all serve to create a fearful inner reality, which is of course, the clear intention. Would we be able to overcome the fear and still function? In actual fact, the aerial gymnastics required on the Tranazium are basic and simple, something that most people would easily accomplish at only two or three feet off the ground. The landscape changes greatly when you're thirty feet up!

The whole of reality is an illusion. But it's a real illusion, which tests how you react to it. What stories do you create in your mind, which do you contract and tighten to? It's in these places where you lose presence and identify. Your body tightens, your breath shortens, and the soul is pulled into the eddy current. You must get into this tightness and explode the myth of your fear by feeling into the worst possible outcome. Then you will liberate your soul from it.

As I stood awaiting my turn, I was recalled a scene from the 70's hit TV series "Kung Fu". The young Caine is being tested by Shaolin priests on his fears of crossing a plank over a vat of acid. A dozen times Caine has easily crossed the plank on the ground, without falling off. But now, above the acid, he wobbles and falls off – only to discover he's fallen into nothing but water: "Life is like a corridor and death but a doorway. There is nothing to fear but our fear itself." The words of Caine's Shaolin priest help me greatly: something clicks – *shifts* – inside me. This is about the fear itself, not the Tranazium. The Tranazium is mostly an illusion. So how did the fear make me feel? Tight and wound up. Can I let go? Well it seems that's all I have to do. All I **can** do. The relaxedness would be by far the best way to cross the aerial obstacle. So I focus instead on the sense of relaxedness.

You were breaking through!

I begin to climb the cold steel, hand carefully over hand, foot carefully over foot, pointed toes searching precariously for something solid. I'm now able to notice how the energy begins to change. As strange as it may seem, everything around me somehow progressively sharpens. Even through the greyish light, the intensity of surrounding countryside becomes stronger. The breath of the person next to me frosts and blends with mine, so I can begin to feel the camaraderie - the oneness - between us. He winks at me, I can feel the warmth inside. Snow prickles my skin as it falls on my face, stimulating the sharpness of the moment and then melting before running down rosy cheeks. The piercing sounds of hands and feet on metal, seem to vibrate right through me...

You were beginning to experience the full, six-sense beauty, of what it really means to be living in the moment – to be breaking through. The purpose of fear is to let you know the reality of the situation, which you can approach essentially in one of two ways: allow it to own you, or accept it, and soften into it. If you allow it to, if you don't avoid it, but walk right into it, then it will bring you fully into the only thing that really exists - the moment of now, as a sensory experience of The One. In this way, fear provides an incredibly instant doorway to the divine, and can be your greatest ally.

Having stepped through the doorway marked 'fear', the further I climb, the more present I become, and the more the fear dissipates. By the time I'm standing at the highest point, on two thin parallel bars, arms outstretched, head seemingly up in the clouds, all fear has dissipated. In its place is the empowering surge of the warrior. As I move onto one foot to step over the hurdle in the middle of the bars - a precarious point, which we had all feared most - I am now feeling rock steady. Successfully completing the peak obstacle, I touch my toes as required, and then stretch my arms out heavenward in a crucifix, shouting out my name and number, "BOURNE 33, Sir." Curiously, I notice the words didn't come from my throat, they emerged from somewhere much deeper than that; a primal scream riding on the outstretched wings of passion. I was indeed unleashing the warrior in my soul. I feel invincible...

Passion is just as much a feature of the soul as surrender. It arises most powerfully when we overcome our fears. It could be standing on the seeming precipice of life like you were, but it could also be experienced in a myriad of life's other possibilities: quitting a job that doesn't serve; ending an outdated relationship; confronting other people's judgments. Authentic living is like this, almost a continual crucifixion – a continual Breakthrough. It takes great passion and courage to surrender fully.

I never considered surrender would get me through one of the toughest selection processes the Army has to offer, but indeed it did. I was one of only three from forty applicants chosen by the Paras to go through to the Regular Commissions Board (RCB) and I was now extremely confident of winning a place at the coveted Sandhurst (Officer Training Academy). However, if I'd learned one thing by now, perhaps it should have been, to expect the unexpected. As I was soon to discover, the Universe was less interested in me becoming an Army Officer and more interested in what I would discover about myself in the process.

LOL! In the abode of the soul, there is no such thing as an 'Army Officer', nor a 'Nurse', nor a 'Teacher' nor any other identity. There's simply you, as a soul, and how you feel to be now.

Suddenly I'm now at the Commissions board in Westbury. I'm standing with a group of bushy-tailed Officer hopefuls, listening intently to the briefing being given before our next timed obstacle test – a finish line 10 metres away, with various planks, boxes and ropes in between. The Directing Staff was just finishing the briefing: "You can touch anything marked blue, but not red, nor the ground in between; you can use the equipment provided, but if you do, you must take it with you. How are you going to do it?" What immediately follows can only be described as a gaggle of seagulls, hungrily cawing and pecking at each other, over a discarded bag of seaside chips. Each candidate 'seagull' needs to be seen and heard to make his mark as a leader (to get the chips!). But how does that work when everyone's trying to be a leader? I clearly remember thinking that at the time.

Somehow, a solution comes to me, and I seize my opportunity during a temporary lull in the feeding frenzy. "Okay Bourne, you're up, how long is it going to take you?" "15 minutes," I positively reply. "Good – you've got ten. Get on with it."

I'd noticed that in our group there was one weak candidate, who always, without fail, made silly mistakes, costing valuable time. Or else he'd ask difficult questions and get in the way. This time was no different – he kept interrupting as I was giving the briefing. So I take what I feel to be a 'command decision' and stand him to one side, with a menial task to distract him, so the rest of us can get on with the job. And indeed, we succeed, just within the allotted 10 minutes. I feel positively elated. How can they fail to see my unquestionable leadership potential?

However, as I looked back on it now, from the perspective of the movie-goer, the situation seemed very different. I could literally feel the impact my actions were having on those around me. Especially in this case, I could feel the disastrous effect on the rejected candidate's confidence. My arrogance had dealt him a crushing blow – the sense of rejection, which probably activated an old childhood wound. Who knows, he might never have gotten over it? Wow, this is what happens when you regress into a life's review.

Yes indeed. You get to feel it all. Especially the impact of your actions on others. That's important. It enhances motivation for development.

Of course this never occurred to me at the time. The fact that we successfully completed the obstacle was, so I thought, good justification. Surely the Army would see it that way too?

But now, as I found myself opening the Commissions Board letter, my mouth sinks to floor, as I have to deal with the emotional breakdown of rejection myself. I'd failed. And I was completely gutted. What had I done? How did this happen? I had all the right credentials, I'd passed with the Paras, how on earth did I fail? Not for one moment did it occur to me that it might have been because I stood that hapless chap to one side. It was only later, when I had the good fortune to connect with someone who'd been involved in officer selection that I understood... What example of leadership is it, if you don't even consider the weaker ones under your care? You were a part of a team, given to work together, and overcome the challenges presented together, including the personal limitations you each hold. Such a team is only as strong as its weakest link – so work hardest with them.

Yes I saw it. My arrogance and lack of empathy demonstrated incredibly poor leadership. I was crushed and humbled by it. And for a while, in the doldrums. Together with the letter of RCB failure, my plans for the 'Corporation Street Great Escape' were crumpled.

So obvious had my arrogance and lack of empathy been, that in the letter, the Army didn't even offer me the opportunity to retake. I was devastated and back in the misery of perceived failure; I was, yet again, unable to recognise the hand of the Universe in the twist and turn of 'fate'. I knew it was in me to lead, because I had done so from an early age, and I felt an inner calling to be an officer, but in order to achieve this, the Universe had conspired an event to show me what true leadership is all about.

Well you did ask to be a leader!

In all people lies the natural ability to lead in given circumstances, where their personality is best suited. In society however, it is all too easy to associate great leadership with rank and position when in truth, you are being a leader when you are being a positive and uplifting example to others (especially those who need it most!).

If you truly wish to lead, don't seek title or position, these are just artificial ranks with which society tries to pigeon-hole you; they limit your true brilliance. Seek instead the light and the compassion inside yourself and be that in every moment. Then you will lead the Universe.

I wasn't completely settled with this from the movie-goer's vantage point however. Surely it's not wrong to go for a particular job or position that inspires you?

The position that inspires you, is a crystallization of a sense of being that you're having. But remember, it's beingness that counts, not the outcome. If you want to create the perfect vehicle to express a particular quality you uphold inside – being an officer for example (or healer or anything else you care to mention) – ask what quality on the inside is that a reflection of? Then be that quality, here and now, wherever you are, in whatever circumstances, with no concern for the outcome. Just be the best example of that quality you can be, right now, where you are. And the rest will follow.

"Wow, yes!"

And here's one of the greatest secrets – the greatest revelations – of manifesting miracles: express the beingness at the core of you now, and the Universe can't fail to create the perfect vehicle to fit your expression. Because that's what it does.

"Incredible. That revelation will change my life. Forever. Thank you!"

From the sky-high altruism of Para selection, then failing RCB, I found myself back at Heathrow International Airport, for a promotion meeting with my new Dow Chemical boss. I'm feeling a bit like a passenger jet, jam-packed with decadent holiday-makers, landing with such a heavy thud, that you feel the undercarriage will give way, as if overloaded by too many hotel buffets and poolside pina coladas. This is it, I'm back in Corporation Street, gone there to find out about my new position - "the job promotion of a lifetime". Despite my lacklustre performance, apparently Dow can appreciate my potential, and want to encourage it, with new bonuses, wage rises and company cars.

'Coincidentally', the day I received notification of RCB failure, **was the exact same one**, that I got my new promotion to field sales.

On the way there my mind is whirring, like a clock with a broken mainspring. Once again, the Universe had constructed an event to test who I really am...

How easily can the soul be bought?

Should I take the job or have another crack at the Army? The Army had seemed pretty definitive. It would be a huge risk to turn down Dow's offer and try again. As I arrive at the meeting, I am increasingly feeling the cosiness of accepting the new promotion. The swish settings of the Heathrow restaurant are a world away from the cold, hard Browning Barracks. The offer is like a mystical temptress, promising alluring hopes and desires.

Lunch is opulent, Dow spares no expense. The Chardonnay is lulling me into a false sense of destiny, but then just as my boss pops the question - "How do I feel about the new position?" - an image flashes into my mind. It is of Daniel Topolski, smiling at me questioningly, back at the scene of my Blue Boat 'failure'. "Did you not resolve never again to take 'no' for an answer?"

In the vision, which I could clearly see as I now looked back, there was the typical sarcasm in his smile, which always pushed my buttons, but this time, I was drawn to his eyes...

Actually, a deep reflection of.... YOU!

There is no mistaking. There, in his reflection, is my soul calling to me. Loud. Unequivocal. Such that I can't ignore it. To do so would make my life a lie: "Don't take no for an answer, give the Army another try."

Becoming a leader in the Army had become my passion, and at that moment, my purpose. Learning to be a leader spoke into the depths of my soul - I simply knew it was something I was meant to do. What followed was like being in a dream.

Reality actually!

"Well actually, I came here to resign," were the words I spoke back to my boss. From the place of the movie-goer, together with the presence, we waited with baited breath. We had just witnessed earth-shattering truth, uttered with profound self-honesty, the one that shapes destiny.

You'd confronted the actual truth of the moment, opened an internal space, and despite the alluring temptation, were speaking with correct discernment, from the heart.

We watch the boss's face turn, ever so slowly, from uncertain amusement at a strange joke delivered strangely, to palpable shock and incredulity, as the steely-eyed resolve becomes crystal clear...

This is clearly no joke!

"Never again take no for an answer." It was all I needed to hear to make my choice. I quit my job at the promotion meeting, left the company four weeks later and reapplied to the Army. Friends and family thought I was crazy. I'd given up a great job, had no alternative lined up, had no savings, and to boot, the Army didn't seem to care...

If you look at your lives at such synchronistic events, it is no coincidence that the Universe frequently creates such difficult and testing circumstances. In these times, it is not about which choice you ultimately follow, but rather what does the moment reveal in yourselves? If you have a genuine passion for something, how easily will you allow that passion to be bought? What commitment are you prepared to make? Would you burn all your boats, just to be who you really are? Someone who is at one with his soul cannot be bought at any price.

This is the measure of true Breakthrough.

And this is true leadership.

Perhaps, for the first time in my life, I was truly learning how to follow my soul.

12

The Universe Works for You

*"If it's truly in your heart,
then you know you're meant to get something from it.
In which case, don't be put off. Don't give up."*

On my journey of discovery, I found myself next at a typically English event, steeped in tradition, piled with aplomb and lofty noses. This is Henley Royal Regatta, the day after leaving Dow. Had I not followed my heart and still been working, I would have missed another superlative moment of divine magic.

Always, but always, follow your heart. And you'll always find the Universe comes to meet you.

Henley was always a great favourite of mine: strawberries and scones, cocktails mixed with rowing, sunshine and smiles - a heavenly concoction indeed. But this time, I was less interested in the day's rowing form, and bored by the high-hatted aloofness. Instead, I found myself drawn to one of the drinks tents, but not to quench any physical thirsting, there was something else undeniably wanting me to go there. Soon enough I discover the reason: an old acquaintance I vaguely know from previous regattas. It feels like something magical is conspiring to connect us. In conversation, it transpires he'd just taken a job as a rowing coach at a prestigious private school in Oxford, and as it happens, they were still looking for another coach.

The Universe works for you!

The conditions were too good to be true. The job provided accommodation, meals in the staff restaurant, just 2 hours of work a day, and ample pocket money. I applied for the job the following Monday and was offered the position a day later. The relaxed working hours would afford me the opportunity to train at Oxford's Officer Cadet Training Centre, to prepare for another shot at the Army. As if this wasn't enough, the icing on the cake was still to be realised. The school had recently recruited a new senior instructor for the School Army Cadet Force. Chris Johnstone had just left the Parachute Regiment, where he'd been responsible for training recruits for the infamous "P-company", the intense physical and mental preparation prior to parachute training. It is widely regarded as one of the toughest tests of endurance in the armed forces. Chris also just happened to be one of the National Judo team coaches. As I looked back on the divinely orchestrated events, I could see it was a match made in heaven - quite literally!

The Universe will work like this when you don't ignore the quiet voice of the soul. Situations and circumstances will simply click into place.

As I looked on, Chris, in all his understated splendour, took form before my eyes. He was a diminutive guy, quietly spoken, but commanding unquestionable authority. You knew instantly that he stood whole-heartedly behind his every word, thought and deed. He never shouted nor became verbally aggressive; he used his words sparingly and carefully. When he looked at you, it felt like you were standing naked in front of him, his piercing and unwavering blue eyes seemed to stare right to the nature of your soul. An expert in human motivation, he could smell insincerity, bluff and fear at a thousand yards. The Paras may have received some bad press over the years, but he exemplified the epitome of undistorted, crystal clear truth.

Chris would never sweep uncomfortable issues under the carpet, preferring instead to tackle them head on, bringing them out into the open. If there was a difficult, unpopular job to be done, no matter how unpleasant, he was the man to do it. It was exactly what you'd expect of someone who'd faced death as a way of life. In Chris, what you saw, was what you got...

When the heart is behind our impulse to do things, if the mind and body are at one with the impulse, NOTHING, BUT NOTHING, can deny the truth. Insincerity, exposed in its presence, has only two choices: to run away and hide or dissolve in its unfathomable light.

Suddenly I found myself on the school parade ground, in front of three platoons of scraggly, giggling, fidgeting, disrespectful, snot-nosed youngsters, who really didn't care much and certainly didn't want to be there. I look on as two other teachers dressed in ill-fitting combat clothing struggle incessantly, and completely ineffectively, to quieten their platoons and gain some attention - "Be Quiet! Stand Still! Shut up!" They couldn't have been more insincere or looked more out of place. But now everyone's reality is about to be rocked by an unexpected earthquake, the narrative about to be changed. The door of Squadron Headquarters creaks slowly open, steadily revealing Chris, in neatly ironed camouflaged smock, mirror-like polished black boots, the wings of Pegasus flying on his angular shoulders, and maroon beret pulled down over the left eye, purposefully presenting the metalled Parachute Regiment insignia, splitting the sunlight, as if through a prism. A hush quickly descended over the parade ground. You could hear young minds whirring - What the f***. Who on earth is this dude? What are we in for now? This is just way too serious!

Chris strides boldly over to the parade, calls everyone to attention, and without hesitation or delay, introduces himself and his purpose for being there. Instantly I knew I could learn something from this guy. This was unwavering, unswerving sense of purpose...

This is the Warrior Energy, and everyone has it. It's the energy of purpose and commitment, which gets the job done. Some people have it already in abundance. Others must look for, and kindle it, in a way that works and expresses best for them.

"How do you kindle warrior energy if you don't already have it?"

Pay attention to those things you do that generate a sense of drive and purpose. Then apply yourself to them as often as you can. Be the Observer of yourself, feel the sense of the energy within, then you can apply it to other areas of your life when needed.

Back in the movie, Chris begins to speak with a calm but purposeful and slightly raised voice... "Today, by way of introduction to me, I'm going to train you on the Assault Course." At which point, one of the boys, Hamid, lets rip a loud farting noise, which shatters the respectful silence into hoots of laughter and boyish bantering. Hamid was well known in the school for challenging authority and had many times come close to expulsion. You can just feel the sense of relief unfold across the parade ground. The status quo was being restored. The mighty Parachute Regiment had been silenced by something as seemingly insignificant as a raspberry, with not even a shot fired.

How humbling!

For any other teacher, this would easily have undermined their sense of self-esteem and authority. But Chris was no ordinary teacher. I knew in my bones this was not the end of the story - just the beginning.

Chris cast the briefest of glances at the hapless perpetrator, just long enough to size up his 'target'. His mind was processing quickly, like lightning.

Indeed this "Hamid" was a maverick... just like you.

"Interesting, yes. I hadn't caught that one at the time."

Having changed into PT kit, the assault course now begins. "Right turn, quick march, follow me," rasps Chris the Para. Hamid doesn't move. You could feel the hesitancy in the platoon. What's he going to do about Hamid? Do we really need to go through with this? Surely he'll give up quickly, just like all those teachers before him. But of course Chris was not for giving up so easily. He strides purposefully forwards and the balance of energy quickly rocks back in his favour. As we break into a jog, all but Hamid have fallen into line. When we get back to the parade ground twenty minutes later, breathless and muddied, but feeling empowered because we'd accomplished something, Hamid was sitting on the grass bank overlooking us, seemingly unperturbed.

There was an unease hanging in the air. Whereas most would have initially sided with Hamid, now the tables had very definitely turned. The rest of the Squadron had pulled together, and you could feel the sense of completeness and achievement. An endorphin rush had helped us transcend mental limitation - anyone who ever questioned the value of leadership needed to feel this. There was just one problem - Hamid - and if it wasn't somehow solved, it would continue to undermine the sense of purpose.

There's something for you to contemplate more deeply though. Yes, you'd found a group harmony, which felt aligned and empowering; but what if we never allow that to be questioned? Who knows where that might lead? - to Passchendaele and the Somme for example. So perhaps Hamid was there for another reason also?

This question began to tug on another revelation, that I simply knew just wanted to land – when I was ready.

Meanwhile the 'cabaret' continues quickly, with Chris the Para right on the case *(did you expect anything less!)*. "Right, gentlemen, normally once would be enough. But one amongst us didn't complete the course. So since we're all a team, and this is about team effort, we'll just have to complete it again for him." The initial shock of silence is soon pierced with groans and grumblings, as the truth steadily lands. I look across at Hamid. The smirk has gone from his face, and for the first time he looks worried and uncomfortable. This is something he's not reckoned with. Those he was 'leading', would have to carry his can.

We completed the assault course - three times! - eating into the school lunch break, and each time Hamid looked on. At that stage, it wasn't clear who'd 'won'. It seemed like stalemate in some 'no-man's-land' until Chris announced that the unfinished business would just have to continue after school and everyone was to return at 4pm. "Is he for real?" I hear one of the boys whisper. He certainly is! I found myself musing. Amidst gasps, groans and disbelief, the Squadron dismisses. When they return, Hamid is present too, only this time looking quite different. A large, shining black eye is doing little to hide his sheepishness. Clearly one of the older boys has decided to metre out some justice in the interests of the whole. The assault course was completed without further drama. It was the first and last time Chris' authority was ever questioned. The incident brought the Squadron together as a team. Now we worked for one another, lifting morale on Pegasus' unrelenting, outstretched wings...

Great, but in all this, did anyone ever stop to think about Hamid? You'd encountered him before you know.

"Where?"

On every games lesson, in every football or hockey team, there's always one who gets chosen last. There's always one who's the maverick. There's always one seeking some kind of attention. Always one....who's been unloved. Remember what happened to you at the Commissions Board?

I was far from getting it at the time, but now the penny was steadily dropping. Yes indeed, I'd met Hamid many times in my life before, and most recently at the Commissions Board. He was the guy I arrogantly stood to one side, whilst we 'got on with the job'.

Yes indeed!

"And how do you work with this kind of person?"

First you have to empathise.

An energy suddenly washes over me, and I found myself, what I can only describe as, at one with Hamid. The feeling was so strong, it was almost as though I had become he.

I can feel his pain, his sense of isolation and alienation. Suddenly I am in some opulent childhood house. His well-dressed, well-spoken parents are speaking very formally about his future, and how they think it best he go to a boarding school. And within me – *within Hamid* – it causes a terrifying sense of foreboding. After all, I am middle eastern, with coloured skin, an accent, and totally different culture. "You'll get on fine with the boys," my mother urges, but really, what I can actually feel, is that I'm a nuisance, cramping her haute couture lifestyle, which she desperately wants to create more space for. I feel dejected, unloved and unlovable, a failure, shunted from nanny to nanny, pillar to post. And now here I am, on some stupid parade ground, abandoned by God and everyone else.

Suddenly I was back in my own skin, looking on at the Hapless Hamid. My heart breaks open, as I weep a river of tears: for Hamid, and for me - how ignorant I'd become. How unforgiving. How heartless.

For some considerable time I felt alone. As if the presence had deserted me. *No. I'd just left you in your own process, to feel what you needed to feel.* And so how do you work with people who've been alienated and abandoned? How can you truly help them?

You mean those that have been trampled on, abused and continually knocked to the ground? There's only one way you can truly effectively deal with them. Yes, you can contain them, yes, you can cajole and martial them. Yes, you can force them into line. But that will never solve their problem. The only effective way, is empathy and unconditional love.

They need you to feel their pain. To know that they've been heard.

"My God. Of course." In that moment, looking from on high, I felt wholly inadequate.

But don't forget the truth in Chris either. It's neither one thing nor the other. In truly balanced states, you don't make one wrong by making the other right. The yin has to be blended into the yang for true success. This leads to another priceless Breakthrough - the warrior of life.

"Certainly, I wasn't one of those yet!"

Don't worry, it takes a lifetime of mastery.

I didn't encounter Hamid much after that (until later in another guise). Instead, I was pretty much glued to Chris, whom I quickly came to admire. Other teachers frequently took offense at Chris' button-pushing antics and challenging demeanour. Interestingly though, it was always those hiding behind some kind of false persona that suffered most discomfort in his presence. Like the once successful Rugby International, living only on his past reputation, drowning out his non-acceptance of the present with bottles of Johnny Walker Whisky.

By contrast, in me, Chris found a willing disciple and instantly we got on like a house on fire. As one would expect, he was as hard as nails, but under the tough exterior, Chris had a heart of gold and took me willingly under his mighty Pegasus wing. We trained together on the assault course, yomped mile after mile along endless meandering riverbanks, and expended countless rivers of sweat in the steamy gym. In between time, he helped me begin to understand (what he felt to be) the true meaning of leadership. I could hear him saying now: "To lead effectively, is to balance three different things at the same time: the mission, the team, and the individual. If you can hold the interests of all three together, you'll be a successful leader. But don't expect to be able to look after all of the team's interests, all of the time. That's impossible, when you've got the mission to achieve."

Maybe he did have some understanding for the individual!

He agreed that whatever had happened previously at RCB, I should re-apply, so I wrote to the Army and just a couple of weeks later got their response. It was not the first time in my life that an apparently insignificant piece of paper seemed to hold the key to my destiny. "Whilst we were not impressed by your sense of arrogance, we value persistence and determination, so we're prepared to give you a second chance." I was over the moon and set about preparing myself with Chris' help.

If it's truly in your heart, then you know you're meant to get something from it. In which case, don't be put off. Don't give up.

"Don't ever – but ever - take "no" for an answer."

Indeed!

As I trained daily with Chris, it was clear that he was a very unusual guy indeed. He'd invested enormous energy and attention in training his body to peak performance, and unlike most people in the Army, he had experimented rigorously with diet. He subscribed to the view that the human body was designed to eat fresh fruit and vegetables and very little else. His diet was based on the famous "Fit for Life" program designed by Harvey and Marilyn Diamond. It is founded on the principle of food combining and eating in harmony with our natural biorhythms. So in the morning, when the body is eliminating waste, you eat only fruit to assist the process. From midday the body is assimilating, in other words ingesting energy, and one of the most efficient ways of supporting this, is through eating raw salads mixed with fats. In the early evening, the body begins to digest, so heavier meals of cooked vegetables and complex carbohydrates or starches are consumed. If meat was to be eaten, it was not to be combined with starch-filled foods.

The idea is that some food types are acid forming and others alkalising, requiring appropriate acid and alkaline enzymes to digest. Since acid and alkali cancel each other out, the food does not digest properly. On top of that, if we eat too much processed food, the liver begins to store poisonous toxins, and amongst other things, becomes less able to metabolise ingested fat. In other words, you put on weight, produce less energy and clog the bodily systems with waste...

Mother nature has it's natural biorhythms for a reason!

141

In training with Chris, I was caused to confront society's conditioning that in order to be strong and fit, we must eat plenty of meat. With the Fit for Life approach, the view is taken that our genes are almost identical to those of chimpanzees and they survive extremely well on a diet of mainly fruit. We're also very closely related to one of the strongest mammals on the planet, the Gorilla, and they eat only a plant-based diet. If you consider that our ancestors evolved over millions of years on a very simple diet, it's likely that our bodies are naturally adapted to that way of eating. It became clear to me that so many of our health problems in life today are caused by over-processed food, full of artificial flavourings and preservatives. If I had any doubts about whether the diet worked, Chris' performance in the gym answered them, unequivocally. I was just 24 at the time, and as a result of Boat Race training extremely fit, or at least I thought so. Chris was 40, and in the gym or on the track, he could destroy me in time for breakfast!

After one training session, which had left me starved of breath and floundering helplessly on the floor, I agreed to try the diet with Chris. In just two months, I went from thirteen stones to eleven, but more importantly, the level of energy in my system went through the roof. During Boat Race trials my time for a 3.5 mile run was around 24 minutes, which left me languishing laboriously at the back. Now, I literally flew around the same course in under 18 minutes, which would have placed me in the top three...

Well I did try to tell you!

"Yes, I know, but it's not at all easy to listen, with all those other ideas, emotions and objectives going on. In society it makes sense to apply logic, and copy what happens in mainstream acceptability."

That's why you've got to directly confront each moment, open a space into it, and let your own soul speak to you.

Back in the movie, as a new leaner me took form, another phenomenon was beginning to emerge. I couldn't put words to it at the time, but I so often felt euphoric, as if floating on air. As I looked on with the presence, I knew it was an expansion of consciousness that I, as Chris, had been experiencing...

When you eat mainly unprocessed food, that is properly combined with your natural biorhythms, the digestive system has to work less hard, and so your metabolism slows down. This is actually a really good thing in terms of consciousness. It makes the internal functioning of your system much 'quieter'; consequently, you are more able to break through the density and 'hear' the quiet inner voice of the soul. As you attune more to the spirit and less so to your bodily functions, the taste of the soul, and its at-one-ment with all life, strengthens. This universal life energy, "chi" or "ki" as it is sometimes known, connects you to your divine birthright, bringing with it increased empowerment, a sense of well-being and a greater level of inner peace. Breakthrough often feels euphoric, like floating on air.

With this new-found energy and the determination to never take "no" for an answer, I literally sailed through the Regular Commissions Board with the Army. Obstacles melted before me. Somehow it seemed like the Universe was willing me forwards. It was as if every light was turning from red to green...

That's what Breakthrough into universal ki does for you!

I was absolutely overjoyed. As my time to leave the school arrives, I have just a few belongings, which easily fit into the boot of my car. It feels tremendously liberating - everything I own in the world is with me. Nevertheless, my heart is heavy at the prospect of leaving Chris. But I can see in his steely blue eyes, that he understands the sense of adventure that draws the warrior forwards. No long goodbyes are necessary. I love him as my father, and it is clear he loves me as his son. Yet still, we are able to let go.

You were breaking through any need of attachment. How liberating!

13

The Sand to Polish the Diamond

*"It's only when you are truly under pressure,
that you can see what you're really made of.
It's only then that there's inspiration
and possibility for lasting change."*

As I arrived at the mighty gates of Sandhurst - the Officer Training Academy - a whole array of thought and adrenaline-induced emotion was surging through me. I was thrilled and excited to be there, but there was great trepidation too. I'd not fully resolved in myself whether I could actually harm another if called to do so, and did I really want to subject myself to all that conditioning?

If I had to summarise the experience in one breath, I would say, most astonishingly, it was a test of one's sense of centredness - the ability to be totally present and focussed in the moment, whilst at the same time, being able to adopt an 'oversight' of circumstances. In other words, to be engrossed in activity but not lost in it - to be more the Observer of myself in life. There are many distorted and judgmental views of the Army, consequently I wasn't prepared for the deeply spiritual experience it turned out to be...

Attention to detail is what the Zen Buddhists call 'mindfulness'. When we can adopt oversight of ourselves in all circumstances - the place of the Observer - then we become less attached to a particular outcome and more able to read the full truth of the moment. If we follow this path to its ultimate conclusion, we become the non-identified, unrestricted, omnipresent "Seer" through all things and events. In short, we unfold into that which we truly are - The Absolute, beyond all illusion.

The quest for Enlightenment may not have been the objective at Sandhurst, but as I looked back, I could see how it invited each of us to step onto the inner journey and uncover deeper truths about who we really were. There were many times when you desperately needed to summon the inner will, to keep going when all seemed beyond hope or possibility; but there were also many others, when you needed to surrender into the pain and to the governance, because you simply couldn't fight it. As I looked back, it was clear, practically every moment offered the potential for a spiritual Breakthrough. Probably none of the instructors would have explained it like that, but I came to see that the daily tests, trials and tribulations helped many find a new centre of completeness, beyond all the aggravation, button-pushing and struggle.

It's only when you are truly under pressure, that you can see what you're really made of. It's only then that there's inspiration and possibility for lasting change.

The chief proponents of the button-pushing at Sandhurst were the Colour Sergeant Instructors. Sandhurst is unlike most training academies, since (in principle), the students outrank their instructors, but even though the Sergeants referred to us as "Sir", no one was under any illusion, whatsoever, as to who wore the pants.

Suddenly I was right back there, right in the thick of it, finding myself standing to attention, awaiting inspection by one of the aforementioned Colour Sergeants. Every muscle in my body is rigid, and yet alive, as if connected up to the mains electricity. Chin raised, shoulders back, chest out, eyes fixed on some distant focus. I am working hard with the dynamic tension of body, fighting rigorously the tired objections of mind, all in order to remain absolutely motionless. Thighs are clenched tight to prevent wobbling knees; pins and needles are shooting through deadened fingers, locked around my rifle, desperately trying to prevent it falling - a fate worse than death! We'd been standing to attention like this for well over an hour - another test of centredness, another chance to let go.

As I'm standing there to attention, the inspecting Sergeant is now standing before me, it is my turn. Not daring to look him in the eyes, I stand ramrod straight, as he picks me over with a fine tooth comb.

Looking back, what are you feeling at this point?

I feel tight throughout my body, in my chest and also my head. I feel threatened and anxious, like being trapped in some very small cage.

This happens to lots of people when they feel under threat. Their souls contract into an inner cage. They're now not able to be fully free, fully empowered, fully them. They become victimised. Your body may be controlled, but it's entirely up to you how you respond in your soul.

I could feel the energetic cage I'd willingly placed around myself. I felt to move, stretch and expand, to breathe deeply. Upon which, I could feel the bars of the cage bending and breaking apart.

A few moments of pause later, back in the movie, my turnout is immaculate, there is nothing to find. I breathe an inaudible, and very controlled, sigh of relief as the Sergeant moves on.

Tim Hemsworth, the next in line, is not so lucky however. He always seems to get picked up for something, and sure enough, today is no exception... "You been cleaning your boots with a chocolate bar again Mr Hemsworth, Sir?" retorts the Sergeant, with very thinly-veiled sarcasm. I can hear a quietly stifled smirk from the cadet next to me, but I dare not release a similar response, even though my sides feel like bursting - I am simply too close to the action for comfort. In fact Hemsworth was well known for his unusual behaviour, and although not generally popular, we came to tolerate him for his slightly weird, but also refreshing humour.

On one previous occasion, where his parade kit had been woefully lacking, the Colour Sergeant had told him to march off to the Statue of Queen Victoria at the bottom of the parade ground and tell her "what a prick he was". Hemsworth dutifully marched off. But then caused total consternation to the platoon as he appeared to begin a conversation with the dear old Queen, and then stretch out on the grass in the sunshine before her. "What the fuck?" I could clearly hear the Colour Sergeant mumble under his breath before quick-marching off in Hemsworth's direction, spouting various undecipherable expletives as he went.

When he got there, apparently Hemsworth had said to the Sergeant... "Well I told Queen Victoria what you said Sarge, to which she told me 'not to worry, take it easy, and put your feet up for a while.'"

Well, what an awesome response. You just have to hand it to him!

"Indeed, he'd certainly mastered a good degree of surrender."

I'd say it's more than that. He'd probably been victimised many times before, just as physically weaker, sensitive or maverick souls often are. Although maybe unknowingly, he'd found a way to tap into his soul, take comfort in it, and not be suppressed or controlled by others.

It's no surprise Hemsworth was singled out by the other Sergeants as a target to be broken down – because he challenged authority in that way.

But there was the rumoured time they'd gone too far, picked on him once too often, and so the courageous Hemsworth took it upon himself to report them up the chain, which saw one of the Colour Sergeants sacked and another severely chastised.

You've seen Hemsworth before of course.

"Really? Where?"

Do you really need me to tell you? Someone who's been trodden down, yet in this case, found something to fight the dejection and alienation with – he'd found humour. Humour can be one of the most disarming and wrong footing gifts of the soul. It can be used to take the seriousness out of any situation. How the apparently mighty can be so easily felled by it.

He's Hamid, all over again.

Back on the parade ground, at the inspection, I can see from the corner of my eye, the Sergeant place his marching stick squarely in the centre of Hemsworth's chest... "There is a piece of shit on the end of this stick Mr Hemsworth, Sir." To my utter astonishment Hemsworth pipes up, "Not on this end, Sergeant!" The rest of us couldn't believe what we were hearing. Amidst stifled smirks, I strain my eyes further to the left to catch a glimpse of the unfolding drama. In the rapidly dying moments of calm before the impending tornado, my focus is drawn to the main artery in the neck of the inspecting Sergeant - a pulsating river of blood, about to burst its banks. Hemsworth was verbally rifted and frogmarched off to the guardroom in double quick time.

Despite his antics, Hemsworth made it through. And as I looked back, although I'd not warmed to him at the time, I certainly did now. Here was someone who just wouldn't be pigeon-holed, who just wouldn't be broken down and stuck in a cage. He just wouldn't take "no" for an answer. Go for it Hemsworth. Go for it Hamid!

You all know the Hemsworths of the world. They're there to challenge judgment, and in-the-box mentality. They're mavericks, and although they may irk you from time to time, pay close attention. For it also needs the sand to polish the diamond.

Sandhurst was indeed a diamond polishing trial. It exposed self-deception and bluff like no other place on earth. We were forced to drag aching and weary limbs from comfortable beds every day, long before sunrise. Much time was needed to prepare for the daily ordeal of room inspections, which began promptly at 6 am. There were photos in the corridor of how everything should be laid out, even those things tucked away in drawers. All uniforms had to be perfectly ironed and hanging neatly in cupboards in the correct order. Every item of equipment was to be spotlessly clean and in its rightful place. Bed blankets and sheets were to be folded into a 'bed block' exactly 18inches square, the bed cover stretched taut so that a coin would bounce at least 6 inches off it. If even the slightest detail was wrong, the risk was to have one's entire kit thrown out of the window and ordered to 'show parade' at 10pm that night - a foreboding repeat performance.

Mindfulness indeed. And not so dissimilar to the Zen Buddhists.

"But is it really necessary?"

It certainly helps bring attention into the moment when you focus on the detail in front of you. Most people have so many things going on in their minds, it's hard for them to focus in this way. Try simplifying your life, take out what you don't need, then focus on what's left.

The daily program was one of absolute precision, not a single minute was wasted. We would run from inspection to the assault course, to the classroom or to the gym. Early afternoons were especially challenging. We'd often do hard physical exercise in the morning and have a lecture straight after lunch. The Directing Staff knew it would be almost impossible to stay awake, but that was part of the test. Could we overcome the natural physical response to give up?

It would also offer the opportunity to explore presence. Can you stay awake and present, even though you feel your body closing down? This is how you penetrate the physical 'box', leading to Breakthrough.

In the beginning I felt the meticulous attention to detail was completely over the top, but the more I got into it, the more I saw it as a possibility to develop my strength of personality.

You had to break through the physical circumstances by feeling into them...feeling through them.

As I reflected on it now, I could see how the attention to detail was actually causing us to be more present in the moment. Something inexplicable was compelling me to do the opposite of what seemed natural - to actually go deeply into the pain. I was learning not to become so attached and identified with the experiences; there seemed literally no choice, you either surrendered or broke down. Although none of us realised it (not even the staff), we were being given a crash course in Enlightenment - to hold the duality of being the One Life (observing experiences) and a finite expression of the One Life (deeply engaged in circumstances) simultaneously in every moment...

It is a paradoxical truth that in times of such exactitude, a person may finally realise that absolutely NOTHING in life really matters. Having reached this place of total surrender, you may also then decide that you can still care about the outcome. To be truly enlightened is not just about being awesomely okay whilst meditating on a mountain top, it is about being enlightened by all events and circumstances.

Apply yourself therefore in stressful circumstances that place great demand on you. Use them as an opportunity to be present, focussed in yourself. Give of yourself to what you're doing, but also expand and relax in the knowing that the outcome doesn't ultimately matter.

Many of the students found the attention to detail, pace of the course and the constant mental, physical and emotional stress difficult to cope with and dropped out. For those who endured however, the rewards were great. Over time, you really began to know your own personality. You knew what conditions caused you to become selfish and focus on your own issues and problems. You knew what made you afraid, how to deal with your fear and rise above it. It became natural to place the interests of others before oneself. The Sandhurst motto is "Serve to Lead" and in trying to serve others, you would constantly push up against the boundary of self-interest.

Pray not for an easy life, but a testing one that helps you grow.

You might be on a squad run for example and be completely shattered, wondering how you would get to the end and yet see others behind you faring even worse. Could you overcome your desire to succeed yourself and instead go back to help a colleague? You might be on exercise in the wind and the rain, having not slept or eaten properly for days, carrying injuries that could put you out of Sandhurst - do you focus on your own problems or do you find the inner strength to inspire and raise the morale of others? The word 'crucifixion' popped into my mind and I could now see, that for me, in many ways, this is what Sandhurst was all about...

A crucifixion of the ego is where you are caused to continually confront all those experiences where you get attached to the need or desire for a particular outcome. Can you be chastised? Judged? Hungry? Thirsty? In pain? Forsaken? Can you suffer these and yet still rise above it all, knowing that you are the imperishable Source that is not defined by any of it? This is what it means to 'crucify the ego'. This is truly polishing the diamond.

"There are a few people to whom this seems to come totally naturally."

They're usually the quiet ones, the unsung heroes of life.

A vision came to my mind of a very talented cadet called Frank Miller. Had he focussed just on self-interest, he would have won most of the tests and exercises and probably gone on to win the "Sword of Honour" for top student. Frank, however, worked tirelessly to make the lives of his comrades easier in many ways that went unseen by the directing staff. He would always be there with a smile when you needed it most. When we stopped on a long march for a few brief moments, he would be the one ignoring his own tiredness and making tea for everyone else. He'd be checking if you were okay, remember what injuries you were carrying - could he do anything to help? Of course as Officers, we were all meant to be helping others, but with Frank, it was second nature, because it came from his heart. Consequently, he was the most popular in our troop, the natural leader. His example was an inspiration to us all, and it would stay with me my whole life...

And this is also what it means to be a 'lightworker'. Many today work tirelessly behind the scenes in the darkest and densest vibrations to help others see the light and all the while receiving little or no recognition for it. A true lightworker knows the best accolade is the simple inner recognition of having given of one's best no matter what the apparent observable outcome.

Finally, after months of grafting and grinding, button-pushing and verbal rifting, cleaning and polishing, we became newly-commissioned Second Lieutenants in the British Army. As I now watch the closing of the parade, slow marching up the steps to the majestic Victorian Hall, led by a dashing white horse, which so reminds me of the mighty Pegasus, I can thoroughly appreciate how Sandhurst had turned out to be one of the most powerful preparations for my eventual spiritual awakening.

Synchronistically, Pegasus is the mystical winged horse that carries spiritual seekers into 'heaven' – symbolic of rising through the dimensions into the hallowed inner temple of The One.

"Yes - but unfortunately I didn't know that at the time!"

Through countless daily tests I had discovered what my personality was all about. I came to know what experiences resonated and spoke to the very core of my being. I had realised how to break through particular situations by feeling deeply into them, which paradoxically rendered the suffering less impactful. Above all, I had learned the utmost importance of retaining a sense of humour, even when the proverbial 'shit hits the fan'...

This form of 'spiritual breakdown' brought you much closer to the ultimate Breakthrough – to "the Seer" in you, which is a pure state of perception. It is simply presence or "is-ness". To be the Observer of oneself in all events, mirrors this experience of the Seer, and is the path to it. Can you stay in the drama but not be defined by it? Sense of humour is a vital characteristic on this journey to the Seer - it requires non-attachment. That's why laughing in the face of life - and death - is so important to everyone.

What I couldn't yet do all the time, was to be fully through the experience, giving of my all, yet not tightening in certain situations - especially where the warrior energy in me wanted to rise.

The soul has many characteristics, and there's the possibility of being 'owned' in different situations by different soul combinations - different 'harmonics' - as they arise within you. For some it will be in deeply challenging physical encounters, for others, through intense emotional ones. The point is to explore what life presents to you, see where you get tight and attached; notice the patternings that repeat, then feel into and through them by honouring them. This way, you break through that particular configuration of reality and set your soul free.

Increasingly, you become able to do this all the time. It's all about confronting and penetrating through the experience into the abode of The Absolute - constantly coming home to that which you truly are.

I would come to realise it's not about fighting the experiences you're having. For this only builds polarity and identity with them – separation from the One Life, which is all-embracing. In time, I would come to realise that to truly master the state of the Seer, I had to blend the will of the warrior - the divine masculine - with the softness and surrender of the divine feminine.

I would need both the Sword and the Rose.

14

The Sword and the Rose

"Each must learn to harmonise the energies
of both purpose and surrender
in order to find true harmony."

So there I was, 'hanging out with the presence', in some obscure farmhouse offices, tucked away in the quiet Hampshire countryside, with nothing particularly noteworthy about it, yet travelling multidimensionally through the movingly profound circumstances of my life. When most people look back, it's probably often through photograph albums - snaps, catching glimpses, inexpertly taken. Yet when you can regress yourself there, actually into the feelings, it brings the movie to life. I had help of course, and I was ready to surrender. I'd experienced far too many of life's broken promises to want to continue the struggle. Now I had a reason to let go.

Each regressive experience revealed another 'layer of the onion' - where I was attached and bound up within the physicality of life. But in seeing and feeling it again, as a deep, conscious exploration, meant I could keep unwinding, unravelling and breaking through...

It's exactly why awakening people often refer to "peeling off layers of an onion". As the soul infuses the bodymind, 'fragments' of it break off and form layers of identification, which get buried in the sediment of life. It's why you can't feel the soul and its interconnectivity. It means most people are only acting as a mere shadow of themselves. When finally you do give up struggling to be something you're not, the compacted layers soften as you bring consciousness into them. You reintegrate soul, and that particular layer peels off. It feels like coming home. It's what I mean by "Breakthrough".

I'd been a warrior all my life – I'd become pretty good at the struggle to get the things I thought I wanted. I was stronger and fitter than most and forever honing the intellect to succeed in this apparent world of dog-eat-dog. But looking back, I could so easily see how this had closed me down, making me often depressed and miserable. It was a sanitized depression, with soft comforts like food, alcohol, boys-toys, and TV to numb the pain. The drudge was occasionally pierced by some joyful 'victory', where I'd attained something. But really, like so many others who are barely alive today, I was on a treadmill, heading to nowhere.

That's why I was so relieved to find this regressive journey of re-awakening. No longer efforting to accomplish something. Just stopping, witnessing and feeling the interconnectivity of my soul, like a soft flower, gently prodding its way through the cracks in decaying concrete, then bathing in warm waves of sunlight; like coming home and being cuddled in a loving blanket. "You've done it! You're breaking through!. You've arrived!"

With each regression, I realised just how important the sweet softness of surrender is. As I reimmersed myself in the experiences, although I couldn't have put words to it at the time, all the while, I was reclaiming lost fragments of soul, all the while reconnecting within. Hotspots in my body *(the chakras)* were coming alive, like a river of warmth, flowing through my body, making me feel overjoyed and at times blissed out. It was indeed a rollercoaster ride of emotion.

Ready for another round?

"Of course. What better is there to do!"

Suddenly I found myself regressed into darkness and fear, as the helicopter hit the surface of the water and tumbled over. We'd been drilled to wait until it came to rest before trying to exit. Icy water is now gushing in, shortening the breath and quickening the heart as the unmistakable pulse of adrenaline fills my veins. Now fully upside down, I gasp for one last breath, as the watery blackness first engulfs my head and then steadily the rest of my rigid body. Drowning in confusion and disorientation, I can still just make out to either side of me, colleagues taking part in the infamous Royal Marine Commando Course. We'd been told to wait until the water had filled the hull of the craft before exiting via the nearest window. The trouble is, that with 30 of us in full kit and only a couple of small windows, there was no margin for error; we wait as patiently as humanly possible for our turn to exit. Although just an exercise, it is hard to maintain perspective in the murky blackness, with the ice cold water rapidly consuming body, mind and spirit.

In such moments, the challenge is always to break through into stillness deep within. And paradoxically, it's the surrender of the divine feminine that takes you there - to be able to accept the disorientation and pain, without needing it to go away. This surrender stops you identifying with the physicality of life.

It may seem almost impossible to do; the increased activity within the bodymind causes you to notice and attune to it, making the circumstances even more terrifying. However, if you can resist this temptation and surrender to what is happening with complete acceptance, then you can pass through the heart of the tightness and attune instead to the sweet expansiveness of the soul.

Like the Paras, The Royal Marines are an elite force trained to be self-sustaining in the fog of war, ready to be dispatched at a moment's notice to trouble spots and deal with chaotic circumstances with the minimum of preparation and equipment. I was now an Army Captain with the Royal Engineers, having switched from the Paras at Sandhurst, feeling it would be more in tune with my science degree background. Besides, I wasn't the kind of 'beast' the Paras were really looking for. The Royal Marines seconded officers and soldiers from the Army to provide specialist engineering and logistic expertise, the combined organisation forming 3 Commando Brigade. These 'Green Berets' have been involved in some of the most challenging campaigns in military history. To serve in the Brigade required one to successfully complete the Commando Course, in which I was now, 'lock stock and barrel', deeply engaged.

You were prepared to throw yourself in at the deep end of life's experiences. You let yourself go over the waterfall, and it battered you in many ways. But you were learning how to surrender into the battering. Thus, increasingly, you were able to become as one with the flow in these occasions. Before long, you'd bob back up to the surface for some welcome breaths of fresh air.

My journey was taking me deep into physical, emotional and mental limitations – *through the layers of the onion* - pushing back inner barriers of non-acceptance, the places where I gave in and became identified with the drama. I was being fully immersed, fully washed through, with the spectacular kaleidoscope of human experience...

Take a look around you at what's happening in the world. Each soul is experiencing a microcosm of the greater macrocosm – of light breaking through darkness – the chaotic evolution of consciousness.

If you truly want to know your completeness and inviolable essence, you have to be able to transcend this darkness – to be able to deal with ALL circumstances that come your way. And to 'transcend', doesn't mean to avoid or suppress. It means to go into the very heart of it, and release your fear of it, so that it can no longer hold you. When you can do this, you connect up with the universal flow, and from this surrendering softness, unleash incredible potential into the moment.

It's why a true warrior has learned to blend both the divine feminine and the masculine.

The Commando Course helped me discover new strengths. In going deep within, I was becoming more frequently the observer of experiences rather than being victimised by them. I became more able to detach myself and as a result, the pain, be it mental, emotional or physical, was becoming more manageable. I couldn't yet do this all the time, and not even at will, but, it seemed like when I needed it most, in the depths of despair, I would somehow slip into this state where time stood still and nothing really mattered...

You were discovering the art of harmonising the sword and the rose - the warrior energy provides the impetus to do something, but once that purpose has been initiated, what is necessary to ensure its successful completion, is absolute surrender into the moment. It is only by surrendering, that you can truly feel the soul and thereby follow Right Action. If you continue to struggle and fight, you can no longer sense the true flow of universal life energy. That's why each must learn to harmonise the energies of both purpose and surrender in order to find true harmony. Paradoxically, you become the best warriors of life when you are most surrendered.

Suddenly, I began to see sports that we might consider masculine 'warrior' type events in a different light. When you consider true greatness, it occurred to me that the very best had found a way (to varying degrees) of harnessing and harmonising both energies. Probably for this reason, the world champion boxer, Muhammed Ali, had so poetically spoken of "floating like a butterfly" before "stinging like a bee"...

Mastering the sword and the rose is not about necessarily becoming some 'gladiator' at the pinnacle of sport. It could be a housewife bringing up the kids, a store keeper at the local grocery or the guy driving your bus. Each and every situation provides the possibility to break through with commitment and surrender - to break through into your deeper sense of self. For that is the only thing truly going on.

It caused me to marvel at the profound sense of humility with which Ali handled his incredibly crippling Parkinson's disease, which, in the twilight of his life, left him pretty much a physical wreck. From the heights of athletic stardom, he was dashed into the physical abyss, and yet all the while, with still the unquenchable glint in the eyes of a warm and embracing smile. Without knowing it at the time, this transition of acceptance was beginning to ignite at key times within me too.

The real heroes of life are often the unseen, unsung ones. Quietly getting on with their challenges, far away from the glitz and the glamour. You'll often see a ready smile and a glint in their eye. Their souls are undimmed by the denseness, and sometimes harshness, of the physical world.

Just a few weeks prior to the course beginning, I met Amanda, a divinely feminine soul who was to become my wife. During the course we were mercifully given the odd Sunday off, a 'generous' 36 hour break; just enough time to make the 5hr journey from Lympstone to London where Amanda was living; just enough time to receive some of the divinely tender side of the female energy, collapse into her lap, sleep for 12 hours, have a hearty Sunday breakfast, treat my blisters and then make the long haul back to Lympstone, ready for Monday morning parade. This was led, very synchronistically, by Colour Sergeant "Rose", who had nothing whatsoever in common with his namesake.

Don't you just love the irony of life! All these little messages sent to wake you up that frequently go unnoticed. The hardness of an unforgiving Sergeant, breaking you down into the softness of the spiritual warrior!

For me, without really knowing it, the Commando Course itself took the harmonisation of yin and yang to a whole new level. Yes you could continue to fight, yes you could apply brute force and ignorance to carry you through some of the tests, but sure enough, there would eventually come a breaking point for even the most macho. We would all have to eventually surrender to pain, cold, saturation, exhaustion, hunger or loss of pride. The longer you resisted, the harder and tighter you became, until at some point, the snap was sure to happen. When the breaking point was reached, you could go one of two ways: give up and leave the course or find a new depth of spirit and become awesomely okay with where you were now at...

Indeed, brute force and ignorance can get you a long way in your desensitised world, but in truth, this approach just heaps on thicker and thicker layers of self-denial, until at some point, the light of the soul is so dimmed, even the most ignorant are caused to acknowledge it is now dark!

The Commando Course mostly took place out in the field where physical and emotional stress is compounded by cold and wet weather, little sleep, little time for food, and endless miles of 'yomping' (trekking) whilst carrying unbearably heavy loads. The attrition rate was high. Many dropped out through injury, although just about everyone was suffering from one problem or another. The directing staff were distant, impersonal at best, and downright abusive at worst. But again, I came to realise this was all a part of the drill. At what seemed like a snail's pace, the weeks crawled by, leaving me just enough strength to make the eagerly anticipated drive on Saturday afternoon up to London to see Amanda. This was the chance of a few brief hours of normality and sensuality in a comfortable, centrally heated, student flat near to Wimbledon. The contrast to the cold, windswept, barren wilderness of Dartmoor, could hardly have been more stark.

In any such arduous challenge you might face, which has some duration to it, think not of the completion, use it only as a target to guide you in the right direction. But then focus intently on each moment. Bring yourself and your presence fully into it. Then the completion – wherever and whatever that is – will naturally take care of itself.

As if to prove the point, I suddenly found myself at the top of a 100ft cliff, dangling by a rope, singing "Ten Green Bottles". This was the Royal Marines introduction to the art of abseiling. Strapped on my back was a full pack with equipment weighing-in at a backbreaking 70-80 pounds. The tautness of the straining rope reflected the whining in muscle and sinew, as I hung powerless a few feet below the cliff edge, held in place by one of the directing staff acting as the brake-man at the bottom of the cliff. It was as if I was hanging by a wafer thin thread of trust.

Whilst singing the song, as instructed, I was constantly kicking off the wall waiting for the moment when the brake-man would let go. Suddenly the break was released, "and if one green bottle should accidentally fall," I plunge backwards down the cliff, heart in mouth, stomach as if trailing a few feet behind. This is it then, the moment of death, this is what it feels like. I come rapidly into total presence, nothing else matters, only the moment. Vision suddenly sharpens as the hardened greyness of the cliff-face streams backwards, colours blurring into oneness, like a time-bending vortex; the rush of the wind roars in my ears, feelings of inner expansion and lightness engulfing all. Strangely, all fear has dissipated...this is it...all coming to an end...no more need to struggle or fight...no need of question, answer or endless mind chatter...no need of justification or self-acceptance...no one here to accept anything...just peace. For me, eternity has unfolded a moment of sheer bliss.

Looking on as the movie-goer, the presence was with me, but no words or thoughts came. There was no need of them. We both knew what we were experiencing together. Time had stopped. Chris the Commando was there, Chris the observer was there, the presence was there. All had merged into a timeless moment. No past, no future, just now. There was an audible click of the fingers...

All three of us are embracing the "Seer".

Then "Thuunkkkkk" pierces the silence. The brake had been applied, the rope had taken the strain, and a sudden, bone-shaking jolt thrust me right back to reality.

Well, back to the illusion actually!

But I remembered the blissful feeling. Even as I was returned brutally to mortality, the memory of the soft expansiveness remained, it had activated something within me. I couldn't say what it was exactly at the time. And it certainly wouldn't have been 'cool' to speak of the divine feminine, even if I'd known that's what it was; but I knew its profoundness, that somehow, surrendering was okay. Of course, especially in the military, it carries so much white flag stigma - that you've lost, given in, and have to suffer the consequences. But within it, I'd found something truly precious. It was like a corridor of mirrors, leading to a hallowed place, that tantalisingly appeared at key times, but a place I somehow couldn't always stay.

One thing was for sure, death and one's proximity to it, seemed to hold a vital key.

If you can surrender each day to the prospect of your inevitable death, then you realise that what you might gain in a physical sense from life, doesn't matter; you start to acquire a sense that there's something beyond all of that, eternal, inviolable through it all, and that's what's truly worth knowing and experiencing. Ultimately, when you master your fear of death, you master your fear of life.

And it's not actually as hard as it may seem. The problem is, practically the whole of society clings precariously to life because of the fear of death. So tight is their clinging, that they strangle the very life essence from it. But if you're prepared to confront all this useless fear-mongering, simply by inquiring within, wherever you are, whatever you're doing, then eventually the myth of death is sure to explode. You'll break through into The One.

It is for no small reason that the Dalai Lama suggests contemplating your death every day. And just look how happy he is!

As I looked back on the abseiling experience, and felt deeply into it again, I was able to feel the sense of surrender within this 'trust fall'. There was literally nothing else to do but let go. In so doing, I felt so much on the edge of life, on the edge of reality, that I became able to step through it all, into that sense of pure presence. It was magical.

Looking back on it now, I realised that the Marines' instruction in abseiling was a powerful exercise in just letting go, trusting and surrendering to the inevitable process of life. I was caused to remember that many times in my life, I had sailed close to death and somehow there had always been a curious side within me wondering what lay beyond and an almost irresistible compulsion to experience it. It surfaced frequently when standing on tall buildings or cliff-faces. Somehow, there was this inner feeling to let go and jump off, restrained only by my ego afraid of the consequences.

Your purpose in life is to fully unveil the soul so that it is no longer shrouded by the restrictions, conditions and limitations of the personality. To truly taste the absolute freedom of the soul is to be surrendered in all things, even, and especially at the moment of death. So the true path of the soul will invite you to confront this at times during your life (providing you don't keep avoiding it). However, the soul seldom causes people to actually take their own lives, for this, in itself, demonstrates lack of acceptance to the state you currently find yourselves in. When people actually commit suicide, it is likely that an inner distortion of non-acceptance drove them beyond what began as an authentic exploration of their mortality.

I would come to face the sense of death many times on my path to ultimate Breakthrough. As I looked on as the movie-goer, it was clear the path had ultimately softened me in that way.

It was now the Autumn of 1990. Earlier that summer Saddam Hussein had invaded Kuwait and it quickly became clear that British Forces might get involved to oust him. Despite there being five Squadrons in my Regiment, as 'luck' would have it, mine was the only unit chosen to go; we were immediately placed on standby at 24 hours notice to move. It meant that whilst still being thrashed on the Commando Course in the cold harshness of Dartmoor, at any moment, I might be summoned out to active service in the Desert. It would be just like stepping out of the frying pan and into the fire.

In the journey of life, it pays to expect the unexpected!

Meanwhile, the windswept, cold, wet and barren moors took their backbreaking toll on the body. In looking back, I wondered did the path need to be so physically challenging for everyone?

No, not at all. It all depends on what your particular soul configuration needs to experience. For some, it will be just as challlenging living in society, bringing up the kids or holding down a busy job for example. In these cases it might be the emotional or intellectual challenges that are needed to forge the soul.

Once more, as I'd discovered many times, if we are prepared to work with our problems and hold an open, positive outlook, it's quite amazing how the right kind of help seems to appear at just the right moment.

Of course! Ever heard the saying "God helps those who help themselves?"

The British Army works on a 'buddy system' where soldiers are partnered to help each other. The Commando Course is an 'all-ranks' one so officers are mixed in with private soldiers. I was now partnered with a Scottish guy, affectionately known as "Jock". Suddenly I was seeing my platoon, yomping in line across some high exposed moor, the rain driving into weary faces, reddened by exertion and the chafing wind. As I floated through their ranks, accompanied by the presence, I could hear their thoughts and feel their feelings. On the surface, there was mostly the steely determination that you'd expect from special forces – it's certainly what the soldiers would only want to show. But underneath the necessary bravado, I found it utterly amazing, there was a soft, child-like vulnerability to many of them.

The soul can demonstrate great courage, commitment and strength. But it is also soft, child-like and vulnerable. In fact it is absolute vulnerability to the moment that makes you best able to deal with the challenges of life. Vulnerability is so often seen as weakness, when in fact this couldn't be further from the truth. It's having the courage to always be this vulnerable, that opens you up to the truth of life, and most importantly, keeps you connected to the natural flow – an awesome, unquenchable river of energy.

My eyes fell once more upon Jock. He was a great guy with a quiet and unassuming personality, yet with this very typical steely determination.

As soldiers we seldom opened up to one another, especially not a Captain to a 'squadie', but the brutality of the conditions made us look to each other for some kind of warm empathy. Jock had that – in bucketloads - through his eyes, there was no concealing the generous compassion of a kindred spirit. But whereas I tended to be more intense, serious and driven, he had a much more easy way of being. He had a quiet inner confidence that I came to greatly respect and admire.

It is no coincidence that the right people in your lives show up when you most need them. Such 'angels' are in fact simply reflecting qualities to you that each possess, but perhaps haven't yet unveiled. The possibility of such encounters is pre-ordained, inherent in the flow - they are meant to happen. A true friend is someone who is drawn to you by this Law of Attraction. They are those who remind you of a buried aspect of your True Self.

Jock was the kind of guy who could take any 'shit' thrown at him, seemed to know deeply that none of it really mattered, and then just get on with the job anyway. Suddenly we were together once more, Jock's smiling, bright and tireless eyes encouraging me onwards, as we dig into grey, stony slate, on a barren, windswept Welsh mountainside. This is the infamous Defence Exercise in the very appropriately named "Black Mountains" of Wales. Beautiful hiking scenery it may well be, but only when you've a warm bed, log fire and nurturing food to go back to in the evening. The mountains take on a whole new perspective after three days without food and sleep, wearing sodden and freezing clothes, soaked through by endless hours of torrential rain.

It is now Wednesday evening; we're digging a six-foot deep defensive trench, which we'd begun at last light the previous Monday. The directing staff have clearly scoured the Welsh mountain range to find the most difficult terrain in which to dig. If that was indeed their intention, they had succeeded well. Jock is using a pickaxe and me the spade. He'll chip away at a couple of inches of slate and stone and I'll scrape it out. My stomach is noisily gurgling with hunger, bleary eyes can all but stay open. Looking back, feeling into it again, was the sense of how do you possibly carry on in such dead-end circumstances?

Surrender, always surrender. As hard as it may seem, if you're attaching, if you're resisting, there's something to gain at a soul level. You can soften more, and in so doing, integrate more.

Then finally, as if by some miracle, we've done it. We've reached the required depth. Now we might stop and eat some warming food. I get out my cooking stove and fumble with freezing fingers, trying hopelessly to light it with sodden matches, watching them fizz briefly before succumbing to the relentless damp. With each dwindling spark, it feels like the light inside of me is dying too. Jock is watching me. Somehow he manages to roll a cigarette, find a dry match, and light up. He smiles encouragingly as he hands it to me, the undimmed light in his eyes say it all. Not being a smoker, I feel to refuse, but something stops me. Perhaps this is something, anything, that could distract me from the appalling conditions and provide at least a fleeting sense of comfort.

Yes, as you grow, you may at times need to distract yourself from the sometimes harsh exterior world. That's why people comfort eat, comfort drink, and comfort smoke. They're reminding themselves of the sense of relaxed openness of the soul that is always there, but may have become buried under the sometimes mountainous labour of their lives. It's not at all wrong to take such comforting distractions from time to time. It's just important not to get addicted to them.

I take a deep, bottomless drag of the roll-up. It's amazing how just the inhale provides comfort enough - anything to contrast with the wretchedness of the surroundings...

During your digging, in the quest for an 'end goal', you'd forgotten the importance of surrender to the moment. The quest of the sword had tightened you to the surrenderedness of the rose, such that you couldn't even feel the simple and yet miraculous beauty of your own breath. In truth, it was all you really needed – a long cool inhale.

Of course when we forget something we're supposed to remember, the Universe always has a way of trying to wake us up - even if we don't see it that way at the time. And sure enough, before I'd barely had time to appreciate the new sensation of relaxedness, there's a sudden, dull, but hard thud to the back of my neck... "What the fuck do you think you two loungers are up to?" rasps the unmistakable voice of Sergeant Rose, simultaneously sticking both the verbal and physical boot in. The cigarette drops from my mouth - a fleeting crutch, trampled under watery foot. "But we've finished our trench," pleads Jock. "We've reached the right depth." "And what about the rest of the troop?" roars Rose. "Have you selfish bastards thought about them for a second? Some officer you are Capt'n Bourne.... 'Sir'. "

Our brief pause ends almost as soon as it's begun. As we climb out of the trench, my eyes lock momentarily with Rose's. A part of me - the warrior - is saying "in any other circumstances you asshole..." and another part - the divine feminine - is accepting the chastisement. Yes, as an officer, I should have thought of the others first. The surrendered part of me wins out, my eyes break the gaze, it's already lasted far too long for comfort. Sheepishly we make our way over to help the others.

The warrior will always win, except that is, when you're not aligned with the truth!

We dig slavishly all through Wednesday night and the whole of the next day, finally finishing at last light on Thursday. By now, several of the troop have dropped out, evacuated by helicopter, having gone down with hypothermia. But the real heart-breaker is still to come; as we were soon to discover, our digging is just the warm up. Having had only an hour's break for the first meal in four days, suddenly we come under simulated attack - thunder flashes are exploding all around us and trip flares light up the blackened night sky over our heads. Hurried commands are being barked out by Sergeant Rose "Your position's been compromised. Everyone is to bug out...NOW! Head for the emergency rendezvous point." My eyes catch Jock's briefly, pleadingly. No words are exchanged, but we each know exactly what the other is thinking: "Please tell me this is not for real." "Yep, it sure is brother," is his unspoken reply.

As lightwarriors you're going to face such challenges in many guises.

The sense of never-ending density - you're in a curious reality that doesn't always work, where people judge you and you have to fight for resources. It doesn't matter if it's the barren coldness of the moor, or the harsh steel and glass canyons of the city, it can feel brutal and unforgiving. It helps not to require some physical outcome, to let go of the need for it to be a certain way. Focus on the breath, let it expand your consciousness, and just keep putting one foot in front of the other.

We speed-yomp the rest of the night through the backbreaking Black Mountains only to end up, on Friday morning, right back where we started from.

Ha! Did you ever really think you were going somewhere? You're always, only, ever right back where you started. It's The One in you which you've really been seeking; and it's always right under your very feet.

"Endex" is finally called. Thank you God! You can clearly hear in everyone's simultaneous unspoken thoughts, as we clamber wearily onto the wagons. We'd come full circle - it was as if all our efforts had literally come to nought.

And here's one of the great lies in human history. It is not the fruits of your labour that count, it is the labour itself; for only there, can you truly find the truth about who you are. It's only there that you self-realise, that you actualise the One Self.

As I looked back as the movie-goer, I could clearly see my ego still hanging on for dear life. And fascinatingly, I could touch that same place inside myself now, watching the movie. It was a twisted feeling in my gut, a buzzing tightness in my head, a sharp stabbing pain in my heart. It was something about what the Green Beret itself represented.

You were still searching for self-acceptance - still pinning it to some badge or accolade. And whilst you do that, the True Self will always remain tantalisingly just out of reach.

"I don't feel I'm ready to get it yet."

Back to the crucible then - the movie - to confront some more layers!

Next I find myself yomping quickly along a narrow country lane, arms swinging rhythmically across the body, with seemingly profound unwavering purpose, like an intercity train not stopping for passengers. With an excruciating weight on my back, lungs pumping, heart pounding and sweat pouring from reddened faces, this is the 12 mile load carry. I can literally feel the steely tightness of determination in my furrowed brow, eyes glued intently on the target - the black piece of tarmac, that seems eternally just a few steps in front.

I was good at marching, my experiences in rowing helped me to get into a rhythm and thereby overcome the pain. My buddy Jock is right next to me. If his surrenderedness had gotten us through the defence exercise, the warrior in me would get us both through the load carry - or at least so I thought.

The march began well for me, but within a few miles Jock starts to struggle, which is unusual, because he too is normally a very good yomper. I assume he's just suffering the effects of very understandable fatigue and so I switch into 'driving mode', the objective to drive him to the end of the march, no matter what the cost. This is a test we each need to successfully complete, and come hell or high water, I feel determined to get us both through.

Powerful sense of purpose - the warrior energy - is just as divine and authentic as the energy of surrender. When you divorce one from the other however, you become unbalanced and sooner or later, if uncorrected, it will push you, or someone else, over the precipice.

I march immediately next to him hanging onto his right ear. I coax, cajole and strongly encourage him, constantly varying the technique to distract him from the suffering. In response Jock courageously digs in, dragging his fractured body through the challenge in the required time, although by the end, finally succumbing to the excruciating pain we'd been fending off for the last twelve miles. I'm now deeply anguished as he's rushed off to hospital where they discover stress fractures in his shins. Shit! He's off the course. I can't believe it. Tears well up, I'm beset with deep remorse and guilt. Jock has been the greatest of friends to me.

Looking on as the movie-goer, the stabbing pain in my heart had intensified. It literally feels like someone has thrust a dagger into it. So much so, I think I'm going to have a heart-attack.

Feel deeply into it, the fullness of it. You're experiencing karma.

Suddenly I'm looking on the faces of many others I'd travelled with, who'd gotten lost along the way, who'd been broken by the path. The pain is beyond excruciating.

Work not to worry. They'll always remain in your heart, they'll always be a part of you. Take the memory of them deep inside.

The pain eases. I just know I'll re-encounter them again, somewhere down the path. I can feel the karma unwinding now. Heat, like hot liquid gold, begins to flood into my heart, healing and expanding it.

That's what happens when you break through karma. You unwind through the tightness all the way back to The One. This unleashes powerful flows of soul energy through your being.

That was the last I saw of Jock. As I looked back, a tear of sadness and a tear of joy ran simultaneously down my cheeks. The fact that I'd reconnected with such a warm and courageous soul, one with whom I'd no doubt travelled with – and died with – on many a battlefield before. One with whom I'd had the good fortune to reconnect in this lifetime.

Try to recognise and celebrate these reconnections with people on the path; for they mean so much in the awakening process.

Unfortunately, any compassionate streak in Chris the Commando was now being tempered by self-interest. In not being connected to what the moment had been telling me, I'd pushed not only Jock, but myself too hard as well, something that was now becoming painfully obvious – I'd acquired deep, blood-filled pressure blisters all across the soles of my feet. Jock paid the price immediately, the cost to myself however, would become brutally clear in due course...

Your bleeding feet were mirroring the bleeding of your soul. No one is saying you shouldn't go for these things – like the Green Beret, writing a book, doing something you're passionate about. It's right to be all-in. However, always soften into it and feel the light of your soul. That's how you truly bring light into the darkness.

It is now a couple of days later, 2 am in the morning, somewhere on the windswept rocky barrenness of Dartmoor. This is the yomping exercise. A hundred miles or so, up hill and down dale across treacherous, clinging peat bog; stripping naked to cross icy rivers. It's exactly what my poor, injured feet don't need - yomping for days on end, crammed into unforgiving boots, battered as raw meat. I notice that the pain would intensify every time we stopped for a brief pause, but soon disappear again once marching. I realise the only way to stay on the exercise (and thereby on the course) is to march on the spot when the rest of the troop are resting...

If you try to remove yourself from pain, you just make it worse. However, if you go right into the heart of it, as if you're trying to make it worse, the tendency is for you to become so familiar with it, that you stop resisting, you stop buying into the drama that it is creating in your mind.

It was an incredible relief to finally make it to the end of the exercise, not least because it meant there was only the final test week left to complete. My relief, however, was very short lived. No sooner had I sat down, than the pain in my feet began to kick in once more. Gingerly I take off my boots - the first time since the beginning of the exercise. I'm horrified at what I see: the whole of the soles of both feet have formed huge blisters, which are on the point of bursting.

The medic comes over and removes several syringes of infected gunge. For a moment this provides a degree of relief, but then he injects iodine into the empty blisters. As the unforgiving chemical violates raw flesh, it feels like I'm going to explode - an intense searing pain leaves me writhing in agony on the ground. I have never experienced anything like this, the pain is shooting through every fibre of my being.

The soles of your feet are reflex points for every part of your body!

It took me many minutes to reconnect with where I was. A couple of guys help carry me to the transport. The senior directing staff comes over to see me, tells me to report to the camp hospital on our return, and that crucially... "You're now off the course, Capt'n Bourne."

As I'm looking back, I can literally feel the sense of loss, even through the incredible intensity. I can feel the sense of impossibility in my battered head, like a roundabout with no exits. With final test week starting first thing in the morning and beginning with a 9 mile speed march, I can see it's an impossibility to continue. I begin to relive the reality of being thrown off the course. I start to slide into self-doubt; I'd failed to get a rowing blue and yet again, when the chips were down, I am failing. I'd hung all my hopes and ambitions on achieving something I considered to be special. But that bubble is now bursting, seemingly taking everything of me, and what I thought I stood for, with it.

Take a look in the mirror. Then take it off the wall, and throw it outside. Get rid of your limiting identity!

So I do. And with that, as I go deep, there is a definite sense that I'm leaving behind something that's simply not me. I'm becoming as nothing. It's a curious liberation.

After some while I find myself back in the drama again, back in identity, beginning to slip off into a world of self-pity. Then suddenly a voice from deep within shouts, "*stop right there!*" Although shouting, it is only barely audible above the din of internal mind chatter and the surging tide of emotion. But clearly a part of me has surrendered just enough to be able to still hear it. The voice recalls the Blue Boat trials when I'd accepted defeat too readily, but then resolved never to take no for an answer - *what is your real passion? Do you really want to give up what you love?* Glimmers of a new possibility begin to take tentative shape. As if from nowhere, arises the feeling that somehow, despite how black things seem, I can get through this.

It's exactly the same on any journey of spiritual evolution, in whatever walk of life you find yourself in. If you can open through the doubting and closing down, the fear and the disbelief, when there's seemingly no light at the end of the tunnel, then you clear a space for truth to arise. You open the potential for all manner of miracles to happen.

Next I found myself face down on a surgery bed, starring at sanitised floor tiles. The first incision of a razor sharp scalpel pierces the burning fire raging through the soles of my feet. The caring voice of a motherly nurse, whispering comfort and support, is the only restraint preventing me from hitting the roof. As luck would have it, the hospital I was taken to is trialling a new type of adrenaline protective tape, especially for serious blisters, and I'm being afforded the opportunity to try it out.

There's no such thing as luck!

The trouble was, it first involved cutting all the damaged skin off with a scalpel. And, assuming a window of possibility of completing the course was to be kept open, it would not be possible to have an anaesthetic. After the operation, the feet would be wrapped in the thin tape, protecting the raw surface to a degree, and the adrenaline would help the wounds heal more quickly. I wondered if the pain would subside enough in time for the next morning? But whether I would be able to walk properly (let alone run), was another question.

Amongst the pain and the seeming impossibility of what lay ahead however, a quiet voice that had connected with me from somewhere was still audible. It was calmly, but insistently saying:

Don't give up, you are more than your body, you can do this.

"It was you, wasn't it?"

Indeed it was. I had been with you many times before. You just weren't always open to listening.

As the sun is coming up the next morning, and I'm once more experiencing Chris the injured Commando, I notice that somehow, the pain has become familiar. There is no possibility of it going away, but internally there's a realisation that I am no longer identifying with it.

You'd stopped creating a drama around it.

The realisation was not in my conscious mind however, it felt like it was coming from somewhere, or perhaps more appropriately, someone else. It felt like a deep knowing. On the one hand Chris was experiencing the pain and on the other, he (or rather his consciousness) was through, above, below and beyond the pain.

In other words 'he' had begun to observe it and if 'he' was observing it, then how could it effect the real him? As I now watched this realisation unfolding, I could see that at the time, Chris had no understanding of what was happening, but the real Chris, the True Self, was beginning to emerge. By experiencing the pain in truth, without judging it, he had accessed the witnessing True Self.

Fascinating isn't it? As you challenge and unwind through the judgments of the False Self, you automatically come back to You.

As I watched this enlightening incident unfolding, I could also see how confusing and difficult it is to rationalise this unveiling process. It is as though there are literally two 'people' acting in the same bodymind and the challenge is to work out which one is which. The presence helped me understand more deeply:

As you shift into the awakening, you'll feel the conflict of the True and False Self, almost as if there are two different beings inside you. When this starts to happen, focus increasingly on the sense of the True Self - the feeling of 'rightness'. Over time, the False Self will dissolve away.

"How do I know which is the False Self and which is the True Self?"

By continual observation of every thought, every word, every feeling and every action you make. In so doing, a pattern emerges, or rather two distinctly different patterns.

In one, that of the False Self, you notice that thought, word and deed are in some way governed by a desire or a need for a particular outcome - one which supports, enhances or glorifies the ego. This also applies when conducting apparently selfless work, such as spiritual service. In this case, the 'imposter of the soul' is particularly difficult to 'smoke out'. You may believe your work is to help others and for the most part this may be true. However, if you look carefully below all your actions to the underlying motivations, often there is at least one motive which supports the ego in some way - financially, for example.

It is not that you shouldn't be supported in your work - not at all - but where the imposter is present, there may be an attached need for this work, arising from a concealed doubt that you won't be financially supported by the Universe when you take a selfless action.

The other pattern that emerges when you examine your motivations, is that of the True Self. The True Self knows no fear. It does not have doubt, trusting implicitly that it will always be supported by the Universe. It understands exactly how that support works. It is not support that furnishes a particular manifestation or material outcome; rather it is unwavering support that reveals the essence of the True Self. That is not to say that the True Self doesn't manifest anything. Far from it, the True Self can move mountains quite literally. However, to the True Self, there is no need to move mountains. Its one true desire, or perhaps more appropriately 'inner longing', is to help unveil the True Self in others. This is the prime motivation, but it realises it doesn't need to do anything to facilitate this objective, other than being what it is. In other words, when you unveil your True Self, you automatically cause the True Self in others to unveil, unfold and emerge.

It also recognises that it does not work alone in this facilitation. Rather it works as one with a vast orchestra of consciousness, subtly shaping events throughout the Universe to reveal ourselves to ourselves.

As I looked back on all of this, my consciousness was shifting yet again. As the deeper meaning for each episode clicked into place, it was increasingly unravelling the previously fixed and 'boxed' relationship I'd had with reality. I was realising the divine majesty of the Universe, which was now overtaking as my new reality. I had heard of so-called miracles, but always doubted they existed. Like many of us, I had read of the miracles of Jesus for example, manifesting food for the thousands, healing the sick and even raising the dead. To me, this was the proof of the presence of the creator that I had longed for, but previously not received. What I felt I needed was a peak experience, demonstrating beyond all doubt, that there is a benevolent intelligence guiding and shaping the Universe.

However, now I began to realise, that there is a very good reason why so-called miracles like these don't frequently happen. The purpose of the Universe is to 'self-realise': to realise every event is designed to reveal ourselves to ourselves. In other words, everything 'out there' is a reflection of everything 'in here' and if I let go of 'out there' then I can feel and realise the whole Universe inside of me. If 'God' were to appear before us feeding thousands from a small basket, we would set that God up as something different to us, something apart from us, something 'out there' in the material Universe, and we would keep looking 'out there' and never discover the truth. The tendency is for people to place Messiahs on a pedestal and then only experience their separateness from the Universe - the polarity - rather than it's awesome oneness.

And still miracles happen in every moment. Have you ever contemplated the incredible energy required to move and shape the Universe in such a way that a chance coincidence - a synchronicity - happens? On earth, the creative Source is manifested in a myriad of forms and most people are busy creating their own reality, with little or no regard for the whole. They selfishly dream their dreams and build their lives using their 'bit' of the collective power of God. Over 7 billion people all pulling in different directions, and in order to bring about one synchronicity, somehow a flow has to penetrate all of that randomness, pulling apparently disparate threads together, in the same time and space. Can you imagine the power behind that? Billions of synchronicities are happening in every moment to people all across the planet, it is like shaping a Rubik's cube with 7 billion variables!

As the awesome incredibility of this flooded my awareness, I felt myself beginning to dissolve into the vastness of the divine. I merged with an infinite ocean of light, so magnificent, so sublime, so omnipresent, and yet exactly because of its omnipresence, so ordinary. So ordinary that most people don't even see it. We are blind to the blindingly obvious.

I wanted to stay in this blissful place of absoluteness for ever, but something inside me pulled me back. There was yet more to realise, understand and ultimately let go of, before this could eternally happen.

And then the question arose... "Why do I need to experience any of this? Why can't I just completely let go and experience the divine completely, all the time?"

Good question. It all depends on the nature of your soul and what is rising to express right now. You have different qualities of your soul, like strings on a guitar that play different chords. In certain circumstances your soul will sound one way – strong, perhaps – and in another, surrendered, for example. Now, in each experience, there is a path to presence – it happens by recognising and aligning with the sense of rightness of your soul. You have to align yourself with authentic beingness that is arising in that moment. When you can be continually aligned with your soul, then you will always be surrendered into The One. This is what's known as "Enlightenment".

I found myself being drawn back to the Royal Marines' barracks at Lympstone. I'd been lying on my bed all night, just staring at the ceiling, steadily letting go – to a degree. But the pain is still intense. The appointed hour for the 9 mile speed march has arrived and from somewhere, I summon the courage to try to put on my boots. I can't simply slide my feet in, so I have to take the laces out and gingerly place my feet in the opened boots and only then, very carefully, tie up the laces. As I try to stand, there seems no possibility of placing the soles of my feet down, but it does seem possible to stand on tiptoes. It creates pain yet again, but eventually I am able to stand with full weight just on the toes. I certainly can't move very quickly however, and I wonder if I'm crazy to even consider marching. Once again though, the quiet inner voice rises, and prevents me going down the path of negativity.

This is your experience. You manifested it. Get the most from it!

We looked from on high as Chris the Commando steadily got dressed, organised his kit for the march and then very gingerly tiptoed to the parade ground. The sense of soft surrender, combined with the warrior, is palpable. We watch on, intrigued as Sergeant Rose catches a first glimpse of the wounded officer, and with sarcastic smile drawls... "That's you out then Captain Bourne, 'Sir'. A crate of beer says you'll never make it." And the rest of the platoon joins in the pathetic cabaret.

Now, looking on, and feeling behind those sarcastic eyes, I could sense the true feelings of my commando comrades back then... 'Poor bastard, that must bloody well hurt. He's sure got some guts'. Yet again it occurred to me how often people hide their true feelings behind a veil of group acceptability.

It's because they want to fit in and be accepted by the 'norm'. But every time you do this, you just plaster on another layer of False Self.

Suddenly I'm back in the march again, which at the gentle starting pace, kind of somehow works on tiptoe. But as the squad breaks into a run, I'm forced to try to place the whole of my feet on the ground. Once more searing pain shoots through my entire body and I'm reduced to a pathetic hobble. It slows me greatly, and I have to move to the side of the group to allow the others to pass. It's now a race against time - whatever happens, I can't afford to drop back too far or I'll get off the pace, never catch up and fail the test. Fail the test and you fail the course. I find myself dropping further and further back. All seems lost. Hopeless. Only a miracle can now keep me going. Perhaps Jesus himself will manifest down from the clouds and take my painful 'sins' away?

Well not Jesus exactly. But never forget, God's 'sons' and 'daughters' manifest in many guises, in all walks of life.

A Land Rover draws up along side me – it's the "meat wagon", there to collect the drop-outs. And you guessed it, hanging out of the window, with sarcastic smile, is the omnipresent Sergeant Rose... "Come on Capt'n Bourne, Sirrrr," with that derogatory slur again, "stop denying it. You're all through. You're never gonna make it. You're just a failed drop-out. Time to get on the meat wagon."

The presence and I were now right there with Chris. It's one of those challenging tests that brings you right into the moment and time seems to stop. As Chris looked into the eyes of Sergeant Rose, we could both feel two different emotions, like two serpents vying for control.

One looked into the eyes of the Serpent and could feel the sense of loss – inevitability – like the Sword of Damocles finally falling. But then there was another, one that still wasn't ready to give up.

It was these eyes that were looking for another possibility, somehow trusting, that if he could hold the space open for just another moment, some miracle would happen.

And happen it did.

Chris' eyes now glanced past the sarcastic Sergeant, to the driver, whose face had been hidden behind Rose's shoulder. And as Chris strained to look closer, finally the face came into focus – it was none other than Daniel Topolski – the Oxford Blue Boat Coach... "Now come on, Chris, didn't you resolve never, but never, to accept 'no' for an answer?" He was smiling at me. He was compassionate to my plight. He had my back. Looking on, I could feel a deep stirring in Chris, like a serpent – *no, a dragon no less* – rising up from my gut.

"Fuck You Sergeant Rose!"

I take off, away from the meat wagon, like a fox running from the pack. As the first step hits the tarmac, searing pain shoots through my body... "fuck it, drive on," the second hits the tarmac, "fuck it, drive on," the third, "fuck it, drive on." As the movie-goer, I can literally feel the mastering of the pain...

Awesome! But what would have been even more effective would have been "feel it, drive through" - with the same level of commitment. You've got to unleash the warrior, but without anger and resentment. Otherwise you get tight again and shut off the universal flow.

"How do I do that?"

The only way is to work at it, like developing a muscle. Work the feeling, let it come through you, express, but notice where something owns you inside and tightens around the expression - like judgment. This is where you must work hardest, where you must soften most.

Back in the drama, the pain did become progressively familiar to me and with the familiarity, the fear of it began to disperse. I was feeling strong but relaxed with it too. I realised the fear of marching had governed virtually my every thought and action during the last 12 hours, and to begin to be relieved of that was awesome.

As I realise what is happening, I begin to feel joy and liberation inside and now the pain begins to subside. I put the whole of my feet down and run faster. Once more, momentarily, the pain intensifies, but not nearly to the previous level. As the pain softens again, the feeling of joy increases and expands until I am in a place of near ecstasy. I find myself running faster and faster. In a few minutes I had caught up the group once more. To which, the Directing Officer looks incredulously at me, his jaw gaping open. Then a smile bursts across his face, "So nice of you to join us, Capt'n Bourne." There was something else in his smile, something familiar. Then it dawned on me, as he came into view - it was the smile of the Para, my old friend Chris Johnstone.

I made it though the march and the rest of test week. The coveted Green Berets were thrown to us, unceremoniously, in a Dartmoor gravel pit, just after completing the final 30 mile test on a grizzly grey day, but nothing could dampen my spirits. I had achieved it – the Green Beret, which had replaced the sense of loss at my failed Blue.

At the time, what was most heart-warming, was that I had some recognition for the efforts I had put in. Finally my peers would recognise, that in some way, I was 'special'. But now as I looked back, I was clearly able to see the illusion in all of this - *because you can feel You beyond it.* Peer recognition is a substitute for lack of self-esteem. Many of us need this recognition in some way. Be it a title on a business card, the brand of clothes that we wear or the personalised car number plate. They are signs to the outside world that we are really 'making it'.

People become distracted by the 'delights' of the material world and then delude themselves that these substitutes somehow adequately replace the inner feeling of completeness. They build external constructs so that they may feel good about themselves - careers, circles of friends, entertainment. They fool themselves that this intoxicating existence is satisfying. Ultimately though, the veils fall and they succumb to the addiction of seeking more physical 'stuff' - more wealth, more possessions, other lovers, different entertainment to replace that with which they're now bored. Drug-induced distractions such as food, alcohol, coffee, tea, cigarettes, promise a momentary release from the boredom – or the pain - but they always end up wanting more.

Big business loves their neediness. It thrives on the addictions, pumping billions into advertising those products that keep people hooked. With their help, people travel the world in search of something new, different, more interesting. But it is a journey to nowhere.

The only place to reconnect with the self-love you are truly seeking is to go within. The journey to nowhere must become a journey to the NOW HERE. Ultimately, you must escape dependency on external things which imprison you.

That evening, the final night of the Commando Course, the successful students were all in a local Lympstone pub with the directing staff. The formality and stiff upper lip were softening with some well-earned respect. But Sergeant Rose was still as crusty as ever. What would it take to penetrate that outer Rhinoceros Hide? I was thinking to myself.

Earlier that afternoon I'd gone into town, looking for a card of 'thanks' (*no thanks!*) to give to the staff. As I passed by a toyshop, I noticed a soldier, no, *a green commando*, lying in typical leopard crawl pose. I couldn't help but go in. It was a mechanised toy, that could crawl. I just knew who to give it to. As I put it on the bar of the noisy, raucous pub that evening and switched it on, gifting it to Sergeant Rose on behalf of everyone, I couldn't believe my eyes what happened next.

Looking on, I notice he is actually deeply touched by it. I can feel the upwelling emotion in him. Tears mist over his eyes, which he clearly has to fight back. I find myself thinking... Here is the harder-than-nails Colour Sergeant, looking like a little boy with a Birthday Toy.

Yes, someone had recognised the pain in him. And instead of hating him for it, had said, "I see you, it's okay, I love you."

Wow, all this time, I'd felt the heart of the Rose was beyond melting. Whatever next?

15

Out of the Frying Pan,
and into the Flame

"Don't deny your love.
Send it out into the world to be felt and experienced.
But always, bring that love back inside yourself."

The next time I was to see the coveted Green Beret was in an entirely different ceremonial situation. There at the altar stood bridegroom Chris, in neat blue uniform, mirror-like boots, crisp nervous smile and ceremonial sword by his side, as an entirely different kind of rose was just beginning to enter the church.

Ah yes, I could remember it well, no sooner had the Commando Course finished, than I was back at my regiment, hurriedly preparing for deployment to the deserts of Iraq. We were due to fly out at the end of the following week. And in between time, a wave of emotion had washed over me... What happens if I don't come back? It was a genuine thought in the minds of probably most of those deploying. There needed to be some outlet for that emotion. There needed to be some tying anchor to bring me back - some sweet softness that would reconnect me to the gentleness of life. As I looked back, I saw it wasn't in me to truly comprehend the emotional rollercoaster at the time. I put it down to the sense of in-love-ness, a need for connection, which my partner, Amanda, fulfilled.

As soon as the Commando Course closed, I'd winged it down to London, and as I passed through the busy village of Wimbledon, although rain was hailing down and bouncing like tennis balls off the pavement, it didn't stop me pulling up on the curb outside the first jewellers I saw, and high-tailing it inside. Wow, I could feel the strength of impulse now as I looked back, so strong was it, so irresistible. Why was that?

Ah yes, who can escape it? This feeling of in-love-ness. Such a powerful emotion. What you're really seeing is the other half of yourself, as a reflection. You're seeing your Twin Flame, that part of your soul which isn't manifest, but stays at the Source, like a homing beacon, lighting the way back. She'll reflect to you in all those things around you - situations and circumstances - and of course in people. It might be in the glint of an eye, the touch of a hand or a sweet smile.

All-too-easily of course, when you get a close reflection of your Twin Flame, in a person for example, the ego confuses them with your Twin Flame. And so now there's a chasing, a compulsive need to lose yourself in them, to bury yourself in them, to be completed by them. The source of your true yearning – your Twin Flame – which was, and always will be, inside, now becomes lost within the reflection - the person in which the reflection is manifested. Of course it's absolutely right and wonderful to be in love, just not to lose yourself in it.

And there she now is, walking up the isle, a vision of loveliness. Hair tied back revealing a slender neck, so vulnerable and gentle. There'd been no time to have a dress made. So she'd borrowed a friend's white tuxedo. It's just too cool. As my eyes fall upon her, my heart just wants to melt. I want to melt into her and never leave her side. As I felt back into it, it was absolutely clear, that was my honest feeling.

And that indeed is the compulsive feeling of the Twin Flame. So wonderful, so miraculous, so alluring. And so easily you confuse the subject with the object. Now you have to possess her, and you can't see her anywhere else, not in one other thing, a bird or a flower, or perhaps in the reflection of a still pond or the swirling clouds in the heavens (which is all entirely possible). You're just lost - all consciousness consumed in a disappearing black hole. Love is such a wonderful thing, and yet when we try to own it, we get lost in it.

"Is there anyway of avoiding this?"

Yes indeed. Of course there is – a very beautiful way. To some it's known as "tantra". It's walking the blade edge of experience – in it, but not lost in it. You appreciate the beauty of life, of being in love; you send your love out, which may touch someone, but, and it's a big but, you recognise that the love you feel is always inside of yourself. It's already a part of you, which you're now activating – it's never 'out there', not in reality at least. It's always 'in here'.

"Yes, I see that, 'it's always in here'. That does help."

So don't deny your love. Let it activate. Send it out into the world to be felt and experienced. But as the connection forms, always, but always, bring that love back inside yourself.

"That seems a bit selfish."

Yes, I see it could. But you accept now that there is only One Self. So if you need another part out there to make you complete, then you're deluding yourself. What's out there may be truly lovely, but they will always only ever be a relativistic expression of the absoluteness within. It's not to say you shouldn't enjoy love – far from it. It's not to say you shouldn't enjoy love with a partner – go for it, absolutely. It's not to say you shouldn't give of yourself – be all-in. But when you lose yourself in them, subconsciously endowing them with the responsibility to make you complete, you're bound to fail. They will never be able to fulfil that completeness, which is only to be found inside yourself – in the completeness with your own Twin Flame. And so the weight you endow the relationship with, becomes an increasing burden, which risks becoming back-breaking. It's a burden your partner can never fully carry.

I'm back in the ceremony now, as the moving Khalil Gibran poem is being read out...

You were born together, and together you shall be for evermore.
You shall be together when white wings of death scatter your days.
Aye, you shall be together even in the silent memory of God.
But let there be spaces in your togetherness,
And let the winds of the heavens dance between you.
Love one another but make not a bond of love:
Let it rather be a moving sea between the shores of your souls.
Fill each other's cup but drink not from one cup.
Give one another of your bread but eat not from the same loaf.
Sing and dance together and be joyous, but let each one of you be alone,
Even as the strings of a lute are alone though they quiver with the same music.
Give your hearts, but not into each other's keeping.
For only the hand of Life can contain your hearts.
And stand together, yet not too near together:
For the pillars of the temple stand apart,
And the oak tree and the cypress grow not in each other's shadow.

"Wow. How moving." I didn't feel it at the time, but I could feel it now - the love I'd handed over and given away, was now beginning to flow back to me, like a cycle. Slowly at first, but then strengthening.

It isn't at all diminished. You give your love out, but then bring it back within again. It means you can love even more!

As I looked back, I could see that the in-love-ness both myself and Amanda felt had obscured reality. In truth, we'd only seen each other occasionally up to the marriage, and each meeting was veiled in the rose-tinted glint of needy passion. The result was we never really got to know each other, especially how we each liked to live our lives. Of course we had many parallels. Like many couples in love, we enjoyed eating out, drinking wine, dancing and celebrating with friends. But we never really got to know the essence of each other - how you live from day to day – in those quiet little moments…

Actually those 'quiet little moments' are probably the most important of all. You remember all too easily of course the 'peak experiences'. But in actual fact, you're likely to spend a lot of your time just 'hanging out', just being there for each other. So how do you get on in those quiet times?

I remembered a holiday we'd spent together, on the romantic island of Corsica, just before the Commando Course. There was a need for me to stay fit, so in the mornings I'd be running up the mountain (conveniently) behind the apartment, or else pumping iron in the nearby gym. At other times, I was content just to stroll, lie on the beach, read a novel and take it easy. And in these quiet little moments, somehow, something didn't quite click. Before long, we'd fall out. It seemed it didn't really work between us, and at that point, we separated. But this was all so easily forgotten back in the stresses and neediness of commando training. And in Amanda too, there was an unquenchable thirst for another 'to make the half whole'. I distinctly recall driving to see her after the first training week away, high-tailing it back to London, as fast as my Escort Turbo would propel me. So eager, so excited, I all too easily overlook that synchronistic Alanis Morissette song that comes on the radio:

"I don't want to be the filler if the void is solely yours
I don't want to be your glass of single malt whiskey
Hidden in the bottom drawer
I don't want to be a bandage if the wound is not mine
Lend me some fresh air

I don't want to be adored for what I merely represent to you
I don't want to be your babysitter
You're a very big boy now
I don't want to be your mother
I didn't carry you in my womb for nine months

I don't want to be the sweeper of the eggshells that you walk upon
And I don't want to be your other half, I believe that 1 and 1
make 2
I don't want to be your food or the light from the fridge on your
face at midnight, hey
What are you hungry for?

I don't want to be the glue that holds your pieces together
I don't want to be responsible for your fractured heart
And it's wounded beat
Show me the back door."

(lyrics by Alanis Morissette)

As I looked back, I could feel into Chris, the words impacting like soft bullets deep into a buried heart. As with most, it was all too easy to simply ignore those resonances.

The mind is just so busy in most people. They don't feel the synchronicity, they don't hear the messages.

And so now we were back at the church, ceremony complete, joined hand-in-hand, strolling back down the aisle, 'till death us do part'. My best man, and Second in Command of my Squadron, had arranged

188

transport back to the barracks. Always with a great sense of humour, he had commandeered an Armoured Personnel Carrier (basically a tank without a turret). And so there we stood, in our wedding finery, sticking out of the top of a tank, cans trailing noisily behind, engine roaring as it carries us away.

I guess I should have taken note of the church wall we knocked down in the process. But in a world of disconnection, you just don't join the dots, you don't appreciate the 'omens'. It's just another good laugh.

Synchronicity is a superlative language indeed. You create it of course. Your inner consciousness manifests out into the world, creating signs and 'omens'. Essentially both the convoluted and aligned aspects of your nature manifest. For anyone who is truly watching, they'll see reflections of both that which is distorted and that which is True Self. It gives you a chance to inquire and reflect – to let go of that which doesn't serve. If you keep reading the signs as feelings inside, if you're committed to being true to yourself (and thereby true to others), then you find yourself making fewer and fewer 'mistakes'. Your life comes into alignment with the Universe – you have to break through fewer and fewer walls.

I looked on with wry amusement...thank you Universe!

I was far from getting it at the time, but I would in due course, as the frying pan of daily married life would ultimately become overwhelmingly hot.

16

Selling your Soul for Sunglasses and M&Ms

"To fully break through is to let go of everything you know –
everything you love or despise.
Let none of it define you."

The engine of the bright red Ferrari is throbbing, like a stallion stomping the ground, straining to be unleashed into full gallop. But we are stuck in a long line of traffic, this being a busy Friday afternoon in downtown Bahrain, just off the port of Al Jubail in the Middle East. It was our first port of call on the way to the deserts of Iraq, and my Squadron's first task was to upgrade the Bahraini airport defences. We'd worked in conjunction with the civilian construction company, Alwardi, and their wealthy sheik boss was so pleased with the contract, he'd loaned us his prized possession for the weekend – the bright red Ferrari 308 GTB, the steering wheel of which, I find myself now gleefully sitting behind.

For many guys, this is a life's dream come true. How many would ever own, or even drive, such a superlative example of mechanical excellence? This is the epitome of engineering, and when you rev the accelerator, it's as if the 3 litre, 12 valve engine is connected directly into your adrenal glands.

I feel like I'm going to explode. And if I'm not going to come back from this war zone (which is how many of us felt), and if the Universe has somehow miraculously manifested this machine for me as the last request of an apparently condemned man, then I am sure as heaven going to make the most of it…oh thank you, God!

Don't you just love the unexpected? You could live your entire life expecting any moment that a miracle could happen. And sure enough, you're bound to have a miraculous life – because life reflects what you believe it to be at your core.

And I could feel exactly what it was like as I looked back. I so desperately wanted to floor the accelerator, to let the stallion in me loose. I could feel how the power and responsiveness touched something deep inside, and at the time, it certainly revved something in Chris.

It is the divine masculine warrior energy – that which is ready to ignite and respond, the fight or flight, which gives thrusting impetus to life, that which makes things happen.

Nothing was going to hold it. The energy in me was somehow going to break through and fully express itself.

It was of course reflective of your soul, one that had been, at times, controlled and limited. In a macrocosmic sense, the warrior energy is all about breaking through the restrictive materialism of physicality. It's like high explosive, that wants to shatter limitation to dust.

Now I'm drawn to the glint – *the initiating spark* - in Chris' eye, as he first looks across to his Sergeant, and then at the empty dirt track by the side of the road. The Sergeant looks back, and although he doesn't utter a word, you can clearly decipher his chain of thought... You're not serious are you Sir? That's a rough dirt track and this is a racing car, with lowered suspension and low profile wheels. But then he isn't too sure he's coming back from this war zone either... "Oh fuck it, let's go for it!"

I shift the stick into a low gear, fling the machine sharply to the left, and floor it. The stallion takes off at a raging gallop, first skidding and swerving from side to side, spewing up sand and dust, all around us, into the air. To the bemused Arab commuters, we must have looked like a whirling dervish in a storm. The Ferrari bounces and jolts, jumps and at times flies; I bang head, shoulders and backside, but boy it was worth it!

Both myself and the presence watched on with amusement, both thinking the same thing... Sometimes in life, you've just gotta go for it, just floor it! And so the first photos I sent back to my wife and folks at home were not of fear and worry, but suntanned, with beaming smiles and of course, the stunning bright red Ferrari...

It just goes to show, always, but always, expect the unexpected.

And as I looked back, there were so many unexpected stories with hidden meanings it would be impossible to take them all in.

I was now out in the desert, with a small reconnaissance party, on my camp bed at night, in the middle of nowhere, looking deeply into the darkened night sky, the stars winking like distant angels. The alluring quietness and vast spaciousness seem to melt me into eternity. Had I been single, I probably would have never wanted to come back. But there was always the thought of my beautiful new wife, that somehow stopped me from completely dissolving...

To fully break through, all the way, is to let go of everything you know
– everything you love or despise. Just let it all go. Let none of it define
you. Because at the highest level anyway, you are all One.

Indeed, my experience in the desert was all about letting go of
expectation – of the quick and ready judgments we make of the
moment. And it was a place of superlative contrast – one moment it's
hot and sunny, miles of unoccupied sand dunes stretching out before
you; the next it's raining, the sand morphing into red sludge, with long
convoys of military vehicles bogging in.

As the Operations/Intelligence Officer, my job was flitting from
place to place, on whatever transport I could commandeer, checking
out resource and supply lines that need to be fixed or upgraded. One
moment I'm in a rugged four-by-four, the next a thundering helicopter,
or else a track bike, skidding and slip-sliding across soft sand. As I
looked back, there was an incredible sense of aliveness to it, an incredible
adventure. My job had real meaning, it was all about resourcefulness,
lateral thinking, coming up with in-the-moment engineering solutions
that might mean the difference between a soldier's life or death.

And we had all the latest 'Gucci' (as we called it) equipment. In
wartime no expense is spared. We had the forerunner of today's in-car
sat-nav. I'd been called out to a rendezvous, deep in 'hot' territory, with
nothing but this new gadget to guide me. Now it's told me I've arrived.
But in the sand storm, peering out through the turret of the armoured
car, I couldn't have seen a battlegroup, let alone a Land Rover. But then
as I step out of the vehicle and up front to peer further forwards, I
suddenly realise I've arrived - we'd practically driven over it, a couple of
metres down in a wadi (river bed), immediately below us.

In the barren, mostly featureless desert, it was a lifesaver indeed – yet
something you buy practically for peanuts today; having it guide you
to your friend's place, the mall or when you're looking for the nearest
pizza takeaway. That, and the new 'mobile phone' we were using, which
was the size of a house brick, yet saved lives, by keeping us in contact,
no matter where we were. As I looked on, what irony I thought – so
much of what took place in the Middle East during "Desert Storm",

would have a lasting impact on all our lives, including the ubiquitous sat-nav and mobile phone. It was a great 'storm' indeed!

Yes, the world changed radically at that point. In ways that most had no inkling of. Not just with the technology that now connects obscure parts of the world, but also with the 'geo-politic' – the West's ability to shape and change entire cultures and economies at will. And you may ask what's driving it all? An insatiable desire by the general public to consume and have what they want. The work you were doing, facilitating supply lines and resources for the battlegroups, was none other than securing supply lines of oil, all the way back to the heart of 'Consumersville, Kentucky'.

"Ouch. That hurts!" To think that's what it was really all about. But no escaping it, I could clearly see the truth in it.

Now I'm standing in a vast queue, in the middle of the desert, behind a snaking line of American GIs, all making their way into the "PX" where you'd get some 'essential' home comforts – M&Ms, sunglasses and suntan oil. Not to mention all manner of other – desperately needed – 'Gucci' products that we all so much take for granted in society. How on earth do the Bedouin manage? I found myself wondering. Right at that moment, President George Bush Snr comes on the radio with one of his 'famous' speeches...

"This is an historic moment. We have in this past year made great progress in ending the long era of conflict and cold war. We have before us the opportunity to forge for ourselves and for future generations a New World Order - a world where the rule of law, not the law of the jungle, governs the conduct of nations. When we are successful - and we will be - we have a real chance at this New World Order, an order in which a credible United Nations can use its peacekeeping role to fulfil the promise and vision of the U.N.'s founders."

Was this the "New World Order" he was really envisioning? Strongly conditioned, nationalistic American GIs, fighting it out in the desert so people can have their sunglasses and M&Ms?

It was one of those thunderbolt moments for me. Whereas up to that point it had been an adventure, and I'd had the sense that I was doing something of truly important significance, here, right before me, snaking across the desert to this vast, iso-container city of home comforts, the real significance was beginning to sink in. Now, as I look and feel back, a distinctly queasy feeling begins to activate in my gut. Something was not wholly right about this 'holy war'.

I had the sense that it wasn't at all about overthrowing 'evil dictators' and 'drawing a line in the sand' against inhumanity. But rather about sustaining the resource and supply line – all the way back to the over-consuming cities of Europe and America.

Of course that was the real reason. Had it been some obscure patch of desert out in the middle of nowhere – with no oil underneath it – then the developed world would hardly have batted an eyelid. And it makes everyone who consumes also culpable. Which is actually a good thing – the effects on the world of increasing economic consumption are being brought home to everyone.

On January 14th 1991, the ground war began. The allied battlegroups swept through the desert in a big left hook, right behind all the frontline minefield defensive positions, painstakingly prepared by Saddam's forces. As engineers, we'd carefully prepared the routes. Sat-nav and the new mobile phones ensured we knew exactly where we were, and what needed to be done – fake movements of frontline troops keep everyone guessing that the allied forces are coming straight up the middle. After months of preparation, the battle is over in less than a 100 hours. So beaten, bedraggled and fed-up are the Iraqi forces, that they're (very fortunately) ready to surrender in their thousands – they even do so to lightly armed supply trucks.

Distorted warrior energy and excessive consumerism stirs up these conflicts. But when that explodes in your face, in a very physical way, fortunately many are caused to question the real value and meaning of life.

Very swiftly, I find myself in the centre of Kuwait City, checking the viability of routes, many of which have been booby-trapped with high explosive – this is the truly dangerous part, and some heroic people give their lives, yet again, securing supply routes for the 'greater good'.

But looking back, I knew it was never a black and white issue - *no war ever is.* The Kuwaiti people had indeed been brutalised by Saddam's forces and they deserved our (anyone's) help. As I pull into the city centre in my Land Rover, with sporadic gunfire going off all around, two young Kuwaiti girls in brightly coloured costume come out to greet us, smiling and waving gleefully, overjoyed to be free. It melts my heart. If many of the reasons for which we went there now stank of hypocrisy, these two little pearls helped justify it for me.

Conflict such as this, mirrors the greater macrocosmic conflict of light penetrating darkness in the cosmos. There are lots of grey areas in the twilight, with sporadic flashes of brilliance – in the microcosm, two innocent little girls standing there, happy and free.

In that moment there is no conflict. Yet again, time and space have vapourised. Chris the soldier, myself and the presence, all connected in time and space, all appreciating the glint of light in an often dark world. Just to witness, be a part of, and to support, these jewels of middle-eastern hope, seems to make it all worthwhile.

Still, something didn't sit right with it all for me. Sometime after my return, I came across a book called, "From the House of War", by the world-renowned journalist, John Simpson, who claimed the American Ambassador in Baghdad had told Saddam, before their invasion, that 'the USA would take no position if his forces were to invade Kuwait'. Apparently, trade deals were being made with the Iranians on the condition that Iraq stopped their ongoing war with them. Kuwait was the carrot. It all smelled decidedly fishy.

In hindsight, after all the other spuriously reasoned middle-eastern incursions that have since taken place, I find it hard to take a definitive view. You could point the finger of blame at the leaders - the powers-that-be - but everyone who consumes is also responsible. Let he in the West who is willing to forgo his tank of fuel, M&Ms, sunglasses, his sat-nav and his Ferrari, cast the first mobile phone…

You are ALL to blame. And no one is to blame. Collective realities are created for the purpose of exploration and growth. What is the truth for you right now? And are you prepared to act on it, or will you turn a blind eye? Each time you consume, there is a cost and a price to pay elsewhere down the food chain.

"So what can any of us do about it? We seem so powerless in it all."

Nothing could be further from the truth. But you must make one essential Breakthrough: to realise that all realities are created from what you're being within, and the choices you make accordingly. Money is just paper. Yet it buys power. And if you spend it with little attention of where your money is going, then you risk placing enormous power into the hands of less scrupulous people.

"But how can one person make any difference?"

This is the illusion by which so many limit themselves. Truth is what makes a difference. If one person dares to stand and express the truth, no matter what the personal consequence, that sends a vibration out into the whole. It may take time to permeate, but if you keep radiating that vibration, permeate it surely will. Within a relatively short space of time you have an unstoppable – peaceful – revolution of rightness.

I didn't fully get this back at the time, but something deep within steeled my resolve now. I wouldn't sell my soul for sunglasses and M&Ms anymore! And another truly important revelation... that sovereignty for my own conscious choice was absolutely paramount. I certainly wouldn't be handing that over to governments and their armies again...

Such a vital revelation for spiritual Breakthrough: that you should allow no one to make your choices for you. Be informed, understand the landscape before you step into it.

17

Mr and Mrs Have-Nothing

"You always get what you need, when you need it.
The question is, are you awake enough to feel it?"

My journey deep into the past continued. With each unfolding episode, I felt like I was coming home to an ever-deeper aspect of me. It was as if there was a different me, a cosmic one, buried under layers, bursting to get out. But brute force wasn't going to do it. I'd used it before, at times in the army or when rowing, but this needed something else - something I was, only by now, through this regressive journey, fully beginning to grasp. It needed surrender and softness; I had to be committed, yes, I had to allow myself into all the nooks and crannies of the inner world. And I needed courage to go there, to see all the things I knew I wouldn't like, forgive myself, and then allow this new essence to permeate through.

That's what defines Breakthrough. It's not a forcing, it's a surrendering. But not the kind that gives up. It requires commitment, courage and persistence. Shall we continue?

"Why not – we've come this far!"

Suddenly I was many worlds away from the desert and armies - far away from oil and M&Ms, far away from lines drawn in the sand by leaders I no longer had any trust in. Where was this peculiar place now? My inner vision began to focus, like clouds parting, steadily revealing an ever-clearer landscape.

The place is Hanover, Germany, and suddenly I find myself watching Chris and wife, Amanda, on their stand at the prestigious Hanover Antiques Fair. A conversation is taking place between Amanda and Herr & Frau Habenicht (which directly translates to Mr & Mrs Have-Nothing). Amanda's step-mum was German, thus she'd become fluent at an early age, and with her very empathic and charming personality, she was the perfect representative to convince customers into buying prestigious English Antiques. My German on the other hand was very sketchy at best, but I had the Antiques expertise, having come from a family who'd sourced and traded them all around the world. We'd left the Army and settled in Germany, following my final posting there.

Now the images and conversation were flooding back in. Herr and Frau Habenicht have just purchased a delightful Victorian hallstand for which Amanda has just closed the sale…. "So Herr und Frau Habenicht, jetz haben sie etwas." Which basically translates to… "Well Mr & Mrs Have-Nothing, now you have something!" Finding myself right back there in it, my sides are literally bursting. She'd said it with such softness and yet a subtle ironic twist – with no harm intended, just a witty sense of irony. My German was basic, but the message is unmissable. It's like watching a slapstick scene from Monty Python.

A good sense of humour on the path is always essential. Never, but never, take yourself too seriously!

Unfortunately Herr & Frau Habenicht didn't have much of a sense of humour, or perhaps more kindly, they didn't resonate with English irony. As I loaded the furniture onto their luxurious Mercedes Estate, they certainly weren't smiling, and I had to be very careful to contain mine. But once they'd gone, Amanda and I laughed our socks off.

Selling antiques to Europe's well-heeled was a very curious experience indeed. It's not what I would ever have imagined myself doing. But there was a recession on in the UK at the time, and I wanted to be self-employed – *you wanted to be self-determining* – so we had brought over a small van load of antiques, towards the end of my Army service, and had taken them to a local antiques market. A recipe of excellent sourcing by my father, friendly empathy by Amanda, and efficient organisation by yours truly, meant our furniture sold like hotcakes and at a healthy profit. From day one, "Victoria House English Antiques" literally began to rocket.

It was easy to see that I'd gotten way too caught up in the success of it at the time, to reflect on the connection with my Gulf War experience. But looking back on it now, it was crystal clear: life in the developed countries of Europe hung so much on a sense of prestige – what car you drove, the clothes you wore and how you furnished your house. Our customers weren't just buying furniture, they were buying a statement…

And the need to make that statement, to prove oneself better than others, or to be singularly interested in one's own well being, is the very selfishness that drives the capitalist economies of the West. It's why you were at war in the Gulf in the first place – the excessive, never-ending need for resource-wealth.

I could now see it all clearly, and how at the time, I was no better. Our business grew and grew, we became financially well-off within just a couple of years. We were riding high on success and affluence. I'd gone into the Army for very selfless reasons. Now I'd become very selfish. Looking on, I'm feeling disappointed *(work not to be harsh on yourself)* - many times I'd either broken through into a deeper sense of spiritual self or was on the point of doing so. Now I was firmly back in the rat race *(don't worry, life is a constant working at Breakthrough!)*. At the completion of only our third year, we moved our business into a prestigious Schloss – a castle – to which people came from all across Germany to visit and buy from us. We felt that we'd really 'made it'. This was the first time I felt truly successful for any lengthy period of time. There'd been the odd goal I'd attained – like the Green Beret – but this was different. I felt like somehow I'd made a meteoric rise into the upper echelons of society. It literally felt like the sky was the limit.

It may have felt great at the time, but as I looked back, the uneasiness grew in my heart. Many times I'd been on the verge of breaking through; now it felt like I was slipping back into the abyss – success was clearly this particular Achilles heel.

But there's something crucial you need to realise: that in every distortion is a hidden truth – the light of your buried soul. In all such situations, work to find the truth and peel away the distortion.

"Can you clarify that?"

Sure. There's nothing at all wrong with wanting to express your gifts and talents – this is the fundamental purpose of the soul, and when you're doing it, you will automatically be successful. It's when you get lost in the outcome of this success – the material manifestation – that things go awry. Many people strive for financial success (or anything else for that matter), but then when they acquire it, they often become owned by it and lose themselves in it. Therefore it's always best to work to focus on pure expression, with no need of an outcome or physical manifestation. Then you'll always be successful, and it will always taste good. And most importantly, it will never come at the expense of someone else. They don't have to lose for you to win.

But success was a potent brew, which I downed very readily. And it became the undoing of me – fortunately…

You've got to go there to come back!

A year or two on, and the cracks have become very evident in our marriage. Seven-day working weeks, always an excuse to work more and play less. We rarely take breaks or holidays, and when we do, it is more a crashing out, before getting back to the 'real purpose'. Success was like some mystical siren, always calling, always being heard and responded to. When our first child, a daughter, came along, there was a momentary respite, a distant melody was activated in my shrivelled heart, but it was, alas, all too short-lived; with Amanda less available, and since I could now speak fluent German, I found myself working even harder and longer hours. Whereas children can bring a marriage together, ours simply split us further apart.

I was rapidly becoming depressed and all-consumed. Something needed to happen. I needed some kind of break before life broke me. I was putting on weight and bags were gathering under my tired eyes. I needed something to rejuvenate me, to wake me up. Then something came along, which surely did.

Look for those special significances, especially when you need it most. Especially when all seems grey, despondent and lost. Open your heart, ask out into the Universe…"Show me!" The Universe can't, and won't, fail to respond. You will always get an answer. You just have to raise your eyelids and look for it.

Flash, crack, bang. The sensei's fist struck like lightning, full-on, into my front teeth! My left front incisor is ripped out instantly, from the roots, and then bounces across the floor, as the onlooking students descend into an astonished, deathly hush.

Well if you're deeply buried, sometimes it takes a big shock to dig you out!

"That big? Was something really so shocking necessary?"

Well you called it to yourself. You manifested it. Just as people manifest

*ALL such shocking circumstances of their lives. Often the first reaction is to point the finger of blame – which is very understandable when you don't appreciate the finer workings of the Universe. But you are master creators. Whether you know it or not, you are **already** creating every circumstance and 'chance happening' of your life – nothing happens by chance! And it all has but one purpose, which you already know...*

"To reveal ourselves, to ourselves."

Bingo. Right on. It takes courage, responsibility and accountability for your awakening to fully proceed; to accept that you're doing everything to yourself in order to reflect your true nature. It becomes easier when you give up trying to get somewhere, to win or attain something. When you switch in the moment from trying to get some material outcome, to instead figuring out what you learnt from it, then your evolution can truly take off. There are no longer any distracting excuses – the finger of blame – to prevent you inquiring into why exactly you created the moment the way you did.

Boy, I was now ready to get this. I could feel this was such a vital revelation. But I could also honestly feel, I wasn't yet ready to fully let go into it.

That's no problem. Profound self-honesty is also vital on the path – so you know exactly where you are. Have no fear, you'll get to that place of true surrender. You just need to regress through some more trials and tribulations of your life first.

Looking back on the experience, I could literally feel my buried soul calling out. I'd been slip-sliding into depression, when out of the blue, a customer appeared in the warehouse who was practising Karate at the local dojo. There again, there it was, that unmistakable "aha" feeling that shifted something deep inside...

You always get what you need, when you need it. The question is, are you awake enough to feel it?

Clearly, enough of me was still awake. I could still feel a degree of soul resonance. And so I followed the pull, whereupon, I met another of my life's gurus – an angel – in the form of Christoph, the Karate sensei, who was to make an impact on my life in more ways than one.

The right person always shows up at the right time. When the student is ready, the teacher will appear!

I quickly felt a deep brotherly respect for Christoph. It wasn't just that he was exceptionally skilled at Karate. He was very charming, but also humble with it. Living purely from his teachings, he was quite poor in a material sense, yet he exuded an energy that made him popular with all his students. We greatly admired and respected him.

Always take special note when you find yourself admiring and respecting someone. It could be a guide or a teacher, it could be a character in a movie or a book – whoever they are, they're there to show you something important: an aspect of your beingness that is waiting and ready to come through. For you can only resonate with something on the outside, which you already have on the inside.

Wow, yes. That struck home. As I now looked on, I could readily appreciate this deep revelation. It was both humbling and exciting. Many other characters I'd admired flashed through my mind, like a collage – friends, rowing coaches, colleagues in the military and in sport - I loved and respected aspects about all of them. Wow. Can this really be true? They're reflecting aspects already in me?

Indeed it is true. You drew them, to remind you, to awaken your soul.

I paused the 'movie' for a moment, upon which, I could clearly feel the integration of soul resonance from characters from my past. Wow!

Back in the drama though, the True Self in me had become buried, ever more deeply. An intense identification with success had led me far from the path. And here was humble Christoph, a living, breathing angel, whose mission it was to wake me up again. He didn't do it on purpose of course – that I knew. But he was a touch short-sighted, and I'd moved faster than anticipated. Which is why he'd made the only mistake I'd ever seen him make, in striking me full-on.

As my tooth skidded across the floor, there was absolute silence. But back in it, there is no pain. I don't even go down. There I am, still looking Christoph in the eyes, watching them turn to shock. But in me something else has happened. I couldn't put words to it at the time, but now as I looked on, it was as though I'd come alive again.

This so often happens – the physicality of life can bring you right back to the precipice of true meaning. You'd been lost in a world of petty, meaningless ambition - a totally unreal world created from the artificial sense of prestige. Many people find that some kind of shock, or accident, brings them right back to what is truly real.

No one knew what to do. They're all just looking on, as I calmly pick up the tooth, and walk out of the dojo headed for the hospital. Now I begin to feel the pain, but somehow, the reality of the situation penetrates it. I'm touching a deep calm, which is now guiding what to do.

Voila. You're right back at the place you came from. Your Cosmic Self!

The tooth was put back in, and the physical pain subsided fairly quickly within a day or two. But something huge had shifted in my life. It felt like I'd been stopped dead in my tracks. It was extremely difficult to re-engage with my former world. It suddenly felt distanced from me – meaningless. And I felt out of kilter, lopsided. Normally quite stable, now my emotions are all over the place. One moment I'm reasonably happy, and the next, in the depths of depression or anxiety. I've lost my confidence - the sense of self-belief. It's now hard to live and work as I used to. Amanda is becoming rapidly worried about me. The situation proceeds quickly downhill, with no apparent cure for the problem; the doctors couldn't help me. As I looked on at the latest episode in my life's review, I wondered what was this all about?

Your problem was not at the physical level. Nor even the emotional. What you were feeling were the effects of an unbalanced energy field. Whenever someone has an accident like the shocking one you suffered, it makes an impact on the biomagnetic energy field around them – their energy body. It's where the karmic imprint of past life events is stored, and it influences every aspect of your physical life.

I was confused, unsure, uncertain. And in looking back, I could feel a distinct upwelling emanate from somewhere deep within – "Is there anybody out there? Anyone who can help? Is there anyone hearing me?" My soul was literally yelling out.

A short while later, maybe even later that day, I was walking past my bookcase when a book fell over. I recall it felt strange. It was probably my weight on the floorboards, I reason with myself, but something seems decidedly odd – poignant – about it. The book is a martial arts favourite of mine. I feel to open it, and the page I come up with is all about biomagnetic energy. It's something I'd not paid that much attention to in the martial arts. It seemed a bit flowery – 'out there'. But now, the idea of it strikes a chord within me, compelling me to read. It relates how the Eastern masters have spoken for centuries about this curious energy and had many names for it, including ki, chi, prana, netter, ihund and 'the winds' to name but a few. In looking on as the movie-goer, I could see that a deep intrigue had been sparked in Chris, and I could feel him 'float' the question, "Perhaps I should seek out an energy healer?" To which there was a strange 'crack' in one of the wall panels, jolting something in Chris…

Synchronicity speaks. When thought and feeling click into the underlying flow, a 'spike' can happen, in which you shift consciousness from a place where everything is disconnected and random, to one where everything reveals a deeper message of importance – because everything is interconnected.

I felt to tell Amanda. Which, despite her worry, proved to be a good intuition – for she'd 'coincidentally' recently heard about a local guy, whom she called 'some kind of faith healer'. That didn't sound at all like what I was looking for, but some 'pull' caused me to explore anyway.

It's absolutely vital to your spiritual growth that you listen to that voiceless inner pull that wants to compel you in a certain direction. And the more you listen, the stronger it gets.

Suddenly I'm standing before the 'faith healer'. "I'm an energy healer actually," he tells me. He's totally blind, having lost his sight at the age of 30. "That's a shame – sorry to hear that." "Not at all," he replies, "that's when my life really took off." At the time I found it hard to believe, but I was soon to discover why.

I'd expected this would be some kind of hands-on massage, but nothing could have been further from the truth. In the beginning he had me just stand there, about 3m away, apparently 'looking on' – he was looking in my general direction, but certainly not with his blinded, physical eyes.

What follows is simply astounding. Breathtaking. He proceeds to diagnose every injury I've ever had in my body: the broken arm for example, injuries I carry from the military, and the dislodged tooth, which as yet, I've not told him about. Not only that, but he is able to talk in general terms about various sports and activities I've done, by noticing the impact it has had on my body. All without even touching me, all from about 3m away, without even seeing me.

Yes, astounding isn't it. But your whole field is like an energetic footprint, which, with the right 'eyes', can easily be seen.

And as I looked back, suddenly it was as if a switch had been thrown within me. Now I could 'see' the energy imprint too. I could see Chris' aura – how amazing!

Back in the experience, the energy healer diagnoses that the Karate injury has generated an energy imbalance in and around my head, which is causing the off-centredness and feelings of depression. He tells me to close my eyes and notice what I feel. I begin to experience a gentle warmth around the level of my heart, which begins to intensify and then spread outwards. After a while, I can feel it throughout my entire body. There then follows a tingling sensation, which begins first in my legs, then spreads upwards, becoming most observable in my hands. And now I'm seeing white light, although it isn't visual; it's more like a knowing of its presence.

You'd accessed higher mind - the place that needs no colour or interpretation. It is simply a place of pure knowing. In most people it is not active. Higher knowing lands in your being as a flash of light compelling you – 'this is the way to go now' - telling you what the moment is really all about. It's a very high vibration, which most people then override with the very clunky lower mind – rationalising what they've just perceived. Within seconds, the flash of genius inspiration is lost under a mountain of pontification.

"Wow. So how do you activate higher mind?"

Essentially, let go of intention and agenda in your life. Let life guide you without over-questioning. If you get a sudden impulse to do something, don't reason with it too strongly. Instead work to figure out how to do what you've now been given to do. Allow natural spontaneity to carry you more in your life. Then witness the energy and synchronicity clicking in all around you. This will lead to a powerful Breakthrough.

Back in front of the energy healer, within minutes, I experience a dramatic mood change. There is a sense of lightness. Somehow, without being able to explain it, I just know I'm cured. Sure enough, as soon as he'd finished and I'd opened my eyes, I felt more or less like my old self again. Except the feeling was also, somehow, different. There's what I can only describe as a 'lightness of being' that wasn't there before. It's like someone has 'turned the volume up' on my senses.

After the session, the energy healer tells me something else - "that an ancient spirit was present with me, caring for and looking after me". As I looked back, I could feel an icy tingle down Chris' spine (*the tingle of truth!*), but also a scepticism. He wasn't ready to go there yet. The idea of energy balancing was one thing – there was a perfectly rational scientific explanation, which you could possibly relate to quantum physics. But the presence of a spirit? Of ghosts? Life after death? That was not in his realm of understanding or acceptance. What I couldn't know then however, was that a short while later, something would happen that would turn this redundant belief system on it's head.

So few people stop to truly question the nature of consciousness and that of 'spirit' (if you want to call it that). There is something inside of you that animates your body and your mind. It is NOT of the body and mind – a simple inner inquiry will reveal that. Just begin to observe all your thoughts, feelings and actions. If you do this diligently, you'll arrive at the point where you realise you are not the body nor the mind, but rather that which is looking on, that which is witnessing. And why would you necessarily blindly accept that just because the body dies, the animating spirit would die also?

Furthermore, you readily accept the density of your body and the world it exists within, which your quantum science tells you is all interconnected energy at various frequencies. So why couldn't other realities exist all around you at higher frequencies? That's exactly where your biomagnetic energy field is, for example, and higher mind, from where flashes of genius inspiration come in.

It's time for people to open their minds to the infinite possibility of the Universe. That the Universe might have a deeper reason and purpose for you, which you've not yet contemplated. One that it is infinitely benevolent, has your personal interests at heart, and is working tirelessly to bring you to the highest revelation of your own being – your Cosmic Self.

Wow. Back at the farm I could feel that. It melted the denseness in me, bringing me intensely alive, with all my senses tingling. My heart was opening yet wider. I simply recognised the benevolent intent of the Universe. I just knew it was there with me, willing me on, encouraging deeper Breakthrough.

It felt like in this new sense of being, this 'Cosmic Self', I was touching a new dimension of existence - something that was there all around me, but I had to progressively let go of the old to touch the new.

There's a vital imperative to Breakthrough which you're now beginning to discover. A shift of consciousness is taking place across the planet into a New Paradigm, in the Fifth Density, one that exists all around you. And for reasons that will become increasingly obvious as the journey unfolds, it's vital that as many souls as possible get on board.

I'm all in.

18

First Contact

*"I've been there for you many times
in the background of your life's experiences."*

Suddenly Chris was alive again, and I was he, with a deep sense of inquiry that I'd never previously experienced. I would be in the showrooms, talking with a customer, not only hearing their words, but somehow, I can hear their thoughts too – and even picking up on some of their feelings. I simply know in advance any objections they're going to have and how much they really want to buy. It feels deliriously exciting. Not because I particularly want to sell – I can feel that need has practically vapourised. My interests in the business itself have all but fallen away.

What is business when you can hear – for the first time – the intricate workings of the Universe?

Sitting in the showrooms again, with antique furniture all around me, I can readily feel the love that's gone into making it. And now I can literally see the carpenters carving and the French polishers polishing; they're all around me, as if their images are somehow projected onto the walls. It's like walking through some virtual reality.

Everything retains an energetic 'footprint'.

Music by Mozart begins to play. Up to that point, I'd no real interest in classical music. We'd used it in the showrooms just to create a sophisticated ambience. But suddenly I find myself transported – it's as if the very bars of music carry me all the way back to the orchestra. I'm not just hearing the music, *but feeling the very essence of it.* It spoke into my heart. This was truly miraculous...

Past, present and future, they're all interconnected lines of energy.

I recall trying to explain this to Amanda, who looked decidedly worried I was having some 'energy regression'. I simply couldn't find the right words and so gave up trying. But I also recall an incredible sense of in-love-ness for her, something that had dwindled between us – especially in those intense business years.

The sense and the feeling of the soul breaking through IS the sense of in-love-ness. The soul is in-love with all life!

Our sex life had become practically non-existent. We'd long since fallen out of love. But now as I looked upon her, it was as though I could see and feel the light in her again – that which we'd both buried under the burdensome mountain of our lives. The warmth in me wanted to express itself – a hug, a smile, a glint in the eyes. And as I expressed that feeling, it seemed to kindle the feeling in her too – an almost extinguished flame, which now wanted to strengthen again. And then we were being sensual and romantic with each other. It felt totally wonderful.

We made love, but in a way we'd never done before. Usually it had always been, pretty much, over too soon. As I looked back with the benefit of heightened awareness, I realised it was because the sense of lack in me wanted to fulfil itself in my partner – to be made whole by her. So there was an ownership, which during arousal, became a desperate need for completion – a sudden explosion, like the big bang.

It's typical of a lot of guys, especially with that strong warrior energy.

Now, however, there was no hurry, no rush. It's like the energy in me was what I really wanted to feel; it's what I was really enjoying, and the feeling of being able to bring that alive in someone else.

You can't take true love from another. You have to have love already inside you – for yourself - then you can truly inspire it in someone else.

I could feel love-making becoming sensual and evocative. It seems to last an eternity, and all the while, the sense of in-love-ness – the energy – is building inside me. When I finally do release, it's totally magical, transcendent - like swirling energy is flowing around me, through Amanda, and out into the room. It is as if we are both transported to another time and space – a higher dimension, all around us.

What you were experiencing was a release of kundalini energy: that which connects you all the way back to the Source. Loving sexual intimacy is one of the best ways to experience it. But you must be totally out of the mind. Not thinking, not controlling. Instead feeling deeply inside - watching, observing - deep into your senses.

That night, although relaxed and fulfilled, I couldn't sleep, I didn't want to sleep. I wanted to bask in this energy for eternity.

Of course you can. Activated kundalini is a totally natural energy. It's your divinely given birthright.

Even in looking back, feeling into it again, the energy begins to rise in me. It's like my focus invokes it.

People are so constantly focussed on what's going on 'out there'. So they miss the real joy inside. What you put your attention on grows.

Very quickly I'm feeling expanded, happy, content and fulfilled. I am relaxed in a way I've never experienced before – all my trials and tribulations have vanished. It is as though all goals have been attained. Any doubt, fear or worry, have dissolved, as if into some distant black hole.

It took me sometime to come back to the movie, but when I did, I remembered it was when 'it' happened. Although it took time to figure out what 'it' was. Suddenly I became aware of some kind of presence in the room, all around me. Amanda was sound asleep, and I felt not to wake her, in case she became worried again. It felt like this presence was not only all around me, but strangely, through me. I felt to ask a question, out into the space…"Are you there?"

The was a creak from the water pipes in the wall that shocked me for a moment. It seemed to answer, upon which I nervously laughed at myself, thinking, how foolish. But it was as if a little child in me wouldn't be deterred and so I asked again "Are you there?" Yet again a creak in the water pipes. Wow, this is no joke, I thought. Suddenly my senses are tingling, I'm fully alive and awake – an intense awakeness that seems to stretch out and explore into every nook and cranny. "Who are you?"

There was no answer from the room, but the feeling and sense of the word 'friend' landed within me. As I reflected back, it was a curious and new phenomenon – like there was a knowing, which popped into my mind.

This is how Higher Mind works. It's not like thoughts are transferred.

There's an activation of energy, within oneself, which then causes a resonance in the one you're communicating with. Lower mind may then interpret the knowing with an idea or a thought or in words.

"Why are you here?" *To help*, was the sense I got back. "Help what?" Upon which, I felt a sense of upliftment, an expansion, an increasing sense of at-one-ment. Wow – yes please! How does this happen? Another feeling landed which my mind interpreted as "follow". Gosh! The rest of the night I played with the energy, and revelled in it, like languishing in a bath of scented water. I was in sheer paradise.

As I looked back on that evening now, a realisation came to me. One that made me feel warm and completely okay with the world – like the Universe was wrapping me up in its arms and giving me a great big hug. "It was you there that night wasn't it?"

Indeed it was.

"It was our first contact."

Yes. I'd been there for you many times in the background of your life's experiences. But this was the first time you recognised me. And it melted my heart too!

When Amanda woke that morning I was really excited to tell her of this incredible experience – how totally mind-blowing it was. That this guide - this guardian angel - exists all around me; the one that the blind healer must have seen too. But I wasn't at all prepared for her response – she looked worried and anxious, asked me if I was feeling okay, and did I need to go and see a doctor?

Yep. That's the usual response, which you'll just have to get used to.

It annoyed me. This was so real, so beautiful, so exquisite. There was something there, in the field all around us. I just knew there was presence there for everyone (*indeed there is*). How awesome if everyone could connect like that? But she wouldn't (*couldn't*) get it. So I had to take off for the day, out in the car.

Looking back, I recall just how magical that day was.

It was like everything was beginning to speak to me – messages on billboards, birds suddenly appearing, clouds moving across the skies. And then my attention would be drawn to sequences of numbers on car number plates. It was as though somehow, my attention was directing me to things. But I just knew it was the presence 'speaking' to me. I saw '59' on a number plate which 'spiked' in me. What does that mean? And suddenly I remembered 59 Commando, which was the unit I was attached to during the Commando Course. *So what does 59 mean?* And I remembered clearly, 'don't give up, keep going'. Then shortly afterwards I saw 95, and more or less in a flash I realised its meaning - 'let go, accept, surrender'. The very opposite of 59 - 'keep going'.

Numerology is a powerful language of the Universe. But here's the key to its interpretation – there are no absolute meanings, no 'rights' or 'wrongs'. There is only what the number means to you. How does the significance of it make you feel?

Reflecting back as the movie-goer, I'm feeling incredible joy and comfort in the sense of rediscovering the universal mother tongue.

Meanwhile, back in the movie, I'm seeing 44s everywhere. Somehow I know it's about 'teaching' and 'guiding' - also feeling into the rightness of the moment. And then I see an image of the Christ.

It's what I resonated for you. The Christ represents a very special energy of the soul (which has nothing to do with the religion). It's about finding the rightness in every situation, one that you feel as a pull of 'Right Action' through the heart. It's why some call it "The passion of the Christ".

This '44 energy' is very important in the world right now. It's the directing force guiding you through the plane of your karma - the Fourth Density - into the New Paradigm of Being.

"How do I pass through the plane of karma?"

Keep following the heart-felt pull. It'll take you on a pathway to unveil and unravel your karma. This is how you make the shift into the New Paradigm - 'heaven' - a journey metaphored in the story of the Christ.

Back in the movie, suddenly I'm seeing 55 everywhere. I didn't understand what it meant at the time, but it seemed to come with an expansive feeling, a much lighter sense of interconnectivity with life - there is a timeless peace to it, that has me looking up into the sky, like floating on air, but which reflects to something inside of me.

Crucially, this New 5D Paradigm is not 'out there' at all, although you may see metaphoric reflections of it. Reality is arrayed through different 'densities' - different frequencies of vibration, which can be found here and now, in this space, like tuning the dial on a radio to get to different stations.

These higher dimensions of existence are to be found inside yourself. When you can touch them inside, it's like you become a movie projector - projecting them outwards to create a new, outer reality.

Looking on as the movie-goer, I can literally feel the wonderful expansiveness again. It's an incredible sense of lightness and relief. All the density and difficulty I'd experienced in my life have fallen away. It's like I've 'tuned' into a different station.

After a while of languishing in that beautiful feeling, back in the movie again, now I'm seeing 22 everywhere. "What's that all about?" Suddenly a song comes on the radio...

"But you are in my head
Swimming forever in my head
Tangled in my dreams
Swimming forever
So I listen to the radio and all the songs we used to know
So I listen to the radio remember where we used to go

Now it's morning light and it's cold outside
caught up in a distant dream
I turn and think that you are by my side
I listen to the radio."
(lyrics by The Corrs)

It feels very feminine, incredibly loving, and like it is inside me. And now my eyes are directed outwards, to a billboard with the picture of a woman on it with smiling eyes. It makes me feel warm inside, whole, completed and loved.

You were seeing reflections of your Twin Flame. The other part of you, which rests at the Source and acts as a homing beacon, to the memory of your completeness. Hence you were seeing the number 22.

That day was so special. So magical. It felt more real than ever I'd experienced life before. Somehow in my heart, I just knew this was how it was supposed to be. In looking back, I knew I wanted to, and could, live this dream. And that ultimately, the dream would be more real than my current 'reality'.

Indeed it is. It can be for anyone. It just requires you to put your attention on it - to watch out for the 'spiking' moments that draw your focus. Follow them. Then you can break through into the greatest romance of your life!

19

Seven Dark Nights of the Soul

*"You have to confront your fears – not retract from them.
Look them square in the eye and go right into the heart of them."*

When I got back from that incredible day it was tough, because Amanda was really suspicious of me and spreading a sense of worry around me, which deflated my mood.

Worry and fear have a big impact on the field around you. They are the very antithesis of the flow. They make it turgid and slow it down. They destroy the romance and contract you back into the density.

The presence and I were looking on together as the movie-goers once more. I knew we could both feel the sense of heightened awareness, as if a quickening of the energy was happening; the 'movie' was building through a new intensity. We looked on as Chris received a phone call. Ah yes, the strange incident with Ingo.

Ingo was a lovely guy, who had developed his own conscious bakery in Osnabrück. He was a bit of a hippy, very warm, friendly and incredibly laid back. It was somewhat surprising therefore, that he should call quite late one evening, and suggest we get together for a walk early next morning in the famous Teutoburger Wald nearby. He was very insistent, not at all like the Ingo I knew. But it seemed important, so I decided to go, taking both Amanda and my daughter with me.

Be open to the possibility of strong connections between people - exchanges that appear out of the ordinary. There are souls who've been drawn into your life for a reason. They may have a vibration that can communicate an energy, which can help you infuse soul and become more of you.

You'll discover this is what the 'game' is really all about – it's all to do with soul infusion. The more you can integrate, the more you can feel your True Self; you come home to who you truly are.

"And there's nothing else going on, right?"

Spot on! But be prepared for some big stories, some big transitions that affect the world around you and your part in what's taking place. Like on Earth right now, which is going through a very turbulent and challenging transition.

Ingo did indeed meet us in the Teutoburger Wald, right at the appointed place, right at the appointed hour. Which was bloody unusual for him - I found myself thinking.

What took place was very curious indeed. It wasn't so much what he had to say, it was more the way he said it. It's like everything he did had a deeper meaning, a deeper feeling. We are now standing next to a map, beside a viewpoint, on one of the highest places. He's explaining to me how, "this location is famous, and of great importance in German history. It's where a group of Germanic tribes defeated the Roman Army in the 9th Century. This prevented Germany being invaded east of the Rhine, and it's considered Rome's greatest defeat". As he was speaking, it was as though the events he was speaking of were not what I was supposed to get - rather the energy of them. Somehow I could feel an invading energy in the field – like a virus – and another benevolent one preventing it.

Indeed you intuited very accurately what I was working to communicate through Ingo. He had a special connection to that area, and you had a karmic connection to him.

What we in the higher realms are working for you all to realise, is that the Earth has been inflicted by a kind of virus, that pits man against man, 'dog-eat-dog', creating all manner of division, aggression and oppression. This German battle was where the people rose up, and the sense of it, is what you're being encouraged to find in yourself right now – to rise up, within your soul, against anything that would suppress you. Not in a fighting or aggressive way, but an assertive one, taking back sovereignty of who you are, in the choices you make.

In looking back, I could see that although I didn't get the exact meaning of it at the time, I did feel an energetic sense of it, rising within me. I felt very maverick and rebellious – that I wouldn't be suppressed and controlled. It felt like I had to break free, to break through and therefore breakout. At this stage, I didn't even fully understand what that meant - "Break out of what?" I just knew something inside of me was wanting to get out - to leave the old reality behind.

All the while, Amanda seemed to become increasingly suspicious of me. Which, in looking back, I could understand. I'd changed quite strongly. I was speaking in a different way, about different things. My motivation in life had almost completely transformed, practically overnight. As we drove back from the Teutoburger Wald, incredible energies were flowing through me, together with many visions of past battles and wars, which I somehow had the sense I'd been involved in. They seemed all interconnected, all working at overcoming this strange virus that I could now feel in the field all around us. And it seemed to exacerbate Amanda's worrisome mood.

Yes, it's a virus – a consciousness – that is drawn to, and clings to, fearful energy. When you look around you at society, you can see it everywhere - in the control of the system, in the subjugation of the masses, addicting them to behaviours that don't serve then. It downgrades people, making them less than who they truly are.

This virus causes the soul to retract inside a shell – that of its own fears and limitations. It means you can more easily be programmed and addicted to base level desires or perceived needs. It leaves you constantly struggling for some kind of completion 'out there'.

That night I had many nightmares of being consumed by a dark, evil energy. But it also felt like the dreams were lucid, and that this energy is all around us – feeding on fears, causing inner repression. It made it hard for me to hear and to feel the presence. I could see that Chris had become confused by it, and so it was only in looking back with the presence that I was fully able to understand...

This is often what's called "The Dark Night of the Soul". Although in truth, it can last many nights. It's where your consciousness has expanded out into the 4D field around you – through your energy body. The energy body contains your karma – past life energy of traumatic memories and experiences; ones your soul has become attached to and fragmented by.

When you expand into the energy body in the 4D, in the beginning it will likely feel pretty amazing – spacious, timeless, expanded. But then at some point, the reconnected soul flows into your karma and activates it – bringing it alive as animations in your psyche and the outer world. Often these images will create fear, that draws in the 'virus' from the field. It's a parasite that feeds off this dissonant energy.

"What can you do about it?"

You have to confront your fears – not retract from them. Look them square in the eye and go right into the heart of them. It's only your fear by which you can be controlled and subjugated. So don't let it compress or contract you down. Stay open!

Back in the drama – the nightmare – I awake, suddenly, with a scream, in a cold sweat, waking Amanda too. This sparks off a deeper bout of worrisome conversation. She is determined I should see a doctor and go to hospital. At first I resist, but the energy seems to grow and consume me, eating me up. I make it through part of the next day, but then at one point, the feelings are so overwhelming, I completely collapse on the floor and pass out.

I came around quickly, but Amanda was beside herself and called a doctor over – a friend whom we both knew. He too was concerned and, although against my wishes, the two of them practically frogmarched me to the local hospital to be checked out.

Looking back on it with the presence, a sense of foreboding was beginning to activate within me. I knew exactly what was to come...

Yes, I recall it too. A very dark night of the soul.

Suddenly I find myself in what appears to be a Nazi concentration camp. Doctors are peering into me with demonic features. An intense and overpowering dialogue is happening. They are insinuating that I am concealing something. That I should surrender and give up. That they wanted to explore into my body and mind. All around me is a sense of foreboding and evil. They put me in a huge machine, which fires x-rays into my body, all of which I can feel intensely, there's a cancerous sense to my field, in the energy body I could now clearly feel.

They put a contraption on my head, which is plugged into the mains, which terrifies me - they're going to fry my brains, I'm thinking. All the while, they're looking for something. And then I get it....they're looking for my True Self. It is as if they - *the virus animating the people - is trying to suppress it, or drive it off.*

My God, looking back, I remember it all too well. It was absolutely terrifying.

Don't worry, my dear friend. Try to see the bigger picture – light is coming into darkness throughout the Universe. But that has to play out into the microcosm of your lives. Your souls come into the darkness to bring light into it. And there are also protagonists – actors – playing out the dark side too. They animate the darkness so you can see into it.

"Is that what fallen angels are?"

Exactly, yes. They too are playing out some kind of distortion – in this case being disconnected from the light, controlling and manipulating reality. These 'entities' are in the field all around you. Where you're not fully conscious – where the soul is not fully penetrating your being – they're able to come in through that blindspot, surreptitiously. Whereupon they plant imagery, thoughts and emotions that drive you into a limiting and fearful reality.

"What's the point? What's their purpose?"

They gain energy that you release. It's how they feed, just as you would eat a physical meal. They're being a parasitic virus - but never forget, they're just souls like you or I, having an experience, playing a role in the drama, the overall purpose of which, is to spread light throughout the Universe.

"Why is it that most people don't see them?"

Because most people are only in tune with the lower three densities of existence, and these kind of entities exist in the Fourth Density. They influence your field negatively, creating all manner of delusion. This then sinks down into your psyche, and, by the time you experience it, the feeling is like it's coming from your own mind and emotions.

I'm on a psychiatric bed now, with some electronic contraption on my head. I just know they're trying to get into my mind; to get rid of the real me. I'm not fooled – the doctor in the white coat may just be some ordinary guy, but influencing him - controlling him - is a demon, and when he throws that switch, my brains will be fried and my soul lost.

This is what they do. These demonic entities distort a truth and make it fearful. So yes, much of the electronic gadgetry in a hospital will lower your vibration and remove the interconnectivity of your soul. The entities play on that fear, blowing it up and dramatising it for you, to exacerbate fear in the situation.

As I looked on with the presence, suddenly the face of Chris the Commando is there again, not going to be beaten, not taking no for an answer, not being subjugated or controlled, not going to be buried in the blackness. Suddenly Chris leaps off the bed, breaks out through the door, and takes off down the corridor, hotly pursued by the doctor and Amanda, who is beside herself with panic.

And now back in the drama again, this feels amazing, empowering and liberating. I don't care what any of them think. As I sprint past bemused and terrified patients in the hospital corridor, it doesn't matter to me just how strange this might seem, they can't see the truth. They can't see with my eyes. They are controlled anyway, dehumanised, zombified. It's bloody well not going to happen to me!

There's truth in everything you saw. Yes they're dehumanised, yes their vibrations are lowered and they're disconnected from the divine, and yes it's intentional. The end effect is no less damaging than being in some concentration camp. It just looks clean, sanitised and somewhat caring on the surface, but it's not crazy to want to escape!

And now I can hear an alarm ringing in my ears – one of the 'prisoners' is getting away. I'm sprinting down a long corridor looking for the nearest exit. All windows are closed, all doors sealed. Up ahead is a hallway – a meeting point of corridors – good, there I'll find a sign, and see the way out. But as I arrive in the middle, suddenly I'm pounced upon by orderlies, who seem to appear from all directions.

I put up a valiant fight, but there's no resisting. I'm wrestled to the ground, face driven into the rough carpet flooring. Suddenly there's a sharp prick in my backside… Shit I'm being injected.

It's my last conscious thought. A toxic wooziness is washing over me, everything slowing down. Reality is bending and waving like some LSD-induced psychedelia. I'm slipping backwards. My last vision is of falling over a cliff edge. And there's a man there, on top of the cliff, dressed in white, with grey and black cloak. His eyes are Asian - Tibetan. He's stretching out his hand to try to catch me. I grasp at his fingers, but alas, neither he nor I can hold on. And now I'm falling, deeply backwards, down the cliff edge, just like Chris the Commando abseiling again. And as I'm falling, one final thought lodges in my mind. It feels like it's coming from the guy with the Tibetan eyes, but his lips aren't moving…

Try not to worry, my friend. I'm still here for you. You may fall asleep again now. But I'll be there for you. It may take a while, but I'll be there…. 2 years. I sense it'll take 2 years.

Thunk! Crack! The rope suddenly tightens, with a backbreaking jolt into reality. I think for a moment I'm about to awaken back at the bottom of the cliff – that somehow I was back on the Commando Course again. But this is very different. I'm not outside, but in a whitened room. Where am I now? I look down. I'm lying on a hospital bed, dressed in a white uniform, strapped by ankles and wrists. What the fuck! I feel alone. So very alone.

It was just too painful looking back and seeing Chris there. I felt like my heart was going to crack wide apart.

How do you feel about what's now happening to Chris - what happened to you?

"I feel tightness in my chest. Anger and rage at the injustice."

Tell me about the injustice.

"Well it's just not fair, not right - what happened."

What is right? What is fair? Why do you need it to be so?

Well, here Chris is - here I am - feeling the light and the interconnectivity, a new aligned way of living and being. It's a feeling of rightness, of justice and fairness for all.

Yes indeed, but the entirety of the Universe is not like that. Where the light is only just breaking through, there are still grey areas - blindspots. Different protagonists occupy those blindspots and play them out - so that souls can decide their truth in it. When you can soften into your need for it to be a certain way - to let go of that and unwind through the tightness it causes - then you will infuse soul. Your soul will become increasingly integral and coherent. You'll begin to shine light into all the darkened corners.

"Yes, I get it. It's actually me - at a consciousness level, that decides to switch off, to give up. I do it to myself."

Sadly, yes. But it is also a necessary part of the great awakening.

At the time, understandably, I was confused, not knowing what was going on inside of me. Maybe I was becoming psychotic? But in looking back, I could so readily see that just wasn't the case. I was having a powerful awakening. I was beginning to see the truth about life and the Universe. I was seeing how disconnected people are from that reality. How soft drugs keep people down, through conditioning, fear and control. How society squeezes people into boxes and wrings the very life from them. And now here was Chris, strapped to a bed, drugged out of his rightful mind, the final injustice, the final humiliation. Tears of anguish are now rolling down the movie-goers cheeks.

Yes, it's a hard one to stomach, I know. And in countries the world over, there are people trapped in society's anaesthetised hospitals, because the so-called 'health services' don't understand, or know how to manage, spiritual awakening. They've little comprehension of the soul, and how it exchanges into the bodymind through chakras. How these conscious exchange points connect into multidimensionality. And they've absolutely no idea how they're being negatively influenced in their practices by this invading virus. In many ways, the health services are an instrument for that dehumanisation and subjugation.

They witness a soul breaking through and call it 'multiple personality disorder' or 'bi-polar'. Then they drug the person to manage the 'condition'. All that does is lock the two states in place, bury the fragmented soul deeper in the psyche, and then subdue the incoherence. Now the soul is locked in a disparate prison cell.

"That is just horrendous. It's institutionalised torture."

Yes. And I remind you, I keep reminding you, to see the bigger picture. You are not this experience – you are the inviolable One having an experience; where the light is breaking into the dark. And break in it will. Right now, your world is on the cusp of monumental change, after aeons of darkness, everywhere people are waking up, even in hospitals like this.

Now back in the drama I'm feeling angry and confused, thrashing around on the bed... How dare anyone do this to me! I was a proud guy, finding it especially difficult being incarcerated, having my freedom removed. Freedom which, like so many people, I readily took for granted. But over the course of a few days, the drugs did their work, pacifying and calming. And the psychologist did his work too – "You were having a nervous breakdown of some kind. Probably brought on by the shock of your Karate accident. It happens to a lot of people. But over time, with the medication, things calm and hopefully everything will return to normal."

After a couple of days I was released into the main ward of the secure psychiatric hospital, whereupon I went on to meet quite a few who'd also described 'expansive, interconnected and timeless experiences'. People who thought somehow they were God (*of course - you are all God!*). There was even someone who thought he'd been Jesus (*people often say that when the Christ Consciousness activates in their heart*).

There were some who described the presence of demons, and others who were just plain confused. Many times though, we'd have powerful conversations of awakening, that is, until the daily cocktail of drugs – 'medication' – did its consciousness undermining work. I felt terribly lost, confined against my will. But amidst it all was a young nurse – a guy who was different to the others. He had punky hair, an earring and a ready smile. When he spoke to me, there was a light in his eyes, which deeply connected in me - it felt warmly healing, like the sun.

There are Warriors of Light everywhere!

One day he hands me a Sony Walkman and smiles – you'll enjoy this…

"I wanna run
I want to hide
I wanna tear down these walls
That hold me inside
I wanna reach out
And touch the flame
Where the streets have no name.

I wanna feel sunlight on my face
I see the dust-cloud
Disappear without a trace
I wanna take shelter
From the poison rain

Where the streets have no name
Where the streets have no name
Where the streets have no name.

The city's a flood, and our love turns to rust
We're beaten and blown by the wind
Trampeled in dust
I'll show you a place
High on a desert plain

Where the streets have no name
Where the streets have no name
Where the streets have no name.

(lyrics by U2)

Suddenly I'm soaring inside. The music rings deep within. It's like it touches the very essence of my pain, recognises it, and expands me out of it… *it's alright, I'm right here with you.*

And looking on, as the movi-goer, the stirring is even stronger... *"I'll show you a place, high on a desert plain, where the streets have no name.* He's singing of the Fifth Density isn't he?

It certainly feels like that to me!

Back in the movie, the experience changed things for me. I was able to surrender to my fate and accept what had happened. Within a short while I was back to 'normal' (*a very 3D 'normal'!*) and was released back into my life.

Sadly, it didn't take long to forget the presence and those other-worldy experiences I'd had - it was all too easy to put it down to some psychotic 'altered state', brought on - as the doctors drilled into me - by my Karate accident. But there was a still a lingering sense that the music had touched deep in my heart. A feeling that I could somehow break through and break out to a more expanded reality. The feeling greatly comforted me.

And there was another thing I remembered – from the dream as I was falling over the cliff edge. It was the feeling – the knowing – that in 2 yrs, the presence would return for me. Somehow that made it okay. Somehow I could accept going back into normal life.

You will break through. You are not alone. You are never alone!

20

Dotbomb

"Whenever you activate your passion,
give attention and energy to it.
Because it's immensely creative."

It's an entirely different scene we're projected forward to now. I'm getting off a train in London, walking under Waterloo Bridge. It's barely six months on from the terrifying hospital experience and all traces of the presence forgotten. Yet there's an enthusiasm and quickness in my stride - a motivation, like that of driving change. I know what to expect under the bridge - the rows of cardboard houses, of the homeless poor; society's disenfranchised, scraping a meagre living from the odd coin, tossed by well-heeled business folk, making their way by the horde, across the bridge and into the affluence of the City.

It was nigh on impossible to settle back into the Antiques business. It no longer stirred my passion and I'd sunk into a fair degree of depression. That was until one day, an old Army colleague of mine came excitedly into the warehouse, like a bushy-tailed squirrel. Charlie, who'd also been an Engineer Captain, had left the Army at the same time as me. He'd always had a keen interest in technology and was now fired by a passion for the internet, which was in its very early developmental days. Synchronistically, it had caught my interest too. I'd gotten the sense that something big was taking off in the world, that would change things beyond measure. I'd love to have been a part of it, but had no technological expertise. That's when Charlie walked in.

Never forget: those 'chance' happenings in your life don't happen by chance!

Charlie had established a fledgling web development company, in the very early days of the craft. He'd come in touting for business, but got more than he bargained for - a lot more. When I discovered what he was capable of, it felt inside like a bonfire was being lit. It's like every sense and sensibility within me suddenly ignited at once. The internet made it possible to access the world at your fingertips. I'd seen a Georgian-style reproduction chair on the Kings Road in London selling at a ridiculous £700. I wanted to trade in reproductions, so had followed a trail, partly on the internet, partly on the road, all the way back to the business that first carved it - in Indonesia.

I'd seen the same chair was being sold to retailers by distributors in the UK at around £300. They had bought it from the importer for around £200, who themselves had acquired it from the eastern exporter for around £75. They in turn had commissioned it from the guy who carved it, for a mere £25. When I showed this to Charlie, his jaw dropped open. The same chair had escalated progressively in price from £25 to £700 over the course of a few thousand miles and a very convoluted resource/delivery chain.

There is indeed massive waste and exploitation in the global supply chain, which is destroying the very biosphere you're living in. It's now become a very hot question as to whether that is possibly reversible. The very positive effect of the internet has been increased communication between people - the escalation of ideas and consciousness. You will come to see how it's becoming a race against time. How will mankind connect, how will he come together to secure his future? Can he communicate the higher dimensional possibilities that exist?

Looking on with the presence, I could feel the sense of excitement that greater possibilities existed, that increased connection might facilitate.

Back in the movie, my conversation with Charlie literally took off - we were like two escapees realising exactly how we'd break out. What began as a casual meeting, lasted several hours and was followed up by excited brainstorming on subsequent days. "The whole of business must be like this," I'd said to Charlie. "That's exactly why they're pouring so much money into the internet," he responded. "You can get millions of venture capital for a start-up." It's then that we first imagined the possibility of "VHO" - Victoria House Online - a global furniture trading platform, that cut out many layers of the middle man.

As I looked back on those early days with Charlie, I could see that in me, the thinking process accelerated exponentially, like shifting quickly through different dimensions of contemplation. It had begun in the sedate world of furniture, but the overburdened logistic chain that I'd discovered, was rife throughout the world in many other forms of business. It was creating enormous wastage and serving only to line the pockets of the fat cats in the middle. What about the poorest in the world? Why shouldn't they benefit from their skills, talents and graft too? And why should people have to pay more than necessary? Why should they have to graft and grind 9-5 to pay for the essentials? Maybe we could change the entire way the global industrial system worked?

In looking back, how does that kind of excitement make you feel?

"Wow, it's passionate, alive, invigorating, electrifying."

Whenever you get that sense about something, whenever you activate your passion in that way, give attention and energy to it. Because it's immensely creative. You're literally sending positive energy out into the Universe, and it can't fail to respond.

As Charlie and I conversed over those early days, we began to feel more and more like renegade mavericks, about to take on the world with a foolproof strategy.

The internet was indeed a major shift, not just in the world of business, but especially in terms of interconnectivity of people. It mirrored the readiness for change in the world that was beginning to ignite within hearts and minds. You have to understand, with utmost imperative, that injustice and inequity cause disharmony within quantum timespace - and wherever that exists, the Universe works tirelessly to unravel and realign. Right now, there is building energetic imperative for monumental change.

Yes indeed. Looking back I know I couldn't have understood it in those terms then, but could readily feel the excitement and adventure for global transformation building in my gut that day, as I was walking across Waterloo Bridge into the City - into the heart of the 'beast'.

My heart is literally bleeding for those in their cardboard houses, whilst a few hundred brisk strides away, on the other side of the bridge, is a vast metropolis of suits, an old-boys club, that vehemently protects the interests of just the few. Fortunately for us (*synchronistically!*) Charlie's brother worked in the City, and just happened to know a fledgling incubator company interested in taking on viable 'dotcoms', helping them win start-up funding from venture capitalists.

Sanjay and Pierce were fascinating souls. Sanjay, was an equities trader and management consultant of Indian descent, who'd attained dizzy heights in the City, before being severely 'stabbed in the back' (in his words) by one of the top consultancy firms. Pierce, his close friend and colleague, had been equally appalled by the treatment and quit at the same time. Both incredibly creative, resourceful and highly intelligent renegades, they'd together established "Cloud9" - the incubator - with a seemingly endless network of connections into the world of business, finance, marketing and now, new start-up companies. They were falling over themselves to put the dotcom jigsaw together. And what drew me to them most of all, what really resonated for me, was their sense of idealism, of altruism. It was clear the money wasn't that important. Like Charlie and I, you could feel in every meeting we had, they were there to light up the world with a new freedom of justice and equity for all.

There are similar souls everywhere, in all parts of the globe, just waiting for a chance to turn the tables and allow in some light.

It didn't stop them cavorting in the City with the well-heeled though - as Sanjay explained it, that was "their patch, their hunting ground". It was clear from the beginning that Sanjay especially had an 'axe to grind' in the city, the sense of betrayal had given him a sharpened edge, a cutting wit, and readiness for 'battle' at a moment's notice.

That day as I was crossing Waterloo Bridge, it did indeed have the feeling of marching into battle - like its Waterloo namesake. My destination was 1 Aldwych, one of the most exclusive meeting venues in the city, and popular amongst the dotcoms, despite the exorbitant prices. But then who really cared, the money was sloshing around like party-time champagne. Sanjay was often to be found there - at 1 Aldwych - he considered it his second office.

I found myself with the presence once more, 'sitting on high', flies on the wall so to speak, as a meeting at 1 Aldwych with potential investors was in mid-flow. They are 'kicking our tyres', testing the VHO value, to see if they can get a better equity deal, when Sanjay, amidst the highflying, in-the-box suits, pulls out his Rayban sunglasses, gets up and walks over to the large windows looking out onto Mother Thames. Feigning disinterest, he begins to make calls to other possibilities, or calling his secretary to see what else is going on of more importance and interest.

It is absolutely fascinating watching the faces of the bemused investors. Unsure how to take this 'cabaret', they are completely wrong-footed by his (apparently) over-the-top slapstick. Shady or not, it worked.

Sometimes a healthy disrespect for the 'way it's always been done' is a very good thing. Like at Waterloo, reality gets too readily bogged down in the 3D. Sometimes you have to pierce right through it. And out in the world, at this moment, that approach is much needed. People everywhere need to stand up and take back their sovereignty - not to be pushed around anymore by the faceless corporations who seemingly have neither care nor responsibility toward the better interests of the world and majority of its people.

It was a heady time for us, venture capitalists were literally throwing money at the dotcoms, many of whom had the simple, and very direct strategy, of "get big fast". We were different though. We really wanted to make it work, to create a solid business, that was resourceful, focussed, fair and just for all involved, including our customers - we were the cavalry, charging with drawn swords at red-tape mentality.

Pulling together an experienced team from around the world (our Chairman had taken companies to public listing on the stock market) we were right on the edge of securing a sizeable investment in the new company, VHO. We were riding high, feeling invincible. That is, until along came the aptly named "Boo.com".

Boo was a highly publicised fashion clothing company, who gobbled up $135 million of venture capital in just 18 months, launching simultaneously on multiple continents with trendy offices and an army of young, inexperienced staff. Despite the massive investment, the website was too slow and clunky, and they burned through way too much money before sales-revenue-streams could catch up. In short they bombed - and unfortunately for us, it was right about the time we were about to secure our own investment. In a flash, investors fled like gazelle across some distant African savannah. The start-up money literally vanished.

Easy come, easy go!

I felt devastated. Here was an opportunity that captured my passion, completely invigorated my life, and had the chance to make a truly beneficial difference in the world. We were on the verge of something big, and it had disappeared in a flash.

If it's truly meant to happen in your life, do not be put off by apparent obstacles and 'failures'. Whatever you want to do, whatever you truly have a passion for, just begin it now, with what you have. It's like that for all light warriors out there. It may often seem like you don't have enough resources or support. You'll wonder how you can possibly get your service going. But creation follows committed, creative passion. So begin it, where you are, and the Universe will not fail to build a vehicle around you.

And when you grow, do so from sustainable creativity, constantly learning, evolving and growing - expressing what's in your heart. If a plant grows too fast, its roots will be weak and it'll often easily perish at the first sign of drought. But if you grow organically, sustainably, with the resources immediately to hand, you'll be in alignment with the way the underlying flow naturally creates. Although there will be many trials, tribulations and tests, you will ultimately succeed.

The next time we caught up with Chris in the movie, he was now back in Osnabrück, sitting quite dejectedly at Victoria House English Antiques, which was definitely NOT online.

Wait a minute. Didn't you resolve never, but never, to take "no" for an answer?

Chris had gone back to sleep after his pre-awakening. But somehow, as we looked on, we could readily feel the spark of higher knowing landing in his psyche. He was reflecting on those challenging moments on his journey, where he was pushed back again and again and again.

Just like the light working to break through the darkness.

And as I looked on, I could feel the thought already landing...

Begin it now, with what you have!

Back in the movie I looked all around me, at the furniture. I had only a small amount of cash, but plenty of money tied up in the business that we'd grown. Somehow, I just had to sell the business. There was a glimmer of hope, yet still it would be tough, since Germany had moved into recession, and exclusive goods like these were usually the first thing people shelved when times got hard.

You only need one buyer. You only need one doorway. You only need one connection to truly make a difference. Never let odds defy the unique possibility that is you.

Looking on, I could feel the upwelling building - the sense that somehow this just had to happen. It deserved to happen. It wasn't just for my own good. I simply knew it was in the interests of all life - that I could make a positive difference in the world. It felt like justice.

Pay attention to these feelings of rightness, give energy to them. For you're aligning with the Universe and harnessing it's energy. All manner of unimaginable possibilities will open up and create.

And that's just when my old friend Marius walks in - also an ex Army guy, who'd gotten into Antique English Silver, and traded mainly by travelling to other antique dealers throughout Germany. Needless to say, he was well-connected. I share my predicament with him, to which he offers to put the word out on his travels. But I wasn't at all prepared for the amazing speed and turn of events that followed.

The Universe can literally turn on a sixpence if you believe. But not blindly believe in anything. It's not about trying to make your desires happen, based on some hidden sense of lack. It's about recognising the authentic upwelling of soul yearning - then expressing that out into the world. If you put your energy truly behind your passion, the Universe will always come to meet you.

Within a couple of days, I was contacted by another Englishman, courtesy of Marius, who just happened to want to settle in Germany and establish his own Antiques business. We meet, and agree a sale within the week. He wants to take over quickly, so as to avoid any loss of business. Within 4 weeks, our whole livelihood in Germany is sold, lock, stock and barrel, and we find ourselves heading back to the UK, in the one furniture truck we retained. Even looking on with the presence, I have to pinch myself several times very hard, just to be sure this isn't all a dream!

Give yourself some credit. You'd broken through many layers on your journey. Yes, the soul was still buried, but nevertheless, aligned impulses were getting through - and so they do for many people on the verge of Breakthrough. So work to trust in your intuition. And if things aren't flowing for you, then feel the tightness that's limiting you inside. Open into it. Unwind it. Look at what's holding you, what you're attached to, and work to let it go.

Then open a space of belief - belief not in some desired outcome, but in infinite possibility. Belief that the flow will ignite and a new opportunity open up for you. You just have to watch for what the Universe is truly inviting and take the step. Then you'll be amazed at just how quickly the Universe can work for you. It always works for those who follow their passion.

"Yes I get it. Thank you. That's exactly what I got from Paulo Coelho when I watched his interview on the plane over to Las Vegas - the Universe works for you when you follow your heart, your true passion."

This message was now resounding loud and clear.

21

High Rise to Nowhere - the "Now Here"

"You're at the beginning and the end…
The now here."

The internet business was simply breathtaking. It was like a billowing cloud of awareness consuming all outdated, in-the-box small-mindedness in its path. We established our fledgling company, "gencon", in a small barn, in the middle of the rolling Hampshire countryside, with just four of us. It couldn't have been a more obtuse, unlikely setting if we'd tried. But we were all thirsty for it. We recruited Zack, an artist turned graphic designer, and Lutz, a Linux programming friend I'd enticed from Germany. Charlie had the internet backbone expertise, and myself a head for strategy - breaking down the convoluted resource chain. All mavericks, all individuals who'd failed to be pigeon-holed by society into some kind of box. Suddenly we were not failures anymore.

That's the problem with society. It has it's fixed ways of doing things - in-the-box logic. And if your greatness doesn't fit within that, you're cast out, a 'failure', hopeless, worthless. The great thing about the internet revolution, was that it opened up the possibility for people everywhere, for generations to come, to simply express themselves. And that's what life is really all about - connecting with the essence of your soul and letting it shine through. This is what will carry you, ultimately all the way into the New 5D Paradigm.

VHO - the online furniture exchange - was launched within a few months of high-intensity, long days of strategising, designing and programming. As the presence and I looked on, we could readily taste the brilliance amongst the team, creating something magical - something entirely new, that the world had not yet seen.

When it came to the launch however, VHO bombed. It wasn't that the technology wasn't good enough - it surely was. It wasn't that the strategy wouldn't work - in due course the cutting-through-red-tape approach would go on to revolutionise just about every industry. The problem was, that in the very staid and sleepy world of furniture, VHO was an idea way ahead of its time. The furniture dealers couldn't get their heads around the internet, and old fashioned buyers wanted to see and touch before they bought. The early internet adopters were spread too thinly to make it successful without a big Marketing budget, which we simply didn't have. It was another one of those 'crashed and burned' feelings I'd had so many times before.

Never worry about those 'crashed and burned' experiences in life. For there to be a phoenix, there has to be a fire!

Now I'm back in the movie, sitting in the office, late one night, feeling quite broken, and lamenting another 'failure'. Yet again the experience of my rowing years comes to mind. No, I won't be beaten. This is now my greatest passion, and I simply won't give it up. It was fast becoming a way toward a new me; to explore new possibilities the world had no minuscule inkling of. It was then, in the quiet solitude late one night, with a sense of creative expression filling my heart, the word "v-creator" popped in; 'v' standing for virtual. But something else resonated about the sound of the abbreviated name - as if "the creator" had pointed his finger down to me and sparked something inside.

When you let go and soften within, when you explore without tightening around the need for some fixed solution or outcome, then you're opening a creative channel into the soul, one that connects all the way back to the Source - the Source of infinite potential. And from there, literally anything can happen.

So what is this 'v-creator'? By now we'd picked up another of life's 'stray cats' in the form of Ethan, who'd been broken down by life and had suffered a nervous breakdown in just his tender twenties. But immediately I met the guy, I recognised a kindred spirit. He had a brilliant - albeit partially broken - mind, and a socialist attitude that wanted society to work for the better of all, not just the well-healed few. Not only that, but he too was an open source - Linux - programmer, having built an internet portal for a group of social workers.

Brainstorming with him the next day, I tell him what's come to me - "What if we can build some kind of modular program, that is quickly adaptable, creating intranet systems for businesses that can connect all parts of the resource chain, thus creating global exchanges?" I was shocked by his response - "There's an army of 'open source' programmers the world over, all working from their bedrooms, producing modular code, which can plug together to create different and variable internet applications." The dots had connected between us, like a flash from the blue.

When you fully express your passion, putting committed energy behind it, then you draw like-minded souls out of the woodwork. They'll literally show up on your doorstep.

But we would need funding to bring it together and create it. That's when another of life's 'chance' meetings changed my destiny.

David Nicholas was one of life's wise old 'silver hairs', in his early 60's. Yet his age had, in no way, diminished the enthusiastic light within; it so clearly shone from his entrepreneurial eyes. He was a 'business suit', working for the local government start-up program, but his traditional attire was where his allegiance with the old and the fuddy-duddy abruptly ended. He had a corking, Irish, self-deprecating humour, and the sense of the maverick rushed through his veins like amber nectar. Without doubt, David was a genius. When most were retiring and thinking of drawing a pension in some quiet backwater somewhere, he'd imagined the "TVC" - The Virtual Company Concept for inventors and social entrepreneurs.

When you're fired by your passion, you're like a fine wine, you just keep getting better as you get older!

His idea was brilliantly simple *(all the best are)*. The problem for start-ups, usually, is lack of funding and poor connections into their chosen Market (like VHO, they have no Marketing budget). I could hear David saying now... "So what if you can bring the entrepreneur together with businesses **already established** in that market, and license the new technology to a TVC - a company created with what would otherwise be your competition?" The UK's Department of Trade and Industry (DTI) simply loved the idea and offered millions of pounds in "Smart Funding", to provide working capital grants to the fledgling TVCs. For the concept of v-creator, this was a match made in heaven. We would be able to build flexible internet platforms to bring the new businesses rapidly to market, with the leanest of infrastructures, connecting different parts of the virtual organisation in different locations.

At a fateful business networking meeting that day, I was drawn to David like a bee to the honey pot. And when I told him of my v-creator concept, his eyes lit up like Guy Fawkes on bonfire night. You could feel it flowing through him - "Jeez, we're gonna light up the world!"

It was a match made in heaven - he was the mentor and father figure my soul badly craved. With his support, I went on to win around £250k in Smart Funding from the DTI to set up v-creator, and then to help a number of other start-ups get going. In the time I was blessed to know him, David always promised me lack of success would not be the problem, but that "we'd be swamped by success!"

You just have to open the mind and heart. Interconnectivity will become the new buzz out in the world. Let the internet join the dots of a new way of thinking, a new way of connecting - ultimately, even to a new way of being.

A venture that touched my heart especially, was the gravity pump invention of Sam Barzanji. He'd had the audacity to invent a pump to raise a staggering 2000 gallons of water a day, to a height of 60m, even from a dirt-filled river, powered solely by the force of gravity. Sam was an Iraqi engineer, persecuted by Saddam's regime, his house blown to bits by a Republican Guard tank, merely because of his Kurdish heritage. In fear for his life, he'd fled to Britain. Now, with TVC expertise from David, and some bright internet strategy from us, he was able to connect up with the right people and bring his much needed invention out into the world - it would go on to irrigate many a barren desert, for some of the globe's most impoverished people.

I was now literally living, eating and breathing v-creator and the new possibility my life could become. Practically every day, David would introduce me to some revolutionary maverick entrepreneur, with some of the best ideas under the sun. Yes, he was right, lack of success was not the problem, but too much of it! It wasn't so much financial success however, since the early stage income would only ever be small, it was more the idea - the heartfelt feeling - that we could bring some of the best ideas on the planet out into the world and make it a more equitable place for more people. This fired the sense of altruism that had ignited in my heart all those many moons ago, when I'd felt disillusioned by the big corporations like Dow.

But little did I know then, that the antiquated system would find a way to bite back.

It always does!

Suddenly, I'm flashed forward to a fateful autumn day in 2001; a day that would go on to change the world forever, in the most spectacular and unpredictable of ways. My attention was sparked by a commotion down in the developers' room, one which caused me to go and investigate. Everyone is glued to computer screens, looking at images of smoking buildings - *the Twin Towers*. Apparently, terrorists have flown fuel-filled aircraft into them. But it is when they collapse that the shock really kicks in. "My God, how is that possible? Is that even possible?"...I remember one of the developers saying as we looked on, mouths wide open, eyes staring in paralysed disbelief. Looking back on the movie, which had just taken another incredible and confusing twist, the presence offered a more illuminated viewpoint...

*Of course it's not possible for fuel-filled aircraft to collapse buildings like that. The fuel doesn't burn hot enough to melt the superstructure - no inflamed building in the world has ever toppled that way. Quite apart from that, take a look at the third building - building 7. Nothing hit it at all, and yet it collapsed. And what's most astounding, is not that it collapsed, **but how it collapsed.***

"What do you mean?"

*It fell at free fall speed, straight down, **just like a controlled demolition.***

"So you're saying it was an intentional demolition? Wow. But by whom and why?"

By those who would come to benefit most from it. By those who could use it to go on to control the world - those who were most afraid of the new shift of consciousness and who needed to stamp it out, or if they couldn't, to control it.

I recall the night of 911 waking up in a cold sweat, after a deeply disturbing nightmare. A gigantic black serpent was weaving its way up the Twin Towers, consuming all within it. But when I looked down, my legs were the Twin Towers, and it was weaving its way up me, steadily engulfing me within it. It was terrifying.

"So what's the significance of the black snake?" I asked in thought to the presence...

It's an ancient energy. One that's been on the Earth a long time. One that is spoken of in the Garden of Eden story. It's an energy of greed and consumption, of control and power. You can call it the 'raptor consciousness'; it pervades the world of capitalism.

"So you're saying it is to blame? I could literally feel that knowing in the field between us."

Yes.

"Why then, would it consume its own 'headquarters' - the visible World Trade Centre of Capitalism?"

A very interesting and illuminating question. Your world is controlled by that ancient of energies, seeping into the hearts of men, poisoning their minds with a virulent parasitic disease to take over the world, its resources and its people. Power and control are what feed it, for which it has an insatiable appetite. If able to, it will consume all in its path. It's a consciousness that exploits, and is bringing the world to the point of destruction. That's why I'm here connecting with you. That's why there are countless higher guides from across the cosmos, connecting with people everywhere on the planet - to make them aware of this rabid infestation in your midst, and what we need to do about it.

"I can feel that. I know it's true. But that still doesn't answer my question - why collapse the towers?"

The powers-that-be in society were beginning to lose control. It's an ancient dynamic of light battling with the dark within the wider Universe. They needed a reason to create fear and panic, to project people's attention outwards, rather than the source of their power within. They needed an almighty distraction. Al Qaeda became that, one which they created themselves, and no doubt many others like it to follow.

"Could the benevolent powers out there not stop it?"

The best way to defeat a controlling force of such monumental power, is to let it topple itself by its own 'success': to let it manifest its darkness out into the light for all to see. 911 was a terrible tragedy, but so is the rape and pillage of Mother Earth's environment that goes on day in, day out, by everyone in society; where sentient life is being brutalised the world over, on a systematic, daily basis.

Whenever such darkness persists in the consciousness of man, it's going to manifest a protagonist to express that for all to see. The powers-that-be are only so, because ordinary people allow them to be so - they continue to consume from corrupt corporations who then buy the ruling parties through bribes and blackmail.

"But how do you unravel that?"

By it's own success. This consciousness becomes so distorted, so perverted, it reveals itself to all by its inflated arrogance. And that is the message of 911. It shows the corruptness of the system you all subscribe to. When you look at it deeply, when the incontrovertible evidence spreads far enough, then enough people will say, "I can't subscribe to that system anymore." Then the system will topple. And we will say of the powers-that-be, just as they deliberately collapsed the Twin Towers to take control, they did it by themselves, to themselves.

And that's what control in the Universe does - it fails by its own 'success'. The beast ultimately consumes itself by its own excesses.

This revelation about 911 shifted something deep within. I could feel the foundations of my intellectual reality wobbling and unravelling. How could I ever take the system seriously again?

Of course, like so many back at the time, I couldn't grasp the deeper significance. I just felt sickened to my core by it. Especially the sense that somehow we'd all been hoodwinked by some larger than life drama - a Shakespearian tragedy - of monumental proportions. It felt like the reality we'd known was beginning to slip from our fingers.

Work not to worry. The machinations of the old reality must come clearly into view for the hopeless redundancy that it is. It will fail and collapse by its own excesses, and thus the New 5D Paradigm will take shape from its ashes.

I simply wasn't ready to get that at the time. It spun me into another bout of depression, especially as 911 seemed to stifle the entrepreneurial flair, making people much more cautious in the world, and so v-creator was not nearly as successful as it might have been. For the next year, through the rest of 2001 and most of 2002, my life took a downward tailspin. Business became shaky, we'd overextended ourselves and gotten into debt by supporting too many cashless start-ups. In my private life, Amanda and I now had another child - a beautiful son - but I couldn't hide the depression and my general disillusion with life. Yes, we had a smart new house, on a typical 'ladder-climbing' executive estate, within commuting distance of London. And at times, I momentarily managed to pacify my discontent with better cars, gadgets, clothes or music. When these failed, adrenaline sports took over and most Sundays you'd find me careering down a rocky mountain pass on my top-of-the-range mountain bike or deeply engaged in my other form of reality avoidance - the martial arts.

Yes, unfortunately, comfortable avoidance is where so many people find themselves. They see the shocking truth behind 911, the sweeping audacity of it all, and yet they close up like clams within their shells, afraid of truly stepping out.

Like the Twin Towers themselves, it felt as if my heart was closing down and sinking into the abyss, in a rising cloud of hazy dust. I was fast losing the reason why we began all this. And the tired Friday night videos, downed with take-away curry and cheap wine, were only making matters worse. Something just had to give.

Depression is a powerful energy. At its source is a deep, soulful yearning for change - of non-acceptance with the way things are, at a core intrinsic level. You just have to work with it. Accept all is not well, but cast your longing out into the Universe with an almighty roar - "show me!"

And that's when it happened that fateful day. When I'd had enough and felt all was lost. I recall just how the day began, driving in my Mercedes, with the curious phenomenon of the broken radio, which just seems to pick tracks randomly, when a song by the Stone Roses comes on and moves me so deeply, it triggers an ancient memory: with a flash, I can recall falling over the cliff edge in that dream a couple of years ago in the psychiatric hospital. And that guy with the Tibetan eyes, reaching out to try to grasp my hand...

"When your heart is black and broken
And you need a helping hand
When you're so much in love
You don't know just how much you can stand
when your questions go unanswered
And the silence is killing you
Take my hand baby I'm your man
I got loving enough for two.

Ten storey love song
I built this thing for you
Who can take you higher than twin peak mountain blue?
Oh well, I built this thing for you
And I love you true.

There's no sure-fire set solutions
No shortcut through the trees
No breach in the wall that they put there to keep you from me
As you're lying awake in this darkness
This everlasting night
Someday soon don't know where or when
You're gonna wake up and see the light."

(lyrics by The Stone Roses)

I pull the car over to the side of the road. It feels like an encasement of concrete has just shattered around by bruised and battered heart. Tears well up and roll down my cheeks. And as I began work that day, with the Stone Roses song still ringing in my ears, a seemingly innocuous email pops into my inbox...

"All-expenses-paid trip to Comdex, Las Vegas."

Looking on as the movie-goer, shivers are now running up and down my spine.

My journey has come full circle. I am sitting at the same desk in the same office. It is only 10 days later, yet in that time, it feels like I've travelled around the far reaches of the Universe and back. And boy how liberating that has been!

You took the 'high rise' to nowhere.
You broke through,
back to the place you arose from
and will always come back to,
You're at the beginning and the end...
The now here.

"That song had reminded me of my connection with you, and my inviolable connection to the whole of the Universe."

With tears of joy now rolling down my cheeks, I knew I'd come home and that I would never leave.

22

The Quickening

"The flow is there everywhere. Look for it.
Soften 'on the breeze', feel for it.
Let it direct you."

I could see it all so clearly now. Like the billions across our planet I'd been lost in a dream, one that I never even realised was actually a nightmare - to be so disconnected from your True Self and not even know it; not even knowing what you were missing. My connection with the presence had opened a channel, something I realised as my birthright - a divine connection to the rest of the Universe. It felt as though every part of it was somehow my brother or sister. And when I looked intently at anything, I seemed to just know the light in it - it kind of winked at me - a sort of knowing that just resonated deep inside... "You're home. You're one of us. We're all connected!"

"So how do I live this now? Everything else seems so pointless. How do I exist from day to day?"

Just follow the pull.

"What, literally? All the time?"

*There is nothing else but the flow of the Universe, which pulls through your heart when you let it. Or else simply fires as a knowing... "this is the way to go now." The whole Universe is interconnected with just one purpose and aim - to reveal yourself to yourself; to reveal you, **as the divine**. And there is absolutely nothing else going on.*

"But all the families, out there, the businesses and the schools, all the lifestyles - they all have objectives, goals and ambitions. What about them?"

They only think that's what they're doing. They have amnesia, believing life's all about achieving some sort of goal, some kind of security or objective to make them happy. They're locked in a kind of space-time warp - an eddy current disconnected from the flow. Yet even there, the light is flowing in, working to reconnect the dots, to bring wayward souls back into the loving embrace of the divine. Even these structures that people build in life contain reflections of the original light of the soul. Literally everything you see, and do, invites a deeper feeling connection inside. When you go to the shops, the school or the cinema, when you're at work or commuting through the city, even when you have an accident in your brand new car, literally everything is speaking to you saying... "Look at yourself, see who you really are at the core of you - be that!"

"So I just follow the pull and live like that?"

Yes.

"But how do I make a living? How do I work, eat and connect with others?"

Everything that you need will come to you. Just give it a try and see.

I can't say I was a hundred percent with it, but so far, this guidance had made far more sense than anything I'd ever experienced playing by the rules of society. So I sat there, at my desk and felt inside. It wasn't easy at all at first. I expected to feel something, to see something or to get some kind of message. All I got was a kind of heaviness, a denseness, and a busy mind that so wanted to fill the moment with ideas.

Put your attention in your heart.

So I do. And sure enough, after a little while there's a tingling sensation, which, as I continue to focus on it, builds as a warmth, which then seems to subtly spread through my body. Suddenly the phone rings, and the feeling immediately dissipates.

It's what you've attuned your consciousness to. So like everyone else, you miss the subtle interplay in the space between the spaces.

I wasn't going to be put off, so I ignore the phone, and when it eventually stops, I go back inside, feeling into the heart once more, the strange but comforting tingling and the warmth, which is now spreading through my entire body again. I was feeling to let go. So I lean back in my chair and stretch my arms out wide. The movement means that I reach back into a beam of sunlight now entering my office window behind me, which warms my neck and seems to somehow connect with the heat inside. A thought comes to me...Why are you facing the computer when this feels so beautiful, so magical? So I turn myself around, and draw myself up to the window, the sun now able to embrace the entirety of me, lighting up my face in a golden warmth.

Wow this is amazing. Just a simple tingling, a very simple commitment to follow the sense, and now I'm literally basking in this universal sunlight, warming my entire body.

Well I did tell you!

What now? A bird suddenly calls, as if to answer. I feel like a walk in nature, and even as the thought lands, a subtle pull is drawing me away from the chair. But what about the office? I'm thinking, and the emails, phone calls and appointments I have to keep? They just seemed so irrelevant at that moment. And even though my mind is struggling to let go, nevertheless I follow the pull, grab my jacket, and even though other colleagues are arriving for the day trying to engage me in conversation, nevertheless, I keep following the flow that now wants very much to carry me. "I'll be back soon," I speak over my shoulder as I hurriedly leave.

Now I'm out in the fields. It's beautiful and expansive. Intense blue of the skies reaching up into the heavens, vibrant greens of the grass, the soft caress of a gentle breeze on my cheeks. There's no question, I just have to take my shoes off. And how wonderful that feels, squidging my toes in the dirt, feeling a part of the earth. Why does everyone stick their feet in shoes? I'm wondering.

Why indeed!

And now a horse in the farmer's field comes over to me. I pat it on the nose as it nuzzles into me. Immediately I notice the smell - a deep primal aroma, that speaks of such depth and power, which I can suddenly feel inside of myself. I nuzzle my nose into its mane, wanting so much to be a physical part of it - at-one with it. "How come I've never seen a horse this way before?" I'm asking myself.

Because none of your senses were fully awake before. You weren't feeling through them with an awakened consciousness.

And now I'm off wandering through the fields. Sometimes the pull quietens, sometimes it strengthens. Why is that?

You're learning to attune to it. Part of the time the mind is kicking in *and still owning the show, thinking it knows what you're supposed to be doing, which makes the flow hard to feel. But when you just let go and <u>trust</u> in the movement itself, then you connect up again.*

Now I'm standing in front of a tree. Not just any old tree.

Is there ever an 'any old tree'? Is anything ordinary?

It's spectacular, huge, reaching up to the skies - a glorious and grand old oak tree, with vast branches spreading outwards; the lower ones graciously reaching down to just a couple of metres off the ground.

I'm standing under them now, feeling the beauty of the tree in my heart. Wondering if somehow I can 'speak' to it. Suddenly there's a gust of wind, which gently rocks the lower boughs, so the branches carefully brush across the top of my head. "Yes of course you can speak to me," it is saying, "just in a different way to what you're used to."

Tune out the old rules, the old way of looking at things, the old conditioned thinking. Instead <u>feel the pull</u>, <u>watch the signs and synchronicity, open a space</u> for it to reveal who you are.

I'm further on now, drawn to another quiet spot, a circle of small trees, a small clearing in the forest. Something's telling me to stop and kneel down. "Why here? What's so important?"

 <u>Stop asking so many questions! Just stop and observe.</u>

So I do. I can feel the quietness of the space, the sense of solitude. Is that what I'm supposed to get? I wonder. No answer. So slightly impatiently I quieten again, and feel deeper within. Again the solitude, again the quietness. My eyes are now closing and the spacious sense of it starts to feel divine - <u>the deep sense of peace and quiet</u> - that 'Fifth Density' experience I'd had before. After maybe five minutes, it feels like there's a natural close, so I slowly open my eyes, upon which I notice a rustling in the bushes in front of me. I'm short-sighted, so I squint to see what it might be. Something brown and furry approaches, moving into the clearing, which I can now quite clearly make out is a fox!

The fox tests the air with its nose, and then begins to walk slowly, carefully, attentively around me. It's totally alive, bristling with energy, yet in this moment, there's a stillness too. I kneel there amazed as it makes a full circle, all the way around me, before disappearing off into the bushes. Wow! This is totally awesome.

And what did you get from the fox? How did it make you feel? What 'medicine' did it give you?

I could feel its aliveness, its attentiveness, its curiosity. It seemed forthright, confident and sure, but when it took off, it literally disappeared into the forest, completely blending, in a flash, out of sight.

This is what the Native Americans - the shamans - would call 'animal medicine'. It brings to you a certain energy of how to be, how to heal the unconscious side of you. In this case, to always be attentive, twitching, feeling, sensing. Be sensitive and alert, soft and gentle in the movement, but when called upon, act with unwavering, sure-footed directness - that's the energy of the fox.

And now I'm walking again, past trees and bushes, when suddenly I'm startled by the loud 'caw' of a crow in a tree next to me. It practically shocks me out of my skin.

Be particularly attentive to crow medicine. It's telling you to be mindful of your shadow side, to watch your distortions, where you slip into lower behaviours. Crow can guide you through your darkness, which you're bound to encounter, as you begin to walk the path of the soul.

Doubt has always been my darkness. Not trusting or believing in myself. And now I'll need to watch where I slip into doubt about this incredible new form of guidance in my life, which seems to be accelerating hour by hour.

Yes indeed. Doubt will quickly disconnect you from the flow.

Now I'm on a hill top, overlooking the farm where I work (and am temporarily living). Suddenly there's a bird - a beautiful kestrel - hanging on the breeze, in line of sight, a little way off in the distance. How magical the miracle of creation that can perfect that. I'm completely in awe of it.

How it seems to be effortlessly riding the flow of the breeze, with all its senses tuned in. It feels like another profoundly deep message indeed.

The flow is there everywhere. Look intently for it. Soften 'on the breeze', feel for it. Let it direct you.

Now I'm in woods, on the way back to the farm, wondering what else I might see, when suddenly there's a young deer. I freeze so as not to startle it. And now we're looking directly at each other.

What do you see?

"There's a softness to it. A vulnerability."

And so you must become softer - vulnerable to the moment.

"Why vulnerable?"

So there's no expectation. No need for the moment to go a particular way. So there's surrender. You can't control the flow, you just have to go with it, wherever it takes you. Even, and especially, when it breaks you down because you feel to be overwhelmed. Soften anyway. It'll take you right back to the Source, from which all authentic action spontaneously arises. And that's the key to absolute vulnerability. From this infinite potential anything can, and does happen. You draw all manner of miracles and magic to you.

Suddenly the deer turns tail and sprints off. I marvel at how the presence, me, the deer and all life around, seem to be conversing in the same dialogue. I have to keep pinching myself, this is just ridiculously amazing!

Now I'm back outside the office. I feel a pull to go inside for the day...

Are you sure that's a pull and not a thought?

I stop, now uncertain.

Breathe, soften.

I expand and open up again. Now my attention is drawn to my car.

There's a resistance, surely my phone will be ringing off the hook by now, and my colleagues will be wanting to confer with me. "Caw!" speaks a crow, up high on the barn to the left of me in the direction of my car: "Watch your shadow side".

I simply couldn't ignore it, and so now I'm off in the car driving. Where to? my mind is already asking, but no answer. None that is, except a bird - a black crow - flying in front of the car.

I get to the next junction. Which way? Suddenly there's a knowing - Go right...

Higher knowing lands in a flash. You can't pre-empt it, or else you simply override it with the dense questioning of lower mind.

And now I'm driving through the local village, where hunger pangs begin to sound in my belly, just as a car reverses out in front of me leaving a car parking space. Somehow it's inviting me in. So I park up. What now? No answer. But suddenly I'm drawn to the colour green on the sweater of a lady walking by. Green for go, right? So now I'm following the colour green, which I'm suddenly seeing everywhere - in clothes, car colours and surrounding signs. It's as if the Universe is laying down a path in that colour frequency.

Now I'm approaching the local convenience store, and with stomach rumbling, I decide to go in. But as I'm about to walk through the door, suddenly I'm seeing red everywhere, and I'm feeling distinctly uneasy. There's a very definite tightening inside. Red means stop, right?

You're getting two conflicting impulses. Didn't crow tell you to watch your shadow side? So now you can feel and connect with the pull, but then society's conditioning kicks in, and frequently overrides it. You're hungry, so you go to the nearest available store to quell the hunger, but crucially, not paying attention to the vibration of the place and the 'food' within it. Nor are you working with the tightness inside that has kicked off. Like most, you all too easily let lower conditioning override your natural aliveness and connection to the flow, without even questioning it.

Notice these automated reactions to life by the tightness they generate inside. Know that's why you created this moment as you did - to expose and feel where your False Self ego owns the show. Get into it, feel into the contraction and unwind it with softness. This allows the soul to break through.

So I back off, and feel inside, to the obvious knot in my solar plexus. After just a few moments, the energy seems to come alive in me again, and my attention is once more drawn to green, on someone's shopping bag, heading back along the main street in the direction of where I parked. I pass the car, and suddenly the local deli jumps out. The energy just seems to want to grab me and draw me into it. But this feeling is different. The only way I can describe it, is that there's an okayness to it - 'a rightness'...

That's it. The flow just feels right. Not 'right' or 'wrong' as in good and bad, in a judgmental sense. But more an alignment of rightness, in tune with the collective learning experience of life, and how it best works for you, how it best teaches you, drawing all the relevant elements around you by the universal Law of Attraction.

"But why didn't I go to there (to the deli) in the first place?"

The flow is how the Fifth Density - New Paradigm - works; it's less concerned with eating, working, walking or any other 'doing' thing for that matter. It's concerned primarily about what you can learn about yourself in the process. So do be prepared for it to run you around in circles a little. Don't worry though, you will be looked after. It's not having some great cosmic joke at your expense - it just wants you to know yourself in the process of life.

In the deli, some green apples and ripe bananas almost jump off the shelves with their vibrancy. That'll be breakfast then! The apples and bananas taste luscious, vibrant and rejuvenating. They seem to bring me more alive.

And now I'm driving in the car again, not sure where to, but there's a definite pull. At each crossroads, as I ask the question "Where now?", my attention is drawn to the movement of a car and the flicker of its indicators telling me what to do...

Your 3D society is consumed with setting intention to succeed; so people automatically write over this beautifully divine flow, which speaks into every situation. But when the mind is open, not expecting or needing things to go a particular way, then the flow, and your higher guides, can 'spike' your attention to the direction. Which as you know by now, is less interested in the destination, and more in how you can learn, evolve and grow in the process - reflections you notice and feel on the path, integrate soul within. Which is the only way to truly change the narrative in your life.

Now I'm driving by an industrial estate, a business park, which the flow clearly directs me to enter, even though the energy of it feels pretty ghastly and is already tightening my solar plexus. So why don't I just immediately reject those places that tighten me down?

Remember, this is all a learning experience. You have to work through your energetic reactions, so that you can genuinely feel the surrounding energy, even where it's unpleasant. You have to still be able to pick up the natural flow through that - because there'll be something you need to see, to let go of, and to evolve through.

All around me I'm seeing waste: overflowing garbage bins, discarded transporter pallets, some old tyres, a skip with junked office furniture and busted computer terminals. There are cars everywhere, both new and old, cheap and expensive. I see people smoking on their coffee break, speaking into mobile phones. Now I'm noticing billboards and some blinking neon sign. It's a sterile, trashy environment. My heart is sinking and my gut feels nauseous. I gun the car engine a little to pull out of it. I realise I've not seen a tree or a grass verge for what seems like ages. Then suddenly there's a verge, to which my attention is drawn - welcoming green grass, but covered in litter.

My self-selecting radio, which now I'm beginning to suspect clearly has a consciousness all of it's own, picks out a track by Coldplay...

"Look at earth from outer space
Everyone must find a place
Give me time and give me space
Give me real, don't give me fake
Give me strength, reserve control
Give me heart and give me soul
Give me time, give us a kiss
Tell me your own politik

Open up your eyes
Just open up your eyes."

(lyrics by Coldplay)

It felt just like Gaia had opened a direct connection right into my heart. She's talking directly to me. I can feel her pain, her sorrow and her tolerance, like an aging mother, unconditionally loving an errant daughter or son. "Give me piece of mind and trust, in confusion confidence." As the lyrics play, my attention is drawn to the person in the car up ahead, throwing their cigarette butt out of the window, not willing to pollute their own car, yet happy to cast it on to the verge... "Just open up your eyes." Then I'm noticing all manner of litter on the side of the road: paper bags, polythene packaging, crisp packets, plastic bottles, the entire contents of a fast food dinner... "Give me strength, reserve control." I feel an irresistible urge to get out of the car and pick up some of the rubbish... "Tell me your own politik."

My mind starts to resist - this is ridiculous, it's just a drop in a worldwide ocean of business parks everywhere. But my heart is ignoring it...do it anyway! So I stop, and begin picking up litter, thinking of Mother Earth and how humanity has trashed her, which brings tears to my eyes. I bend down to pick up the final sweet wrapper, when a gust of wind blows it away in front of me. So I pursue it until I finally grasp it. It's a "Star Bar", and I just seem to know it's a message direct from Gaia - "Thanks for thinking of me, you're a star!"

This is the mother tongue of universal synchronicity. It is the language of the Fifth Density, speaking through all 3D circumstances and situations, beyond mind, and directly into your heart. When you feel it, who can deny such a divine vocabulary?

As I'm driving away, the feeling is bitter-sweet: my heart is heavy, yet I'm also joyous for the beautiful Gaia connection. I notice the bushes by the side of the road are seeming to wave. "Give me heart and give me soul, wounds that heal and cracks that fix." I could literally feel her consciousness. She is alive as much as you or I. "How can we continue to do this to her?" I implore out loud.

It's a very good question indeed. One which everyone would do well to consider. Open up your eyes!

Now I'm leaving the industrial estate, pulling up to a roundabout - Which way? A car with 44 in the number plate (which feels significant) enters from my right, followed by another with JC on the plate. They go nearly full circle and then take the exit North. I notice a strong feeling in my heart, as if some old wound is being activated...

It's the Christ Consciousness. Not of a religious kind, not the way it's been so often depicted. It's that of non-judgmental discernment of Right Action felt as a pull through the heart. It weaves through the consensus reality you've all created, connecting up the dots and finding the path through the field that is in the best interests of all. It's purpose is to carry as many as possible 'higher', into the 5D.

The car radio is on, because I just love music, especially now that lyrics and sounds seem to speak into the heart of me. As I take the exit north, just behind the JC plate, the radio is doing its self-select thing...

"When you're down and they're counting
When your secrets all found out
When your troubles take to mounting
When the map you have leads you to doubt
When there's no information
And the compass turns to nowhere that you know well

When the doctors failed to heal you
When no medicine chest can make you well
When no counsel leads to comfort
When there are no more lies they can tell
No more useless information
And the compass spins
The compass spins between heaven and hell

Let your pain be my sorrow
Let your tears be my tears too
Let your courage be my model
That the north you find will be true
When there's no information
And the compass turns to nowhere that you know well

Let your soul be your pilot
Let your soul guide you
Let your soul guide you upon your way..."

(lyrics by Sting)

At this point I just can't hold back the tears. The song is seeming to touch an ancient time, a great sadness for me and all humanity - a symbol of everything wrong, the lack of compassion with which man treats his fellow man. I feel absolutely **not** religious, but I also immediately know there is great truth in the Jesus story.

Indeed there is. And much to be learned from it. But it was never about one man, one religion, unfortunately used to control people's minds. You are all the sons and daughters of God - The One. The character Jesus showed you, in many ways, what you're all capable of, and the transitions you can come to make on the spiritual journey. His very life was a journey of unfolding and discovery, one of "Ascension", into the Fifth Density.

I've reached a roundabout with the M4 now - Which way? No answer, but the sign M4 is still engaging me. And as a flash I suddenly get the 'M' speaks for 'messiah'...

Follow the 'messiah' in your heart.

And that was one of the great things I was picking up - the flow would stop, and when it did so, it was wanting me to get something. When the appropriate knowing landed, it would engage again.

Which way now? A car with 59 on the plate enters the roundabout from the right, circles, and heads north... "Fuck it, drive on!" I'm laughing to myself, reflecting on the 59 commando experience. I take that direction and my attention is immediately drawn to a sign - "The Oracle". It's a shopping centre in a busy city, Reading (pronounced 'redding'), which chokes me up with laughter...

Are you reading this?

"Yes, I most definitely am!"

And now I pull up to another roundabout with '59' in front of me, which I'm clearly supposed to follow, so I "fuck it, drive on" again. Up to a set of traffic lights now, which are on red. I wait. "Which way?" Immediately my attention is drawn to a bird in the sky, which I allow my gaze to follow. It lands on the steeple of a church - on top of the cross. Immediately a song comes on the self-selecting radio by a band called Faithless, "God is a DJ". "Sure is!" I shout out loud:

"This is my church
this is where I heal my hurt
It's the world I become
Content in the hum
Between voice and drum
It's in change
The poetic justice of cause and effect
Respect, love, compassion
This is my church
This is where I heal my hurt
For tonight
God is a DJ.

(lyrics by Faithless)

I turn off the dual carriageway onto a one-way slip road with the music still playing. As I approach the Oracle shopping centre a sign reads "car park full". So now what? I'm wondering if my guidance has somehow broken down. But then suddenly another car with '59' on the plate leaves through the barrier, so I "fuck it, drive on!" I enter the car park following the driveway upwards. Which floor? the number 3 pops into my head, but 3 turns out to be full. I follow it anyway, and just as I enter, a car with 'JC' on the plate reverses out in front of me leaving a space. As I pull in, the car I park in front of has an 'M' on it, the car to the left a 'J', the one to the right a '44'. My God. Is this really real?

It's the 'quickening'. It's when you finally let go of the life of control, of logical in-the-box solutions and answers. It's when you let go of the system and all its conditioning. Then the natural flow just floods in. You see and feel it everywhere!

"Why is this 'quickening' happening to me now? Why so strongly?"

You've confronted, and broken through, many repressive inner layers in your life, because you'd been 'all-in', you'd thrown yourself into plenty of challenges. You'd confronted the density of doubt, fear and disbelief, all the things that retard the flow of the soul through you. It's an inner movement that reflects out into your world: as you break through 'in here', you break through 'out there'.

I take the lift down to the shopping centre. Which way now? My attention is immediately drawn to a girl in front with a Waterstones bag in her hand. Waterstones, the book store, is straight on. The pull is, by now, literally blowing me away with its awesome organising power. It's as if somehow, higher guidance is reading into my thoughts and feelings, relating them to everything around - I'm having a dialogue with the whole of life. "This is just totally awesome!" I yell out, jumping up and punching the air, as a young woman shopper looks me up and down. Whose this crazy psycho? I can hear her thinking. But I'm given to ignore the closing down sarcasm, as my attention is immediately drawn to a sign behind her, on a shop being renovated...

"Still Open"

Indeed I am!

And now I'm in Waterstones, my attention immediately drawn to the bestseller section in the entrance. Suddenly a childhood hero is there, Bruce Lee, staring me right in the eyes, as if ready to pounce off the bookshelf in one of his Kung Fu stances. His book is about 'Jeet Kune Do' (JKD), the martial art of 'styleless style' that Bruce himself developed. Some very direct knowing carries me to page 12, and although it's speaking about martial arts, between the lines, it feels very much like it's speaking about the flow itself too...

"JKD is not a system; it is not a style. Bruce Lee rejected the notion of 'style' as it necessarily brought on ossification. When martial artists pledge allegiance to a style, they tend to see it as complete and in need of little or no modification. They tend to defend the style dogmatically. Then when they find another fighter they cannot deal with, they panic. How can their 'complete', 'perfect', 'best in the world' style be beaten? What do we do now?

You can look at religion and spiritual dogma in exactly the same way. Such fixed and conditioned ways of looking at reality, often mean your mind is too full to pick up the natural spontaneity of the free-flowing soul and its interconnectivity with the whole of life. If you expect it to always happen a particular way, how can you possibly appreciate it when 'God' comes to you in the unexpected?

This spoke loud and clear - to avoid rigid and over-disciplined approaches to divine connection. Then another truth rang loud and clear in the pages...

"This may seem like an odd thing to say, but a true JKD player seeks out failure. A true JKD player looks for the situation that s/he does not know how to deal with. Then when the situation is met, s/he looks for a solution. By repeatedly finding internal weaknesses, and then finding solutions, the JKD player improves as a fighter and becomes a better person. This constant need to grow by testing limits takes a very secure person. Anyone feels better by clinging to the illusion that he or she has all the answers. It is not easy to let go and realise you can be beaten. But, in this humility, the only path to self-perfection lies."

The path of the divine will open up to you by connecting through the heart and surrendering to its guidance. But when you do this, it's going to guide you to all the places where you get stuck - especially by identification with the physical 3D. The flow wants you to succeed - meaning to evolve, ascend, and become all that you can be. So you must confront all those places where you descend into doubt and feel disconnected or 'less than' - that somehow you're not worthy, and don't deserve this divine gift that is rightfully yours. You have to break through such moments, where you feel you're 'failing'. Feel deeply into, and open out through them. Then your path will naturally lead into the New Paradigm of the 5D.

I buy the book, and as I leave the shop, above the chatter and bustle of busy shoppers, I notice a song which I recognise by the band Oasis...

"And all the roads you have to walk are winding, and all the lights that light the way are blinding."

I can't help smiling at hearing the 'words of God' spoken through the mouth of Liam Gallagher, whose probably best known more for his four-letter expletives...

Why would not the divine speak through all people and in all ways? It's only either arrogance or ignorance that says it can only be like 'this' or 'that'.

Yes, I totally get it. "Sing on dude," I say to myself as I enter the store.

This time I'm drawn to the DVD shelves, where my attention suddenly fixes on a little-known (at the time) film called "The Matrix". I instantly recalled Lutz back in the studio talking to me about it, but at a time when my mind was much too full to pay attention to the obvious spiking in the field that wanted me to take note. This time I wasn't ignoring. I would watch it later.

As I'm leaving the store, another track from my youth is playing - it's "Spirits in the Material World" by the Police...

"There is no political solution
To our troubled evolution
Have no faith in constitution
There is no bloody revolution

Our so-called leaders speak
With words they try to jail you
They subjugate the meek
But it's the rhetoric of failure

Where does the answer lie?
Living from day to day
If it's something we can't buy
There must be another way
We are spirits in the material world."

(lyrics by The Police)

It felt to me like this and The Matrix film might be speaking about something similar. As my eyes surveyed all around me, I felt distinctly uneasy about the conspicuous consumerism. There was a clear sense it was heading toward some apocalyptic abyss, and that 'spirit' was trying to speak to us all, as loudly and clearly as possible.

I'm just about to take off when another Police song kicks in...

"Just a castaway, an island lost at sea, oh
Another lonely day, with no one here but me, oh
More loneliness than any man could bear
Rescue me before I fall into despair, oh

I'll send an s.o.s. to the world
I hope that someone gets my
Message in a bottle, yeah

A year has passed since I wrote my note
But I should have known this right from the start
Only hope can keep me together

Love can mend your life but
Love can break your heart
I'll send an s.o.s. to the world
I hope that someone gets my
Message in a bottle, yeah

Walked out this morning, don't believe what I saw
A hundred billion bottles washed up on the shore
Seems I'm not alone at being alone
A hundred billion castaways, looking for a home

Sending out at an s.o.s.
Sending out at an s.o.s.
Sending out at an s.o.s."

(lyrics by The Police)

As Sting's words resonate through me, I can't help looking around and wondering at the vast number of lost souls out there "just looking for a home". But the home they are really looking for is inside. All they have to do is look within and inquire. Now I'm feeling a powerful urge to shout out, "Wake up, wake up, and see the truth. God is there for you; it is not a dream, not a wish nor a promise. God is real, inside you and everywhere around you. You are breathing God, seeing her, feeling her. She is loving you through the words of the songs you are listening to, through the sights and smells, through touch and feeling. She is your breath. She is everywhere - wake up and see her!"

It was right at that moment that a passionate calling within my heart awakened and wanted to reach out to other souls and help show them the way home. Somehow I needed to find a way...

Be patient, my dear friend, for all will come. Many will have their own break through days, and like the countless other warriors of light out there, in your time, when you're ready, you'll help too.

23

Spiritual Emergence

"A Great Realignment of energy is coming to the Earth.
It will become such a crucible of catastrophic change,
that many will have no choice, but to truly let go,
to start to question and wake up."

I watched The Matrix that night, and as for many, it fires just about every cell in my being. It's as if 'God' wanted to reach down and speak directly into the minds of people - "This is the slavery you're really living in. This is how the wool is being pulled over your eyes to blind you from the truth. There is so much more to life that you can touch, beyond the confines of body and mind."

"The Matrix is everywhere. It is all around us. Even in this very room. You can see it when you look out your window or when you turn on your television. You can feel it when you go to work, when you go to church, when you pay your taxes. It is the world that has been pulled over your eyes to blind you from the truth."

(Morpheus from "The Matrix")

I look around me: computer screens and electronic gadgets everywhere; unnatural materials in the carpets, curtains and furniture we sit on; mobile and cordless phones that seem to buzz inside the head. In the kitchen, all lights are on standby just waiting to cook up a meal or make a cup of coffee. And then there's the microwave, for those pre-packed meals, especially when you're in a hurry. It dawns on me, that only the other day, some bright spark inventor had approached us with a "revolutionary new device for cleaning surgical instruments in hospitals" - he'd unveiled a household microwave cooker before us - "because it kills all organic matter, stone dead!" And what does it do to the nutrient content of food, I'm now thinking...?

Not to mention the impact on lowering energetic vibration - how such dissonant frequencies contract consciousness down. In fact practically your entire lifestyle would seem purposefully designed to do that - to disconnect you from the natural flow of the divine, as Morpheus so eloquently says, "to turn a human being into a battery."

"How does that work exactly?"

Because these dissonant vibes in the field all around you dampen the natural flow and infusion of soul. It makes you controllable - more easily susceptible to conditioning and programming; to accept a lesser lifestyle; to set you on the treadmill of the endless quest for some kind of pacification, gratification or 'entertainment'. In this state you're so easily bought.

In fact the system - the matrix - is so effective at doing this, you'd have to assume it was deliberately designed that way to enslave people.

My God. The full scope of it is now landing deeply within me. It very much mirrors the feelings I had those many moons ago in the hospital I'd been shunted to, which also seemed perfectly designed to drain the very life energy from me. We have to do something about this!

It's early morning now, the birds outside my window have just finished their wonderful dawn chorus, when suddenly there's a loud grinding noise - a large and powerful engine is firing up. Not a car, maybe a tractor. It's not unusual of course on a working farm, but something about this attracts my attention for some reason. And why so early?

I go outside to investigate, but can hardly believe what I'm now seeing. I have to rub my eyes, my mouth has fallen wide open. It's a bulldozer, belonging to our landlord, bulldozing down the trees in the orchard next to the office, scattering crows everywhere, with raucous protesting 'caws', which are nevertheless ignored and drowned out by the aggressive roar of the tractor's engine.

I don't know what to do. I'm beside myself, practically jumping up and down on the spot, working desperately to contain the sense of injustice and bubbling rage, like some pressure cooker wanting to boil over. I go over to the driver - the landlord's groundsman - who tells me, "Ah yes, the boss wants to create a parking overflow area, which he's leasing to the BMW garage in the village." I'm so dumbfounded by the ignorance of it, I simply can't respond; my mouth is moving, but only like some fisherman's catch stranded on the bank and no words would come. I stare on as fruit trees are mercilessly ripped up, birds' nests ridden roughshod over, not to mention the countless other wildlife who'd made the orchard their home. My God, is humanity really so ignorant?

What you've sadly witnessed is going on in every village, every town and every city around the world. More and more trees and wildlife are being mercilessly obliterated to make way for the ever-expanding matrix. The Earth has been around for billions of years, and yet just in the last couple of hundred, since the beginning of the industrial revolution, a staggering 50% of the trees have been cut down. Not to mention the astronomical cost to wildlife.

I staggered away from this murderous scene, unable to look on, shocked to the core by the knowing that this is happening the world over. Yes, in truth, I had suspected something like this, but like everyone else, I drove it by, daily, in the endless need to get somewhere or something - I have my bills and my family to worry about. And besides, I'm just one person in billions. What can I do?

And that's the problem. Too many people think that way. They're all waiting for governments or organisations to do something about it. But what's really needed is an expansion of consciousness; an elevation in how you witness and consider life; to realise that you're all interconnected, and what you do to another - or allow to be done in your name - you do to yourself. It has to start with one person. It can only start with you.

I'm now sitting in my own car, shutting out the din of the nearby tractor, mercilessly carrying out its murderous work. Suddenly a line from the Matrix film pops in, again by Morpheus, "We don't know who struck first, us or them. But we do know it was us that scorched the sky." Wow - that feels deeply poignant. It's resonating inside me...

The way humanity is currently heading, is set to entirely destroy the 3D biosphere and natural eco-systems of your planet. In fact you're already well into the sixth mass extinction of wild life. You're all a part of an interconnected, self-sustaining natural system. When the wildlife goes, and you've poisoned the soils, oceans and skies, you all go!

Wow - that felt heavy in my heart - the impact of such dramatic upheaval and catastrophe. Even though a big part of me was still denying it and didn't want to embrace it, nevertheless, I could definitely feel the truth in it.

Most people don't want to know the truth. It's just way too impactful on their sensibilities. It means they'd have to question every single action within their lives and the effect on their families. Most aren't ready or willing to go there.

"So is the Matrix film some kind of prophecy?"

You could say that. Some artists are open enough to connect up to the natural underlying flow of life and to express it. Many are now feeling the sense of urgency of the Earth's predicament, here in the 3D.

I'm now driving in my car, back through the village, where I need to make a stop for breakfast. As I get out of the car, the smell of burning petrol fills my nostrils from the car parked next to me. As I enter the deli and buy my fruit, the lady behind the counter is telling the customer in front how unpleasant it is, with her shop being next to a busy road, and how the fumes have given her daughter asthma. When will we all sit up and take note? When will we actually do something? Somehow, the thought seems wasted...

Not at all! Keep having those thoughts. Keep questioning reality. Do not ignore and pull the wool over what you see. The injustice of it, the ignorance of it, will stir deep inside and send the energy out, as a roar into the ether. It's a vibration others will pick up. It'll gather in strength, like a building wave. It's such deep yearning inside that ultimately changes things - that's how evolution happens. Not from logic-based answers, but from a deep upwelling of Unity Consciousness. That's how realities are shaped and changed.

But you must learn to trust. If you don't trust, the natural flow inside of you turns off like a tap. You've got to stay open, even when everyone around you is closed or telling you it just can't be done - "there is no New Paradigm". Never, but never, take no for an answer!

I'm now low on fuel. In fact the orange light had come on during the drive back from Reading the day before. So I pull into a local petrol station, but as I'm driving onto the forecourt, something very strange happens - it seems as if the sudden movement of a couple of cars in front, wants to block my entry. But I'm learning quickly by now, not to react to the surface level of such 'spiking' events - rather to look for some deeper meaning.

Perfect!

So I look around me, and suddenly I get the message from a couple of billboards..."You don't need this." I knew it was meant for me.

"What do you mean 'you don't need this'?" I asked? The lyrics of that Coldplay song echo through my head, "*Give me peace of mind to trust, in confusion confidence.*" You don't need the fuel! A bird flies across the front of the car and upwards drawing my attention to the sky. *The car will run on air, trust me.*

The way onto the forecourt is still being blocked, and I'm now feeling an irresistible urge to drive on. It's really strong, like some volcano building in my gut. But my mind is frantically resisting... Really? It can run on air. No, that can't be real!

At which point, another quote from The Matrix pops in... "What is real? How do you define 'real'? If you're talking about what you can feel, what you can smell, what you can taste and see, then 'real' is simply electrical signals interpreted by your brain."

And now I'm suddenly projected back to quantum physics at Oxford. I know that matter is mostly space, that if for example, you took out all the space from between the atoms in a human being, there wouldn't be enough matter to fit on a pinhead. And that matter really only exists as waves of interconnected energy, that only take form from the 'quantum soup' when someone or something is observing them.

Reality becomes what you expect it to be. As you believe, so you create.

"I recall trying this 'mind over matter stuff', breaking through bricks as the young 'Karate Kid'..."

No, this is not mind over matter. This is opening the mind to the natural flow of energy. And especially an upwelling of soul that yearns for something more aligned than this. When such an upwelling is in natural alignment with the mainstream movement of underlying consciousness, when you're beset all around with injustice and inequity, then from the building need for righteousness - for realignment - literally anything becomes possible.

Now it feels like my mind has slipped out of gear and jumped into the back seat as I drive out of the petrol station on empty. Take it out into the country, lands the knowing. And although my mind is still sceptical, it's still in the back seat, and anyhow, my heart reasons...What have I got to lose?

So I drive on, until some 40 miles later, when the car should clearly have run out of fuel and suddenly I start to have doubts again. This can't be real, I must be in some kind of dream world. At which point, the car judders to a halt.

"Fear, doubt and disbelief," to coin a phrase from Morpheus, will kill the flow almost immediately. "Free your mind!"

So I let go of the doubt, of the disbelief, and to my utter amazement, the car fires up again. I'm out driving practically the whole day, with little or no thought about work. How could you possibly be thinking about that when you've just discovered you can run a car on air! With each passing mile, I'm getting more and more uplifted. This is just spectacular. It's too crazy to be true, but hey, I'll go with it!

All through that day, and into the next, the car is running on air still. Each time I switch off the engine, I'm not quite sure it will fire up again, but each time it does. And now I'm steadily slipping into a different sense of being - there's a sense of openness. It's as if I can observe my mind, and as it's closing down around the old beliefs, the old judgments, the old model about how this reality supposedly works; I can open up through those judgments and keep realigning with this incredible flow.

That's it. That's exactly it. Your whole reality is coming to a dramatic crux point, an almighty climax. There's no time to waste anymore. You've got to test what you believe to be real.

When the car's done about 180 miles, and I'm still in 'wonderland', I'm literally punching the steering wheel... "I must be a God that I can do this. Just wait until I tell the media." Suddenly the car begins to shudder again, before grinding to a halt. I sit back in shock, hands off the steering wheel, as if somehow it's been electrified. What have I done? No answer. So I look within. I'm feeling excited, in a kind of rush, which in many ways feels good. But I also feel very disconnected from this reality, very ungrounded. So I breathe deeply and work to calm myself down.

Watch for a careful balance - between the strong building of energy, which is initiated by the realigning flow, and staying connected to the reality around you. You can't influence what you're disconnected from.

Feeling much calmer now, but still energetically revved inside, my attention is drawn to an advert on the billboard next to me. This time I notice not the words, but the picture - that of a football team. Then I'm drawn to the number plate of an oncoming car, particularly to the number 1. So what's it telling me?

Your ego considers that it's you creating the 'miracle'. But the miracle is life itself, which works as an interconnected flow. Most of the time, you only witness 'small miracles', ones that you've accepted and become used to - something as simple as breathing, being in a body, being able to look out onto a green meadow or hear a bird singing. You pass them by daily as somehow ordinary.

And sometimes, especially in times of great injustice - as on your planet right now - there's such an upwelling for realignment, that reality itself will bend, working to wake you up to the truth. In fact many people around the world, in all walks of life, are experiencing peak miraculous events just as you are - especially now, with the world facing such a perilous predicament.

The point is, you're driving a car on air, but it's not 'you' doing it. The flow itself is. You're just not getting in the way of it, with doubt and disbelief overriding it - to how it 'should be', or 'how it's always been'. You're becoming a channel for a movement of energy - you're opening up for that energy to infuse into this world through you.

And sometimes, like now, when something 'big' happens, the ego wants to own it, and make it about you. Like Christianity made the flow of miracles about Jesus. The number '1' that you're seeing, and the football team, are telling you the Universe works as one orchestra of activity, pulling together as a team - when the ego lets go of control and ownership.

The arrogance in me softened. I surrendered once more into the oneness. Upon which, the engine fires up into a purr once more.

By now, it's becoming crystal clear to me that a major shift is wanting to happen to the planet - *is happening on the planet*. Suddenly my phone starts to ring. I guess people will be wondering where I am. It's Amanda, inquiring after me, hearing that I'd not been at work, and concerned about 'strange' behaviour that Charlie, my business partner, has told her about. Despite her worry, I felt to go and see the children. I so much wanted to hug them. That seemed far more important than anything else going on - in light of what I'd been witness to these last few days.

It's so important that when you awaken to this energy, you begin to share it with others. It doesn't have to be some 'great story' though. Just a hug, or a caring look into their eyes, the sense of love. Let them feel the emergent soul in you.

I adore seeing the children - it's so lovely, all smiles, happiness and hugs. They don't care about business, they're just enjoying the moment. I can see it clearly now - *they just live it, and the energy flows through them.*

And I was feeling love toward Amanda too, even though I can instantly feel her worry and concern, threatening to close the field down around me. I can't help but blurt out to her how I'm being guided by a benevolent presence, which is speaking to me through the events and circumstances all around us - that life is speaking that way to **everyone**, if only people would stop, breathe and take notice. And then the biggest mistake - I tell her about the car and driving on air.

At which point, I notice the energy between us take a very abrupt, and deep, tailspin. Now there's contracting concern in her face; she's ushering me away from the children, and strongly suggesting she call the doctor for me. And suddenly I'm concerned about being interned in some hospital again. So I make my excuses and leave, as quickly as possible.

Be forewarned. Most people are just not ready for the wider expanded reality. They'll happily read about the miracles of Jesus, and even though he said, "what I can do, so shall you, and more," to them, it's just a story about one man - the "Son of God". And just look what the sceptical did to him!

I'm back outside the office now, knowing that at some point I just have to face the music from the others. There would have been appointments and schedules I'd missed. As I enter, I can feel it all around me - concern, worry, scepticism and even anger - it's like a thick veil, cloaking the very atmosphere of the place.

Somehow, I'm feeling the only thing I can do is speak the truth. So I try to share with them the sense of the guiding Christ Consciousness on the way to the Oracle the day before, and now being able to drive the car on empty. Surely someone will get this; surely someone will be able to wake up and see the truth - even just the guiding flow that speaks to you about who you really are? But alas, I am simply met with a barrage of scepticism.

You can't blame them. It's just too big a reality shift to take all in one go. When you think about it, when you look back at the story of your own life, you'd been testing the edge of reality since a very early age. Even if you hadn't broken through at the surface level of mind, even if you wouldn't have considered your revelations as 'divine', you'd been constantly testing reality and your part within it. That's why you are ready to experience what you now are. But you have to give those that haven't pushed the boundaries so much, time to come to these realisations themselves.

A Great Realignment of energy is coming to the Earth. It will be powerful, but also progressive, over time, such that the mirrors of the deeper truth will get ever stronger. It will become such a crucible of catastrophic change, that many will have no choice but to truly let go, to start to question and wake up.

The tempo is now definitely hotting up. I can feel it, just as my car runs out of fuel and I'm left stranded on a roundabout...

The planet is running out of fuel. Humanity is stranded at a roundabout!

But why can't we have cars that run on air or at least water? Wouldn't that do a huge amount to save the environment? As the question arises, I reflect back on a recent meeting, about someone claiming to be able to run a car on water, but that the big oil companies were trying to close him down, fearful of the impact on their business...

And should everyone get a car that runs on water? Because to truly change things, they would need to be mass-produced. Where does the water come from? And what about all the parts needed to make them? What about the discarded parts you have to throw away? The planet was never designed to take so many people, all living the way you are, all exploiting the Earth and steadily bleeding it dry.

"I can feel the truth in this - there has to be some other way."

Your reality is starting to unwind - just as you've been witnessing. The Earth's consciousness is moving into a higher vibrational reality, in the Fifth Density, where cars, engines and fuel are just not necessary.

Yet again, I can feel the truth in this, although my mind is struggling to grasp it. "What exactly does that mean - 'a higher vibrational reality'?"

Remember, it's like tuning the dial on a radio. You can pick up all manner of channels at different frequencies, some higher, some lower. Reality is exactly the same - there's an undeniable pull that wants to take you on a journey, through the outer circumstances of your life, but this is simply a mirror, reflecting an inner journey, drawing you back toward the Source, through the next reality - in the 5D.

But now I'm disturbed by a knocking on the window - a concerned commuter. "It's okay, I've just run out of fuel." "Want to borrow a phone?" - he asks politely. "No it's okay, I have my own." The only person I can reach is Amanda, who has a friend pick me up some while later.

When I get back to the office - where I'm living - Charlie makes a bee-line for me. He's now practically beside himself, all worried and flustered. He'd called my parents - I guess I couldn't blame him. How do you blend these two realities when others have always known you in the old way?

It's a challenge indeed. But you will find a way. Right now, you're integrating so much energy, so much infusing consciousness, it's becoming increasingly hard to relate to the world the way you've known it. In time, you'll integrate it all, you'll be grounded, and you'll have a new vocabulary, that can placate the people in the 'matrix'. You'll find a way of relating to them, without denying your own truth. But it does take time.

Eventually I acquiesce to Charlie driving me north to Stoke-on-Trent, to where my parents live. Although I didn't at all feel I needed it, at least it was a kind and caring thought. And perhaps my parents might be able to grasp something of what's going on for me, without thinking I was going crazy.

I'll be there for you. Working with you. But know that only YOU can integrate higher consciousness into YOUR being. I can reflect, I can resonate, but that part you have to do yourself.

"I understand. I think!"

All the way up to Stoke, I can feel Charlie's worry and fear, the sense of negativity. Clearly there's compassion, but also the sense that he just wants to get me off his hands. So as we arrive at my parents, I'm feeling glad to be out of the car and away from his negative energy. However, if there was some optimism that everything would be fine at my parents' home, then this was quickly dashed at the doorstep, with my mother immediately breaking down in floods of tears, and my father looking on with deep concern in his eyes. Clearly they'd been 'forewarned' that "something was seriously wrong with Chris". They'd found it extremely difficult to let go of my experience in the German hospital, and to them, this was another bout of breakdown raising its ugly head.

Unfortunately your society, and the people in it, witness breathtaking Breakthrough, but all they can see, is breakdown. For a seed to unleash its finest expression, the shell must crack, it must come completely undone, before the new shoots can emerge. But all that most people see, are the cracks, not the new shoots.

To make matters worse, the house - on a typical middle class estate, with all the gadgets and widgets - now feels like a dense fog of constricting energy. In every room I go, I can feel electrosmog, like a grey blanket, wanting to close me down. Computers, cordless and mobile phones, countless gadgets on standby, the stink of unnatural cleaning materials. And to add to that, the near constant droning of the TV, which feels like it's seeping into my psyche, like some purposefully torturous white noise.

Everything is vibrational - your body and mind, your emotions and the energy field all around you. Your society has been perfectly configured to throw a big, debilitating, downgrading blanket all around you, to cut you off from your soul sovereignty and divine connection.

The food is mostly packaged and processed - I'm now looking at the ingredients of everything I eat. It's so full of chemicals and substances that I don't know or understand. I can't even pronounce them - you could be literally eating poison. Yet this is considered 'normal'...

Most of it literally is poisonous. Take a look around you, at the 'health and well-being' of most people, especially as they're getting older. Their bodies are breaking down, their minds so often confused and befuddled - many living in fear and worry. So often their lives are only perpetuated, for any length of time, because of a cocktail of prescription drugs. Humanity in general is very sick. And his sickness is destroying the planet too. And all the time this continues, he's drawing ever nearer to a very drastic wake-up call.

And what is it that I can feel all around me? What is it that I somehow know from way back? I'm feeling an energy, a consciousness, that somehow seems to feed off this energetic incoherency...

It's that energetic 'virus' I've spoken of before, which thrives off such disharmony; especially worry and fear. There are entities that populate and 'feed' from people's dissonant vibrations, just as you or anyone else would eat dinner. I call it an "Opposing Consciousness", because its purpose is to oppose the elevation of consciousness that you, and many others across the planet, are now beginning to feel. It is resisting the shift into the 5D paradigm, spreading dissonant vibrations so that it can maintain control.

And now when I see my parents, I can literally see shadows behind and around them, drifting in and out of their fields. Even though I still feel expanded and connected, it causes me deep concern.

You're 'seeing' - more perceiving - the energy field and what some people would call 'the aura'. You've expanded your consciousness into your energy body - in the Fourth Density - and so now you can see the entities that pervade it, the virus that is controlling people and society for its own agenda.

"My God. People need to be made aware of this. They need to be helped to make better choices, to escape the influence. How do we do that?"

You have to be patient, take your time. If you simply blurted out what you're now seeing, in the wrong circles, they'd call you crazy. You have to understand the depth of how this virus works. Most people can only perceive what's happening in the physical frequency - their physical body - and in the mind. As far as they're concerned, everything that happens inside themselves is coming from them - initiated by them. But this energy - this virus and the entities that pervade it - come in on different frequencies, which can only be perceived when your consciousness is expanded and vibration elevated.

In most people, the influences flow in unseen, and are then condensed down into just a couple of channels of information, which they pick up. By the time they perceive it, they're just under the impression it's their own energy, their own consciousness. They have no inkling as to what is influencing their every thought, feeling and emotion (and how it is doing so). It's as if this Opposing Consciousness has become a part of them.

To them, this is reality, which everything they consume confirms for them, from the poisonous toxic chemicals that pass as 'food', to the tabloid newspapers that fill their minds, to the judgmental soap-operas they watch as entertainment on TV. It's all conditioning, designed to dumb down, to limit and thereby control.

It's so people release dissonant energy from which the entities feed.

The truth was obvious. The scope and magnitude lands inside me with a jolt, like an overladen passenger plane, as it hits my inner 'tarmac'.

My heart feels heavy, as I can all too readily appreciate how their choices are being negatively influenced - almost as if they're zombified.

That's actually very close to the truth. The majority are totally blind to it. Which is why the planet is so overexploited and in such a mess.

I wake up the next morning feeling nauseous. My head is cloudy and fuzzy, as if I've drunk too much alcohol the previous night on the town. My body is aching and tired, like I'd just run a marathon. "Why's that?" I'm asking out loud...

Most people don't really feel their bodies - neither have you up to this point. As souls, they're not fully infused into them; they're living mostly in the mind. And so they don't feel the tension and trauma they're building up. This is one of the reasons there's so much cancer in society. Cancer is much less widespread in nature, where creatures live in tune with the natural vibration. But where there's such out-of-alignment with Unity Consciousness, as we're witnessing in society, you build dissonance, creating illness, energetic disorder and dis-ease. Cancer is a prime effect of that.

In your developed world, many have all the comforts of life. And even the 'have-nots' have been conditioned to aspire to this consumeristic 'heaven'. When in truth, it's a living hell.

I simply know that, I just have to get out, get far away, and somehow find a place where I can live more in alignment, more connected with the natural flow of life. Living here, even after just a couple of days, I'm concerned I'll fall into some dense abyss - just like them. I can literally already sense that virus surreptitiously creeping into my consciousness. I'm feeling the influence on thought and emotion. It causes a momentary panic attack.

Be careful. That's what it does. And it can all too easily flood your consciousness with negativity. It's good to be aware of it, to see it, but you certainly don't want to be languishing in it for too long.

So now I'm in a car I've borrowed from my mother, heading south, feeling I need to get away, just as fast as possible. I'm following a pull in the direction of my old university town of Oxford. And even though the car is borrowed from my mum, even though there's no 'self-selection' on the radio, the first track that's playing when I switch it on synchronistically speaks right into the heart of the problem...

"It's no secret that the stars are falling from the sky
It's no secret that our world is in darkness tonight.
They say the sun is sometimes eclipsed by the moon
You know I don't see you when she walks in the room.

It's no secret that a friend is someone who lets you help.
It's no secret that a liar won't believe anyone else.
They say a secret is something you tell one other person
So I'm telling you, child.

A man will beg, a man will crawl
On the sheer face of love, like a fly on a wall
It's no secret at all.

Love, we shine like a burning star
We're falling from the sky... tonight."

(lyrics by U2)

All the way down the motorway, one song after another is speaking to me, all creating a picture of what's truly going on - unseen - all around us. I'm passing car after car, commuters on their way to work, vans and huge articulated trucks, thundering their consumer goods to the next town or city. I'm surrounded by wall-to-wall density. And the more I think of it, the more I can appreciate how this is going on through every town and city practically throughout the world. This industrial consumerism - *this rampant beast* - is totally accepted as 'normality'. I can hardly take it - this mechanised madness, all rushing full speed over a cliff edge, into a giant abyss. And the sad fact is, that none of them can see it. Or even if they can, the magnitude is just too great to believe they can do anything about it. So they drink it all in, and let it consume them - I'm thinking this just as a Coca Cola truck passes by.

And in me, it's almost too much to take.

Stay with me, stay connected. See it, but feel your soul through it.

I'm feeling pretty ungrounded at this stage. I'm guessing the movement of the car and the sense of floating along, whilst in an expanded state, can begin to disconnect you from the density of the world, especially as the enormity of it has suddenly washed overwhelmingly into view.

You've got to be careful how quickly you unfold. You're almost completely shifting from one reality to another.

So I pull into a service station. But the sheer volume of traffic, noise, bustle and conspicuous consumption is even more overwhelming. I go inside, into a wall of dissonant, confused energy - distraction everywhere. There are queues - reams of people - outside KFC and MacDonalds, waste packaging and rubbish is literally oozing from garbage bins, like some overflowing sewer. The noxious smell of junk food fills my nostrils. Endless chatter, like some slot machine arcade fills my ears. It's like an energetic tsunami is ripping through my field. After just a minute or two, I feel completely drowned by it, and have to leave.

Every town, every city, every motorway, the world over.

And now I'm sitting in my car, just watching people going in and coming out of the service station main doors, as if they're entering and leaving some enormous, all-consuming, satanic beast - some relic dinosaur from a bygone, extinct time. Except this is very much here and now, thriving, devouring, but sanitised and distracting, so you can't see it - the flashing neon lights are blinding with their repetitive messages of "Buy all you can eat for only £9.99." A warning sign if ever I've seen one.

I need to get away, as fast as I can, concerned that I'll be devoured myself. I'm now heading south, not too far from Oxford. Every song is singing to me, and I assume to other drivers too, passing by in their cars, sadly oblivious, even though the messages are coming loud and clear...

"Open up your eyes, just open up your eyes."

Tears begin to flood down my cheeks, my heart feels like it's bursting, pounding with compassion for them. Can you not see?

"Open up your eyes, just open up your eyes."

Energy is welling up from within me, as I'm feeling their plight and that of the good Earth, across which their cars are thundering. Wall-to-wall trucks are surrounding me. Do they not get it? Am I the only one seeing this?

More tears, more heart bursting, and now I'm feeling like I'm in two distinct realities at once: a peaceful, harmonious higher one, and this decadent, decaying one that I'm driving in. Now, as I look on, something spectacular happens. I'm seeing the Earth from up above...

"Look at Earth from outer space"

I'm seeing it turning and turning, faster and faster, changing colour from blue to orange and then a smoky red, like it's steadily being consumed within a fiery cauldron. And through it, people rushing around in panic...

"Everyone must find a place"

I'm seeing the dark energetic virus they're consumed within, being burned away by the fire. I simply know - it lands in my heart - this is what the Earth is coming to, this is the direction she's heading in. There's just no question. It's the stark-staringly obvious outcome for this mechanised madness.

The presence is trying to connect with me, but I just can't take it anymore. The visions and the emotive feelings are just too overwhelming. And in amongst the flooding emotions, I can feel that virus vibration, seeping into my psyche - "You're going crazy. Mad. End it all now. It's all pointless. It's coming to an end anyway. Why wait?"

The situation overwhelms me, it's hard to stay connected to this place, to this Earth, to this reality. I believe I know exactly where it's going and what that means for everyone around me - all life on the planet - all these people driving their cars on a motorway bound for nowhere. It all seems so pointless, no meaning to it.

And so in this confused, emotive state, with the shadowy influence of negative entities now all around me, I do the only thing that seems to make sense - I completely let go. I let go of everything. I let go of every goal and ambition, I let go of everything I love and cherish, I let go of everything I hate. I let go of my family and my lovely kids; with tears flowing as ceaselessly as a flooding river, bursting its banks down my cheeks, I just totally let go. And now, through the tearful visual distortion, I see my former life on the windscreen, like a movie, flashing before my eyes... the young Karate student, rowing at Oxford, Big Business civvy street with Dow Chemical, the Commando Course, out in the Deserts of Iraq, Victoria House, the English Antique warehouse, and then VHO, it's online virtual evolution. I let go of it all. Until finally, I let go of my own life, and with that, my hands fall from the steering wheel.

This is it then. I've been here before, it seems a thousand times before. Nothing to be afraid of then, nothing to fear, just let go.

And now I can feel the car veering off the motorway to the left. This is it, death is close. But it doesn't matter, it's all going anyway. And amidst it all, a thought flashes through my mind...

What is there that remains?

Just then the car hits something hard, a speed barrier, angled down, and so the car rockets up into the air, thrusting sharply to the right, back across the motorway, directly perpendicular to the speeding oncoming traffic. I let go deeper, because now I know it's all very close. Literally only seconds remaining.

Come on Chris. What is it that remains?

Suddenly, as I'm flying along with the car, arms stretched out to the sides of me, a wave flows through me. It's a wave I recognise from the roof of the Hilton Hotel, that incredible morning after my awakening at the Grand Canyon. It's a wave of unconditional love, coursing through me, seeming to lift the car with it.

Then there's that song again, but I can no longer tell if it's on the radio or just in my head. Wait a minute, it's neither; it's literally all around me...

"And give me love over, love over, love over this, ahhh
And give me love over, love over, love over this, ahhh."

I can feel the love, sweeping everything that's negative away. I don't mind dying. It's okay. I can feel my connection to the Source and to the whole of life.

Then an almighty "thunnkkk" stops my chain of thought and feeling, as the car plunges head-on into the barrier of the central reservation, and bounces back, side-on into the fast lane.

I look up to my right. There, just a few tens of metres away, is death, coming for me in the shape of a fast approaching car, with yellow driving light peering into my cab and into my eyes. This really is it then! I throw my head back, a final letting go, it's time to pass on.

And then suddenly, from up above, the sense of wave upon wave of unconditional love, as if someone is sitting over me with a big bucket, pouring it down. Time now grinds to a halt; reality suddenly freezes. And then I'm expanding, like some mystical genie from a dusty bottle, in waves of loving light. I'm in higher dimensions again, looking down upon the Earth, but this time the view is very different.

She's rejuvenated, vibrant greens in the fields, deep blue oceans, clear blue skies. She's reborn, positively pulsating with life energy. This New Earth is overlapping the remnants of the old, which is being consumed within a molten fire. And I see sparks of light - souls - rising out of the debris, also taking on new, glorious form in this renewed 5D reality. My heart is practically overwhelmed and bursting with the sense of love, joy and timeless interconnectivity. I'm rejoicing at Gaia, coming back to life, in all her magnificent beauty and perfection.

I literally feel I've died and gone to heaven.

Which is why I wasn't at all expecting what happened next.

The driver's door of my car opens, and there's a guy crouching down by the side of me, asking if I'm okay. At this point it's hard for me to tell what's really real. Maybe I truly am in heaven?

He leans across and undoes my safety belt, helping me climb out of the wreckage of the car. And now we're walking across the motorway, toward the hard shoulder. But wait a minute, I'm thinking, what about all the other cars? Especially the one with the yellow lights that was fast approaching mine? And the thought crosses my mind, with a touch of ironic humour...We're going to get run over! This causes me to look to my left - my attention being guided that way. I'm completely shocked by what I now see...

Every single car has stopped. And just as if Moses himself had come down and parted the Red Sea, there was a perfect dividing line, along which we were now walking. On a busy midday motorway, with traffic travelling at its usual breakneck speed, not one car had crashed into another.

And neither was any of the cars trying to drive around the wreck, as usually happens. It's as if someone - 'God' - had reached down a hand, stopped time, and brought all the cars to a sudden halt.

I'm not supposed to die then? was the next thought. It was followed immediately by an exchange with the presence, who now seemed to be much closer, all around me and in me...

No. You're not meant to die; you're meant to live! To share a message of what you've seen. For all those who have the ears to hear. A message about the world they're really living in - the hazy wool that's been pulled over their eyes to blind them from the truth.

The truth about what the Earth is now really coming to. But most importantly of all, just like others across the planet, in all walks of life everywhere, how each of you can break through, into your God-given birthright - your intimate connection to the divine, as a living breathing child of the Universe that you all are.

You're meant to share your visions of the new reality - the New Earth - in a higher dimension of being, that is all around you, that you can all access, when you go inwards and peel away the restrictive density that is blocking you.

No matter where you are, how you're living, whatever circumstances, every single moment offers that Breakthrough opportunity.

Begin with the tightness, whether it be in your mind or emotions. Feel deep into your body. <u>Watch, observe, witness</u>. Then know yourself as that which is beyond, that which is witnessing. This disassociates you from the lower density. Then your consciousness will steadily expand, into the New Paradigm, the new reality, which is in you, but then unfolds from you, all around you.

In some, it will be more dramatic and sudden, through a life-threatening event or some apparent tragedy. For others, it will be more gentle and introspective. How ever it is for you, whatever feels right for you, keep inquiring, keep exploring. Don't rest with the limitation that keeps you locked and subjugated to a lesser life.

Know that you have a choice. The whole of life is a choice. To live every second as if nothing is a miracle, or as if everything is. Every single one of you can break through! You just have to reach within, soften, and take what is rightfully yours.

I was in a bit of a haze, now in the back seat of the guy's car, who had a strangely angelic sense to him. The police arrived first, then the paramedics to check me over. The medics pass me with a clean bill of health, and strangely, the police don't even inquire as to what had happened. They give me an incident report and recover the car to the hard shoulder.

Within about 30 minutes of the crash, I'm in a taxi, which is taking me back down south to Hampshire. And as we're driving, the taxi driver turns, and with a glint in his eye, asks if I'd like some sounds? "Sure, why not, it's been a helluva day." I should have known they'd be lyrics by the omnipresent Coldplay...

"Look at the stars,
Look how they shine for you,
And everything you do,
Yeah, they were all yellow.

I came along,
I wrote a song for you,
And all the things you do,
And it was called "Yellow".

Your skin,
Oh yeah your skin and bones,
Turn into something beautiful,
Do you know,
You know I love you so,
You know I love you so.

I swam across,
I jumped across for you,
Oh what a thing to do.
'Cause you were all yellow,

I drew a line,
I drew a line for you,
Oh what a thing to do,
And it was all yellow.

Your skin,
Oh yeah your skin and bones,
Turn into
Something beautiful,
Do you know,
For you I'd bleed myself dry,
For you I'd bleed myself dry,

Look at the stars,
Look how they shine for you,
And all the things that you do."

It felt like the song was singing just for me.
But I knew it was for everyone.

Epilogue

It's several days later now. I'm at The Oracle once more, having a quiet cup of tea, watching the world go by, and the busyness of the shoppers. But I can handle it all now. I've seen it for what it is. And I've seen what is to come. And I'm not afraid.

All of life changes, evolves and grows. All realities come and go. We are merely a speck of dust in a wider Universe, that's constantly changing. Why should it be any different here?

Yes, I've seen what the world is coming to. I've seen the catastrophic breakdown of the old reality, but I've also seen the miraculous Breakthrough of the new - Gaia rejuvenated in all her heavenly glory.

I feel totally unattached to life, and with that, I feel immortal, invincible - but also humble, definitely not arrogant.

And the presence is very much with me now. All around me. In my thoughts and my heart. It's a constant dialogue - a constant loving exchange with a dear old friend. It's like the presence has literally infused into me and become a part of me.

As I'm sitting there, a question comes to mind... "What do I call you?"

My attention is immediately drawn to a shop doorway, then another and another in quick succession...

Open

"Well that's original!"

It's what it is. It's more a way of being than a name - open to the natural flow of the Universe and my right action within it.

"And why are you here?"

I came to help you, to help share a wider message for humanity, about this incredible shift that the world has now begun to undergo.

"My heart is already in the New Paradigm. I'm done with this place. It's my soul's yearning to pass on."

Yes I can feel that, and so, like many others, in due time, you shall.

"When?"

That all depends on you.

"If that's the case, I'd like to go now please!"

It doesn't work like that, my dear friend. There will be a reason why your soul is keeping you here for the time being. But when your purpose is fulfilled, you will indeed pass on and join the new dawning in the Fifth Density.

"What might that purpose be?"

Now everywhere around me, my attention is drawn to the number 5. And then doorways.

Well gateways to be more precise.

"5GATEWAYS then?"

5D Shift Project

The consciousness of the Earth is shifting into the Fifth Density, which will leave no stone unturned. How can you join this phenomenal transition? A vast army of higher dimensional support is gathering to facilitate the shift. Openhand's 5D Shift Project is a bridge into the higher densities, supported by the benevolent hand of the Universe. It is a sequence of writings and courses, sharing direct personal experience, to support your own personal shift into the Fifth Density.

The 5D Shift Project contains three levels of inquiry and exploration:

Level 1 - BREAKTHROUGH: an epic journey of awakening that reveals how to break through into your deeper divinity, told through a true life story, that can relate directly to your own. It is supported by a 3 day experiential intensive retreat.

Level 2 - 5GATEWAYS: provides a way of attuning your personal spiritual compass and a spiritual route map through the inner dimensions into the Fifth Density. It is a text book, that you can continually refer to through your journey. It is supported by a 5 day retreat.

Level 3 - DIVINICUS: regresses you on a journey through humanity's past life karma, where did he really come from and exactly why is the 5D Shift necessary? It will help you process your own karma and activate your spirit-light-body. It is supported by a 7 day course.

Openhand

Purpose

Openhand is a Higher Benevolent Presence, the purpose of which, is to catalyse spiritual evolution, by helping people dissolve conditioned behaviour patterns and limiting beliefs. Openhand is empowering people to find their true beingness and ascend into a magical new reality in the Fifth Density, based on unconditional love, joy and mutual respect for all life.

Openhand Foundation

Openhand Foundation is an organisation led by Open, supported by a team of facilitators, which operates as a not-for-profit organisation. Its purpose is to harness and express the energy of Openhand, here in this realm, for the benefit of evolving people.

Worldwide Seminars, Workshops and Courses

We are given to spread the message, tools and advice contained within this book, as far and wide as possible. In line with this calling, we conduct seminars, courses, workshops and retreats around the world. If you would like us to run a seminar or course for your organisation or private group, email courses@Openhandweb.org

Join our growing community - Openhandweb

It brings great joy to our hearts to witness the miraculous expansion of consciousness taking place across the planet. It is within our purpose to join together a virtual community of ascending people to share advice, resources, transformational tools, philosophy and above all, a common bond of unconditional love. Our website provides a platform for this growing community.

To find out more, visit...

www.Openhandweb.org

CPSIA information can be obtained
at www.ICGtesting.com
Printed in the USA
FSHW01n1946191018
53161FS